C0-AOH-077

WITHDRAWN
SAINT PETER'S COLLEGE LIBRARY

PRAGMATICS AND SEMANTICS

An Empiricist Theory

PRAGMATICS AND SEMANTICS

An Empiricist Theory

CAROL A. KATES

WITHDRAWN
SAINT PETER'S COLLEGE LIBRARY

Cornell University Press

ITHACA AND LONDON

Copyright © 1980 by Cornell University

All rights reserved. Except for brief quotations in a review, this book, or parts thereof, must not be reproduced in any form without permission in writing from the publisher. For information address Cornell University Press, 124 Roberts Place, Ithaca, New York 14850.

First published 1980 by Cornell University Press.
Published in the United Kingdom by Cornell University Press Ltd.,
2–4 Brook Street, London W1Y 1AA.

International Standard Book Number 0-8014-1288-9
Library of Congress Catalog Card Number 80-16742
Printed in the United States of America
*Librarians: Library of Congress cataloging information appears
on the last page of the book.*

P
37.5
C64
K3

To my esteemed
colleague
Joyce Elbrecht

Acknowledgments

It is probably impossible to be fully aware of one's intellectual debts. Without the help I have received over the years from teachers, students, and colleagues, I could not have written this book. I am especially grateful to Charles F. Hockett for his generosity and patience in explaining the intricacies of linguistic theory. I could not have found a more brilliant teacher, and I am greatly indebted to him for the many hours he spent reading and commenting on earlier drafts of this book.

I also thank those whose suggestions and criticisms have been helpful to me in preparing the final draft. In particular, I am indebted to Edward Ballard for his enormously useful comments on the manuscript. I am grateful to Lydia Fakundiny for meticulous scrutiny of several chapters and for many valuable criticisms. Joyce Elbrecht and Susan Graetz elucidated many puzzles I encountered along the way. My thanks also go to Lois Bloom for her comments on several chapters and on portions of an earlier draft, and to Linda Waugh and Alan Shaterian for their suggestions. I also thank Dorothy Owens for typing portions of the manuscript and Allison Dodge for valuable editorial assistance.

I began my research in 1973 as a research associate at Cornell University; my work at that time was partially supported by a grant from the National Endowment for the Humanities. In 1976–77, when I completed the manuscript in approximately its present form, I was supported by a fellowship from the American Council of Learned Societies. I owe a great deal to these institutions for their assistance and to Ithaca College for allowing me to take needed research leave and for providing a grant that covered some of the cost of typing the manuscript.

I wish to thank the editors and publishers of *Man and World, Research in Phenomenology,* and *Forum Linguisticum* for granting permission to publish (as Chapters 9, 11, and 12) slightly revised versions of the following articles: "The Problem of Universals" in *Man and World* (vol. 12, no. 4, 1979); "An Intentional Analysis of the Law of Contradiction" in *Research in Phenomenology* (vol. 9, 1979); and "A Pragmatic Theory of Metaphor" in *Forum Linguisticum* (vol. 3, forthcoming).

To those who were patient and understanding while I was writing this book I am deeply grateful.

CAROL A. KATES

Ithaca, New York

Contents

9

Contents

Introduction

This book explores the nature of communicative competence, or the cognitive prerequisites for speaking and understanding. It is essentially a philosophical investigation of language and speech which is deeply indebted to Husserlian phenomenology. At the same time, it is an interdisciplinary study of the exciting research on the nature of linguistic competence and the process of language acquisition now being done in linguistics and psycholinguistics.

A theory of communicative competence must explain what speakers know about a language that enables them to produce and understand a theoretically infinite number of novel utterances. The widespread conviction that linguists and psychologists should investigate linguistic competence is, of course, a result of Noam Chomsky's influence in these fields. Though I do not accept Chomsky's theory of generative and universal grammar, I agree with the opinion of many scholars that his focus on competence has been enormously fruitful and his rationalistic theory has stimulated a valuable theoretical controversy.

In Chomsky's view, the creative ability of speakers is based on a tacit knowledge of a transformational-generative (T-G) grammar. A generative grammar is a system of rules which describes ("generates") the set of all and only grammatical sentences of a language. A T-G grammar is a generative grammar composed of phrase structure and transformational rules. These rules generate sentences in two stages: first, phrase structure rules generate "deep structures" (renamed "initial phrase markers" by Chomsky [1975]), and, second, surface structures are derived from deep structures by means of transformations. Chomsky's claim is that competent speakers are able to produce and understand novel sentences because of an unconscious knowledge of a T-G grammar which assigns the correct structural and semantic description to the set of all and only possible sentences of a language. Since children do not appear to learn, in any ordinary sense of the word, such a grammar, Chomsky posits an innate, a priori knowledge of a universal grammar, with its component linguistic universals, as the genetic basis for language acquisition.

I shall argue that this rationalistic model of competence should be rejected for at least three reasons. First, empirical tests of the theory have not supported it. Second, the rationalistic theory cannot accommodate the pragmatic relation between speaker and sign, which is fundamental in determining both the grammatical acceptability and the meaning of an utterance. Third, the theory of universal grammar has unacceptable metaphysical implications unless it is interpreted in a way that is consistent with empiricism.

I propose, as an alternative to the rationalistic theory, an empiricist account of communicative competence. An empirically based model of speech has emerged from recent work in linguistics and psycholinguistics, indicating that speakers acquire linguistic structures as a function of general cognitive development and individual experience of referential speech. Cognitive models of language acquisition view semantic structures as cognitive schemas mapped into the forms and patterns of a language. Recently developed models of semantic grammar have been particularly useful in describing the semantic structures acquired at various stages of cognitive development. Speakers who have acquired these structures must also learn to use the patterns of a language in a communicative situation to indicate a topic and express a comment in some context.

Although the grammar of a language provides information essential for the interpretation of contextual meaning, I shall argue that utterance meaning (that is, the intended meaning of an utterance in context), as well as the grammatical acceptability of an utterance, is ultimately determined by a pragmatic relation between speaker and sign which is not reducible to a system of pragmatic rules. If fundamental linguistic intuitions about the meaning and acceptability of utterances are in part a function of nonsystematic contextual variables, it follows that utterances may not be, in effect, reduced to tokens of sentence types described by a generative grammar.

My basic aim in Part I is to establish a broadly empiricist model of language as a system of structures that provide a foundation for communicative competence. I begin my discussion of competence by considering, in Chapter 1, the rationalistic theory of T-G grammar proposed by Chomsky. In Chapter 2, I evaluate semantic grammar and the contribution it has made to an empiricist model of communicative competence. I then examine empirical data bearing on the acquisition of lexical (Chapter 3) and grammatical (Chapter 4) paradigms. In Chapter 5, I discuss the essential pragmatic structure of speech and argue against the possibility of an adequate generative grammar. In Chapter 6, I summarize the role of linguistic structures in the interpretation and creation of novel utterances.

In Part II, I give a philosophical elaboration and defense of the theory that utterance meaning is a function of the referring intention of a speaker in some context. In Chapter 7, I introduce a theory of phenomenological or radical empiricism which explicates the concept of a referring intention, allowing a distinction between essentially private and contingent individual psychological states (such as images, associations, or other sensory material which may accompany a referring act) and ideal intentional structures which may be called the "meant" as such. In Chapter 8, I develop an empiricist account of intentional objects as ideal structures within experience and defend this theory against philosophical objections to classical empiricism. In Chapter 9, I consider the bearing of the philosophical problem of universals on the rationalistic theory of universal grammar and argue that claims about a priori linguistic knowledge entail an unacceptable metaphysical position unless that theory is interpreted in a way that is consistent with a broadly conceived empiricism. In Chapter 10, I explicate the utterance meaning of logical truths and show how a phenomenologically modified empiricism avoids psychologism. Finally, in Chapter 11, I examine the utterance meaning of metaphorical statements to show how novel intentional structures may be created in a language as a way of increasing its expressive power.

PART I
PRAGMATICS AND SEMANTICS:
THE NATURE OF
COMMUNICATIVE COMPETENCE

CHAPTER 1

Transformational-Generative Grammar

The study of language—its structure, acquisition, and influence on perception and cognition—is, and for several years has been, a vital area of interdisciplinary research. The so-called Chomskyan revolution in linguistics created a somewhat virulent but exciting controversy between transformationalists and distributionalists, which focused attention on language as a system only partially expressed through an actual speech corpus. Speech as an observable behavior needs to be explained by a theory of linguistic competence, describing what a speaker knows about the language.

Distributional grammars focused on regularities in speech which seemed to be productive within a given community of speakers, and thus were structures of the language at a given stage of historical development. A grammar was empirically justified if it presented a somewhat idealized representation of structures abstracted from a corpus of utterances acceptable to the speakers of the community. The distributional grammars written by such pioneers as Leonard Bloomfield (1933) described phonological and grammatical (syntactic and morphological) structures, avoiding or at least postponing the investigation of semantic and pragmatic structure in language. Bloomfield was a behaviorist who did not wish to posit any unobservable mental entities that might endanger the objectivity of structural analysis. The alternative to the sort of mentalistic semantic theory he rejected was, he thought, a behaviorist account; he defined the meaning of a linguistic form as "the situation in which the speaker utters it and the response which it calls forth in the hearer" (p. 139). Unfortunately, such an account of meaning effectively ruled out the possibility of an adequate, scientific description of semantic structure. In Bloomfield's words: "The situations which prompt people to utter speech, include every object and happening in their universe. In order to give a scientifically accurate definition of meaning for every form of language, we should have to have scientifically accurate knowledge of everything in the speakers' world. The actual extent of human knowledge is very small, compared to this" (p. 139). Bloomfield concluded that semantics was the "weak point" in language study, and would remain so until general human knowledge made a considerable advance.

Despite the absence of a strictly verifiable semantic theory, linguists were constrained to use semantic clues in reconstructing the grammatical system of a language. Bloomfield acknowledged that linguists had to use such makeshift devices as ostensive definition, circumlocution, and translation into a second language to elicit informants' judgments about the name of some referent or the equivalence of some expressions, or to discover what semantic function was served by a particular grammatical construction. Bloomfield's behavioristic model of semantics has been restated more recently by Charles F. Hockett (1958), who defined linguistic meanings as associative ties between morphemes and morpheme-combinations and types of things and situations in the world.[1] In Hockett's view, it is not the business of linguistics to investigate or describe these associations. However, since they will be "more or less the same for all speakers of a language" (p. 139), the linguist can make a fairly accurate use of semantic criteria to discover the distributional structure of a language.

Distributional grammars might be said to provide a model of competence in the sense that they describe the most productive patterns in the speech of a given community of individuals. Pre-

---

1. Since 1958, Hockett has adopted a slightly different definition of "meaning," derived from the work of Eugene A. Nida, as follows: "The meaning of a linguistic form is the concatenation of properties of a thing, situation, or state of affairs by virtue of which the form can appropriately be used to refer to the thing, situation, or state of affairs" (personal communication, July, 1978).

sumably, regularities in speech reflect the grammatical as well as semantic structures that have been internalized by speakers as the result of exposure to a particular language environment. Of course, speakers do not have a conscious knowledge of the distributional structure of their language. Nonetheless, they have acquired, possibly through some complex form of associative learning, a stock of linguistic forms which may be used habitually, in certain types of situations, to communicate certain intentions. On this account, it is the task of the psychologist to provide the learning theory and that of the linguist to describe the speech patterns that reflect the most widely developed linguistic habits.

Chomsky's (1959) review of Skinner's *Verbal Behavior* was the beginning of an argument against distributional grammar and the behaviorist psychology on which it seemed to rest.[2] Chomsky argued that linguistics must provide a theory of competence that accounts for the creativity of speech. It is an essential fact about language that speakers are able to produce and understand novel but appropriate and acceptable utterances, and it is precisely this fact, he claimed, that behaviorism cannot explain. If competence were simply a matter of associative learning or habit formation, then speakers could never produce or understand a previously unheard sentence. Chomsky echoes Descartes in his argument that the obvious independence of most utterances from any definable set of stimuli and the unpredictability and creativity of speech are clear evidence of the autonomy of the human mind. Thus Chomsky proposes a "mentalistic" and rationalistic theory of transformational-generative (T-G)

2. For a defense of behaviorism, see Hugh Lacey (1974) and Kenneth Mac-Corquodale (1970). Chomsky (1975) has replied to more recent attempts to develop a behaviorist model of speech. For example, he responded to Quine's attempt to find stimulus conditions governing verbal behavior and to characterize linguistic competence in terms of "dispositions" as follows: "If a child learns most of language by hearing and emulation, and—as Quine elsewhere insists—learning a language is a matter of learning sentences, then the child must learn most of his sentences by hearing and emulation. But this is so grossly false that one can only wonder what Quine may have in mind, particularly since elsewhere he observes correctly that a language is an infinite system characterized by a generative grammar, and further, that conditioning, induction, and ostension do not suffice for language learning" (p. 193).

grammar which he claims will provide an adequate model of competence.

I believe that to evaluate Chomsky's criticism of empiricism one must distinguish between an empiricist learning theory in a general sense, and, for example, behaviorism as a special type of learning theory. An empiricist might agree that there may never be an adequate behaviorist model of language acquisition (for example, a Skinnerian model characterizing language learning as a type of operant conditioning, defining the reinforcers for speech, and discovering stimulus conditions that control "verbal behavior"). Certainly there are at this time no convincing behaviorist theories of language acquisition. Further, an adequate model of semantic structures may in fact involve mentalistic cognitive structures. Behaviorism, however, is not the only possible type of empiricist approach to language. An empiricist model would require only that there be a fixed connection between linguistic forms and patterns and experiential schemas such that the latter provide an adequate foundation for the creativity exhibited by speakers of a language. The question of how experience shapes linguistic competence can be resolved only through the empirical study of language acquisition and, more generally, of the speech process.

Bloomfield and Hockett, among others, have attributed linguistic creativity to a process of analogical construction (Bloomfield, 1933, p. 275; Hockett, 1958, pp. 356–57, 425–26). For example, if one understands the terms and the construction involved in the sentence "Mary is riding a horse," and if one knows the meaning of 'tame' and 'tiger', one can easily produce the (previously unheard) sentence, "Mary is riding a tame tiger." Similarly, if one grasps the meaning of the plural suffix '-s', one can easily fill in the missing term in the following analogy: 'chair' : 'chairs' :: 'table' : '_____'. The difficult point is to describe the basic paradigms or productive patterns of the language and to explain how they are acquired.

Chomsky has rejected this sort of empiricist account of creativity, because, in his words, the concepts of habit or analogy are used "in a completely metaphorical way, with no clear sense and with no relation to the technical usage of linguistic theory"

(1966b, p. 12).[3] In contrast to the "vague" notion of analogy, then, Chomsky wishes to introduce the "precise," explicit, and technical notion of an abstract grammatical rule. Speakers who know the rules of grammar are competent to produce and understand any possible sentence of a given language.

According to Chomsky, the rules of grammar are of two types: "phrase structure" rules and "transformational" rules. The former are "rewrite" rules[4] that assign the syntactic "deep structure" appropriate to some sentence. For example, a simplified phrase structure grammar might include the following sequence of rules: S (sentence) → NP (noun phrase) + VP (verb phrase); NP → Det. (determiner) + N (noun, singular or plural); VP → Verb + NP, and so on, ending with "terminal strings" of words and morphemes of the appropriate syntactic category. The strings, or sequences of symbols, which repeated application of these rules produces are called phrase markers, or hierarchically structured, labeled bracketings conventionally represented by tree diagrams. These deep structure phrase markers provide syntactic information essential to the semantic interpretation of sentences.[5]

The deep structures that are the "output" of the phrase structure component of the grammar may, in turn, undergo one or more transformations before emerging as "surface structures": the strings of words and morphemes which constitute the set of acceptable sentences of a language. Transformational rules de-

3. Of course, this assertion about the theory of analogy is one that linguistic empiricists would dispute. What is true is that the Bloomfield-Hockett model of analogy has "no relation to the technical usage" of Chomsky's theory; that is, it does not "make sense" in the terms Chomsky prefers. But, as Hockett has observed, to offer this as a reason for preferring Chomsky's theory to that of analogy is simply to argue in a circle. I would agree, though, that a model of linguistic knowledge adequate to account for creativity must describe the cognitive structures that underlie semantic interpretation of a novel arrangement of forms.

4. A "rewrite rule" is an instruction, such as one might give to a computer, to rewrite what is on the left side of some symbol (→) as what is on the right side of that symbol in a program.

5. As I shall observe presently, Chomsky (1975) has slightly modified his earlier theory that deep structures determine semantic interpretation. The new theory is that "enriched" surface structures, to which initial phrase markers have been assigned, determine a semantic interpretation.

SAINT PETER'S COLLEGE LIBRARY
JERSEY CITY, NEW JERSEY 07306

scribe a set of operations, such as deletion, embedding, permuta-
tion, and so on, that "transform" the abstract deep structures
generated[6] by phrase structure rules. For example, "Mary hit
the ball" and "The ball was hit by Mary" have the same deep
structure, but the passive form has undergone a transformation.[7]

Chomsky characterizes a grammar, in the broadest sense, as
having three components: a syntactic component, including
phrase structure and transformational rules; a phonological component, which provides a phonological interpretation of morphemes (converting surface structures into a phonetic representation); and a semantic component, which provides a semantic
interpretation on the basis of (deep) syntactic information. Because of Chomsky's original claim that the semantic component
of grammar serves an interpretive function in relation to the deep
structures provided by the syntactic component, Chomsky's version of T-G theory has been dubbed "interpretive semantic"
grammar, in contrast to the "generative semantic" position I shall
describe in Chapter 2.

Chomsky has proposed several versions of T-G grammar and
has recently changed his mind about one difficult aspect of the
relation between syntax and semantics. In the model he presented in *Aspects of the Theory of Syntax* (1965), Chomsky argued
that semantic interpretation of sentences operates on the syntactic deep structures generated by the phrase structure or "base"
component of the grammar, and that semantic interpretation is

6. John Lyons (1971) has given a particularly clear account of "generative"
grammars. "When we say that a grammar generates the sentences of a language
we imply that it constitutes a system of rules (with an associated lexicon) which
are formulated in such a way that they yield, in principle, a decision-procedure
for any combination of the elements of the language (let us call them 'words' at
this juncture). . . . The grammar not only 'decides' whether a given combination
is grammatical or not (by generating or failing to generate a combination of
symbols which can be tested for 'identity' with the utterance in question); but it
provides for each grammatical combination at least one structural description"
(p. 156).

7. According to Chomsky, kernel sentences are always active. The basic justification for passive transformations is that they simplify grammar and provide
a significant generalization about language, known intuitively to native speakers.
The alternative would be independent phrase structure analysis of active and
passive forms of all sentences, although such sentences are clearly related in
some systematic way. The "rule" makes the structure of the relationship explicit.

not affected by transformations. His proposal was that semantic interpretation is *not* based on surface structure and that an adequate deep structure analysis of a sentence should provide sufficient information for interpreting the sentence, for specifying multiple interpretations when it is ambiguous, and for showing that it is equivalent to some other sentence whenever they have the same deep structure. As a case in point, consider Chomsky's most famous example: "Flying planes can be dangerous." If one simply assigns phrase markers to (or performs an immediate constituent analysis of) this *surface* structure, one gets the following hierarchical structure:

(((flying) (planes)) (((can) (be)) (dangerous)))

But this sort of analysis does not differentiate the two possible meanings of the sentence and thus does not provide an adequate basis for semantic interpretation. What does show the difference, according to Chomsky, is a transformational analysis that derives the same surface structure from two different deep structures. In one case, phrase structure rules are applied to the kernel sentence: "Planes which fly [or, "are flying"] can be dangerous," and in the other case to the kernel sentence: "To fly planes can be dangerous." One interprets the ambiguous surface structure by analyzing its possible deep structures.

Chomsky (1975) has modified his theory of semantic interpretation in response to a number of counterexamples that seem to show that such interpretations are affected by transformations.[8] The more recent "trace" theory posits an "enriched" surface structure, which retains "traces" of what were formerly called deep structure interpretations, as the object of semantic interpretation (pp. 81–82, 116–17). Chomsky has also decided to drop the term "deep structure" in favor of "initial [i.e., first stage] phrase marker," first because the former expression (falsely) implied to many that the other aspects of grammar are somehow "superficial, unimportant, and variable across languages" and, second, because, in the standard theory, deep structures initiated transformational derivations and determined semantic interpretations. At this point, Chomsky no longer be-

---

8. Examples of such transformations are "No number is both even and odd" from "No number is even and no number is odd," and "Every man voted for himself" from "Every man voted for every man."

lieves that deep structures give all the information required for determining the meaning of sentences. Thus, he now distinguishes between the initial phrase markers (the former deep structures), which initiate transformations, and the syntactically enriched surface structures, which undergo semantic interpretations.

The essence of Chomsky's criticism of distributional grammar is that it does not provide an adequate theory of linguistic competence. In Chomsky's view, the fact that speakers are able to produce and understand novel sentences demonstrates that they have a knowledge of the system of language, which explains those regularities in speech described in distributional grammars. The proper task of linguistics is to describe the underlying system, and to do that is to describe the set of syntactic, semantic, and phonological rules that generate (assign structural descriptions to) the grammatical sentences of some language.[9] Chomsky's hypothesis is that linguistic competence (that is, tacit knowledge of rules) underlies and accounts for a native speaker's intuitions about the grammatical acceptability or unacceptability, the ambiguity or equivalence, and, in general, the meaning of any subset of an infinite set of possible grammatical sentences.

It follows from Chomsky's view of competence that to acquire a language signifies constructing, in some manner, a representation of the set of rules that generate those utterances to which the language learner is exposed. Since the sample of utterances is necessarily finite, and since moreover it may contain ungrammatical, incomplete, or in some other sense degenerate data, the language learner must be engaged in a complex pro-

9. Actually, it is tautologous to say that a descriptively adequate grammar generates all and only grammatical sentences of a language, since, by definition, a sentence is "grammatical" if and only if it is generated by the grammar. The assumption is that an adequate grammar will generate all and only utterances that are found acceptable to native speakers. The judgment of acceptability is intuitive, and, according to Chomsky, intuitions reflect a tacit knowledge of the grammar of a language that the linguist is trying to capture in a description. One problem with this assumption has been that Chomsky has occasionally changed his mind about whether a given sentence is or is not grammatical (for example, "Colorless green ideas sleep furiously"), and many of the grammatical sentences allowed by Chomsky's theory are not, in any obvious sense, intuitively acceptable. For example, consider the doubly embedded sentence: "The floats that the parade that the children enjoyed contained featured Donald Duck."

cess of hypothesis testing. Furthermore, on Chomsky's account, the structural relationships and ambiguities of which speakers are intuitively aware (and which must, therefore, be captured by explicit rules), can be fully described only by a transformational grammar, which posits a distinction between deep structure and surface structure. The competent speaker must, then, make inferences from the surface structures directly available in speech to more abstract phrase markers that may describe other kernel sentences. Thus, one cannot assume that language is acquired simply through exposure to the distributional structure implicit in speech. Distributional grammar is, again, said to be inadequate as a model of competence.

If Chomsky's account of competence is correct, it is clear that language acquisition is an impossibly difficult task. Not only must the learner contend with noisy data, but she must recognize something about the nature of the task as a process of theory construction and hypothesis testing, and she must discover the crucial difference between underlying phrase markers and surface structures to construct an adequate grammar. Furthermore, of course, the language learner must do all of this at an age when there is no reason to believe human beings are capable of such sophisticated conceptual feats. In short, an adequate T-G grammar would seem to be, for children, and perhaps for most adults, unlearnable.

One might conclude from this argument that Chomsky's view of competence must be wrong. But the theory of competence as knowledge of an adequate T-G grammar is justified by the argument that such a grammar accounts for creativity, since it enables a speaker to generate an infinite number of possible sentences. Thus, he says, if such a grammar cannot be learned in the ordinary sense (or in a way made precise by some learning theory), yet speakers must be assumed to have such knowledge, then there must be an innate basis for language acquisition. This suggestion is reinforced by the observation that language acquisition appears to be uniform across the species. All human beings acquire language—unless some physical defect prevents them from doing so—regardless of differential intelligence; limited, frequently degenerate, and widely variable speech data; and absence of formal instruction or apparent reinforcement. Moreover, the onset of speech activity is fairly constant, and, in

Chomsky's view, the acquisition period strikingly brief.[10] All of these factors seem to point to a genetically based, specifically linguistic, cognitive ability that Chomsky characterizes as an innate, a priori knowledge of universal grammar.

Universal grammar (UG) is said to provide "a schema to which any particular grammar must conform (Chomsky, 1968, p. 76). It includes what Chomsky calls formal and substantive universals and an evaluation procedure or "weighing device" for selecting one grammar from among several possibilities. Formal universals specify the abstract or formal structure of the rules of any grammar. For example, it is a formal universal that grammars are systems of rules that assign a pairing of sound and meaning and that grammars include phrase structure and transformational rules.[11] Substantive universals such as the concept of a sentence, phrase marker, noun phrase, and so on, provide the "vocabulary" or elements of particular T-G grammars. Chomsky has made various proposals, and at times changed his mind about the content of universal grammar (for example, the role of deep structure), but his general strategy is to posit an innate, a priori knowledge of any linguistic structure that cannot plausibly be said to be learned by speakers. In his words: "If a general principle is confirmed empirically for a given language and if, furthermore, there is reason to believe that it is not learned (and surely not taught), then it is proper to postulate that the principle belongs to universal grammar, as part of the system of 'pre-existent knowledge' that makes learning possible" (1975, p. 118). Knowledge of universal grammar facilitates language acquisition by providing an a priori knowledge of the essential elements of any grammar and narrowly restricting the range of grammars that might describe the speech data available to the learner. Chomsky (1968) summarized this view of language acquisition as follows:

> Suppose . . . that we can make this schema [i.e., universal grammar] sufficiently restrictive so that very few possible grammars conforming to the schema will be consistent with the meager and

---

10. Chomsky has claimed that the language acquisition period is essentially over at a very early age (about four or five years), though recent studies of the use of relational terms by older children have led to dispute about this claim.
11. See note 1 in Chapter 9 for examples of formal universals.

degenerate data actually available to the language learner. His task, then, is to search among the possible grammars and select one that is not definitely rejected by the data available to him. What faces the language learner, under these assumptions, is not the impossible task of inventing a highly abstract and intricately structured theory on the basis of degenerate data, but rather the much more manageable task of determining whether these data belong to one or another of a fairly restricted set of potential languages. [p. 76]

Chomsky is not simply arguing that there is, in some general sense, a genetic basis for language acquisition. No one would dispute such a claim. At a minimum, a certain brain capacity as well as articulatory and vocalizing mechanisms seem to be necessary conditions for the development of language.[12] Further, it would be plausible to argue that language acquisition reflects a general pattern of cognitive development which may, in turn, have a genetic basis. This proposal has been made by developmental psycholinguists who have been influenced by Piaget or by other developmental theorists.[13] Chomsky, however, has postulated a specifically linguistic capacity that reflects an innate, a priori knowledge of universal linguistic structures, although there is currently no genetic theory that supports this proposal.[14] Chomsky (1975) has dismissed this objection on the

12. See Philip Lieberman (1968), Eric Lenneberg (1967, Ch. 6), and Norman Geschwind (1970).
13. For recent discussions see Bärbel Inhelder (1978) and Hermina Sinclair (1978).
14. Eric Lenneberg (1967) investigated biological factors governing language acquisition with specific reference to Chomsky's model of grammar. He gave the following account of the relation between genetic endowment and linguistic abilities: "It is not strictly correct to speak of genes for long ears, for auditory acuity, or for the capacity for language. Genes can only affect ontogenesis through varying the cells' repertoire of differentiation, but this, in turn may have secondary effects upon structure, function, and capacities.... enlarged heart and lung may improve the ability to run; an enlarged liver, the endurance for prolonged intake of alcoholic beverages; a thinning of the fingers, the capacity for assembling electronic equipment" (p. 241). Further, Lenneberg has commented on a hypothetical genetic basis for a language acquisition device capable of constructing a T-G grammar through induction from random input from some natural language. Asked if he knew of any genetic mechanism capable of transmitting highly specific grammatical information, along the lines of Chomsky's proposal, Lenneberg replied that he knew of nothing like it. (See Smith and Miller, 1966, p. 271. See also Chomsky's discussion of Lenneberg's thesis in Chomsky [1978]).

27

grounds that it simply points to a limitation on current theoretical knowledge but does not disprove the hypothesis.[15] His proposal is that the language faculty may be one of several systems of knowledge which make up "common sense understanding," and that speech performance will reflect the intimate interaction between these two systems. Nonetheless, language acquisition is not determined by any general learning strategies (Chomsky, 1975, pp. 41–2, 214), but rather by an "autonomous component of mental structure": the genetically based language faculty with its component universal grammar.

As Chomsky has emphasized, his "theory of mind" has "a distinctly rationalist cast. Learning is primarily a matter of filling in detail within a structure that is innate" (Chomsky, 1975, p. 39). The T-G grammar the language learner must construct to achieve linguistic competence is, in Chomsky's (1975) words:

not a structure of higher-order concepts and principles constructed from simpler elements by "abstraction" or "generalization" or "induction." Rather, it is a rich structure of predetermined form, compatible with triggering experience and more highly valued, by a measure that is itself part of UG, than other cognitive structures meeting the dual conditions of compatibility with the structural principles of UG and with relevant experience. [pp. 43–44]

Chomsky's rationalistic theory of a priori linguistic knowledge, which he has explicitly linked to Cartesian and Leibnizean theories of innate ideas, has been extremely controversial.[16] Perhaps the most damaging criticism made by linguists and psychologists is that the proposal is not verifiable. Chomsky has countered this claim by describing an experiment which would

15. Chomsky (1975) rejects the argument that his proposal is wrong because there are no known genetic mechanisms that could account for innate linguistic knowledge. He says, "[the argument] is correct, but irrelevant. The genetic mechanisms are unknown, just like the mechanisms responsible for such learning as takes place or for the development of physical organs" (p. 91).
16. For statements of Chomsky's views on universal grammar and innate linguistic knowledge, see Chomsky (1966b, 1968, 1971a, 1971b, 1972, 1975). For an imposing array of arguments against the innateness hypothesis see Putnam (1968). Chomsky (1972, 1975) has replied to these and other objections to universal grammar.

test the theory of UG. One need only construct an artificial language that violates some principle that has been postulated as an innate linguistic universal. If such a language were not "accessible to humans in the manner of natural language" (that is, "under comparable conditions of time and exposure to data, with comparable success, and so on" [Chomsky, 1975, p. 209]), this fact would tend to confirm the theory of UG; and if it were "accessible," or learnable, in the way that natural languages are, this experiment would disconfirm the theory of UG.

The difficulty with Chomsky's proposed crucial experiment is that success in learning such a language would not really disconfirm the theory that speakers have *some* innate linguistic knowledge, but only, at best, that the specific rule violated by the artificial language was not a component of UG. On the other hand, failure to learn such a language would not necessarily confirm either the general theory of innate linguistic knowledge or the specific rules violated by the artificial language. First, the conditions of language acquisition would not be comparable to the ordinary case, since the language learner would not be surrounded by native speakers of the language in question who would use the artificial language as a primary or at least critically important means of communication. Chomsky says such a language might be learnable in the way that physics is learnable, so one assumes that the parents of the unlucky experimental child would find the artificial language difficult to use. (Obviously, the experiment is purely hypothetical.) Second, though Chomsky has not proposed any examples of such artificial languages, one might always argue that failure to learn them would reflect the fact that they were somehow inconsistent with normal (biologically or culturally based) cognitive structures or "strategies," and were thus not easily grasped or useful in carrying out communicative functions. To use an analogy, one might learn to use a hammer while wearing glasses that reversed the visual field, but since the glasses would interfere with normal vision, it would require a conscious mental effort to do so. In fact, there is no obvious need to posit innate linguistic knowledge to account for the accessibility of linguistic structures or principles to which we are cognitively attuned, or the relative inaccessibility of those that are not in some way cognitively motivated.

29

It would seem, then, that the strongest argument in favor of the theory of innate linguistic knowledge is that the learning task that would be involved in constructing a T-G grammar is simply too difficult to explain along empiricist lines. The other aspects of language acquisition—uniformity across the species, developmental pattern, absence of reinforcement or instruction—might be explained by a theory of cognitive development, positing a minimal level of cognitive capacity, a universal maturation schedule of some type, and the crucial importance of acquiring a communicative system that can express those aspects of experience which become salient to speakers at a given point in development. If, as I shall presently argue, there is an alternative model of grammar which can account for the creativity or linguistic competence of speakers and which is learnable in an empiricist sense, then there would remain no further reason to posit innate, a priori linguistic knowledge.

Since linguistic competence is said to consist in knowledge of the rules of language—that is, of a T-G grammar constructed on the basis of innate knowledge of universal grammar—descriptions of the grammar of a language are at once descriptions of such competence. The evidence used to confirm or disconfirm a particular model of competence (hereafter called a "C-model") is the intuition of native speakers concerning such matters as the grammatical acceptability, ambiguity, and equivalence of sentences, on the theory that such intuitions reflect a speaker's knowledge of a specific set of rules that generate the possible sentences of a language. However, the way in which such partially innate knowledge is acquired, represented in the mind or brain, and used by speakers is unknown. Chomsky's claim is that competence "somehow" underlies performance, but the nature of that relationship remains to be clarified, and is, on the face of it, quite mysterious.[17]

Chomsky has proposed a set of formal criteria for evaluating generative grammars or C-models. A grammar is said to be "descriptively adequate" if it accounts for linguistic intuitions by "correctly" generating the structures of "all and only" grammatical sentences (acceptable utterances) of a language,

17. See Kates (1976) for a discussion of this point.

providing multiple or identical initial phrase markers for sentences that are ambiguous or synonymous, as well as providing "significant generalizations" that explicate the underlying regularities in a language. Since there can be more than one descriptively adequate grammar for a given language, a linguistic theory achieves "explanatory adequacy" when it provides a theoretical basis for selecting the best grammar from a set of descriptively adequate grammars.

Chomsky has said that the ultimate goal of linguistic theory is to account for language acquisition by showing how a speaker selects one most highly valued descriptively adequate grammar on the basis of linguistic data and the internal structure of the (innate) language acquistion device. He has also suggested, however, that it may be too much to ask linguistic theory to provide a discovery procedure or method for constructing the grammar internalized by the native speaker on the basis of innate knowledge of universal grammar. It may also be too ambitious to require a decision procedure for selecting the best (and thus correct) grammar from among the set of descriptively adequate grammars. Linguistic theory may be able to provide only an evaluation procedure for selecting the best grammar from a proposed set—the one that provides the most intuitively satisfying and, in some unclear sense, "simplest" description of significant structural relationships within a language.[18] The working

---

18. Chomsky (1971b) has said that the innate language acquisition device includes "a method of evaluation that assigns some measure of 'complexity' to grammars" and which then "selects the highest valued grammar compatible with the data" (p. 126). Such statements suggest that the grammar selected by the language learner from the set of possible grammars will be that which provides the simplest account of the significant structural features of the language. The task of linguistic theory is, presumably, to create hypotheses about the nature of the grammar selected by a native speaker, and thus to find the simplest and most significant set of rules. Chomsky has also said, however, that there is no "a priori" notion of "simplicity" and that one must decide on empirical grounds which grammar would be selected by the evaluation measure included in the language acquisition device. For example, Chomsky (1972) writes: "When I speak of 'simplicity of grammar,' I am referring to a 'weighting function,' empirically determined, that selects a grammar of the form permitted by the universal schematism over others. . . . I am not using the term 'simplicity' to refer to that poorly understood property of theories that leads the scientist to select one rather than another. The evaluation measure that defines 'simplicity of grammars' is part of linguistic theory. We must try to discover this measure on

assumption is that language learners are able to select the best grammar for some language on the basis of a certain innate evaluation measure included in the system of universal grammar. An accurate model of UG would include a description of this measure. Despite doubts that one can verify the correctness of any theory of competence, Chomsky and Halle (1965) leave no doubt about the ultimate purpose of linguistic theory: "A linguistic theory meets the level of explanatory adequacy insofar as it succeeds in describing the internal structure of [the language-acquisition device] and thus shows how the descriptively adequate grammar arises from the primary linguistic data" (p. 100).

Charles F. Hockett (1968) replied to Chomsky's rationalistic views from the perspective of empirical linguistics. His major argument was that language is not a rigid or mathematically well-defined system that can be described adequately in terms of some finite number of syntactic patterns or rules, that is, by means of a descriptively adequate grammar. Hockett's view is that grammars can describe only some of the most productive patterns in speech. Furthermore, since productive speech patterns change through time, Hockett sees models of grammar as descriptions of the major patterns or regularities in the speech of some social group at some point in time, rather than more or less accurate pictures of an abstract, entity-like (perhaps reified) set of grammatical rules. Hockett argues further that the attribution to speakers of an unconscious knowledge of certain linguistic rules (that is, a T-G grammar), with no independent empirical verification beyond the intuition and speech

---

empirical grounds, by considering the actual relation between input data and acquired grammars" (p. 189).

The problem with this position is that there is in fact no way to discover which evaluation measure might be included in a hypothetical language acquisition device. Speakers have no conscious knowledge of grammar, and any descriptively adequate grammar could "account" for intuitions in Chomsky's sense. Thus, Chomsky actually makes a "decision" to favor shorter grammars with fewer rules over more "complex" grammars, providing that the former reveal "significant" properties of language. Once again, the question of determining what is "significant" remains vague. See also Bruce Derwing's (1973) discussion of this point (ch. 5.2).

performance that is said to reflect that knowledge, violates the canons of scientific method and enters the area of metaphysical speculation.

Hockett's remarks reflect Bloomfield's assumption that linguists should describe regularities (or structures) within speech. A grammar of this type might be said to characterize "what speakers know about a language" (and thus provide a limited explanation of speech performance), insofar as it describes the forms and patterns by means of which speakers are able to produce and understand novel utterances as analogical formations. Distributional grammars, however, which focused on syntactic and morphological regularities, were never intended to serve as a complete C-model in the sense of a theory of the cognitive prerequisites for speaking and understanding. In his more recent work, Hockett (unpublished material), as well as such theorists as Dell Hymes (1967), Victor Yngve (1975), and others have discussed the need for an expanded empiricist model of what Hockett calls the theory of speaking and understanding.

Clearly, communicative competence must involve a knowledge of paradigmatic semantic-syntactic and morphological structures, as well as an understanding of the complex effects of intonation patterns, gestures, contextual factors, and other elements that affect the interpretation of utterances. If linguistics is the study of speech, then it should be the study of the entire system of human communication, including the mental structures that underlie speech and make communication possible. Such an approach grows directly out of the empirical tradition of describing patterns or structures within speech, but it supplements distributional grammar by incorporating semantic and pragmatic structures in a model of essential linguistic knowledge. In particular, a theory of communicative competence would not merely describe patterns in *behavior,* but would attempt to characterize a semantic deep structure constituted by those cognitive structures mapped into lexical forms, or classes of forms, and grammatical constructions. Descriptions positing such structures would, of course, be subject to experimental confirmation by psychologists.

Obviously, such a reformulation of the goal of linguistics raises questions about the autonomy of the discipline, and specif-

ically about the relation between linguistics and psychology as well as, less centrally, between linguistics and anthropology or sociology. The emerging fields of psycholinguistics, ethnolinguistics, and sociolinguistics might properly be viewed as aspects of a single empirical science: the description of communicative competence. One can still make a distinction, however, between C-models, which describe a speaker's knowledge of language, and P-models (performance models), which describe such things as the way linguistic knowledge is acquired, stored in memory, transmitted through the nervous system, tied to perceptual mechanisms, and so on. In general, C-models describe cognitive structures that reflect essential linguistic knowledge, while P-models describe aspects of the acquisition or use of such knowledge.

Models of paradigmatic (syntactic-morphological, semantic, and pragmatic) structures of a language would, I think, explicate the nature of the "analogies" or productive patterns speakers use to produce and interpret novel utterances. Such a grammar would not simply describe morphological-syntactic regularities, but would provide a semantic motivation for the selection of a given arrangement of forms. A speaker possessing the requisite set of paradigmatic structures would, then, be competent to recognize or intend such structures as the invariant aspects of novel combinations of forms. I shall summarize this view of creativity in Chapter 6.

A model of linguistic (structural) knowledge would characterize only the systematic aspects of what speakers must know to produce and interpret novel utterances or to pass other sorts of linguistic judgments. I shall argue in Chapter 5 that, in fact, no grammar is "descriptively adequate," because a speaker must also take into account unsystematic, contextual factors that condition linguistic intuitions in an essential way. It is for this reason, I think, that it is not possible to describe in advance all of the surface structure regularities of utterances or to define a set of possible sentences of a language. On this point I agree essentially with Hockett's argument that languages are not rigid, mathematically well-defined systems. However, it is possible to describe the linguistic structures that place constraints on the acceptability and interpretation of utterances and that compe-

tent speakers must therefore know in order to interpret novel utterances in context.

In the next chapter, I shall consider the contribution generative semantic theory and the psycholinguistic research stimulated by that theory have made to an understanding of semantic structure.

CHAPTER 2

Semantic Grammar and Communicative Competence

Chomsky's theory of transformational grammar assigns an interpretive function to semantics, in that syntactically enriched surface structures undergo semantic interpretation. The theory is that speakers are able to interpret sentences and account for ambiguity, equivalence, and other systematic structural relationships among sentences on the basis of knowledge of underlying syntactic structures. Further, the theory explains intuitive judgments of grammatical acceptability by providing a structural description of only those utterances that are acceptable. To satisfy all of these requirements, however, the syntactic component of grammar must contain a great deal of information that many critics have judged to be semantic.

In an attempt to meet formal criteria of adequacy, Chomsky and his associates have included in the base component of grammar lexical information, context-sensitive rules of strict subcategorization, and selection rules governing lexical insertion into specified syntactic "frames." For example, the lexical component of grammar might be indexed to provide the following sort of information: 'steak' = (+N, (Det)____, ±Count, −Animate, −Human, . . .), which informs the speaker that the word 'steak' is a noun, that it may be preceded by an optional determiner ('the', 'a', etc.), that it may be used both as a count and a mass noun, and that it is neither animate nor human. Other context-sensitive rules and indices restrict the linguistic contexts in which certain lexical items may appear and prohibit certain transformations under certain conditions. Thus, "They goes" is ruled out because one does not add a third person suffix to a verb unless the preceding noun or pronoun is singular; "They throw" is rejected because 'throw' is a transitive verb; and "The steak ate Sally" is unacceptable because the noun preceding 'ate' (actually, "the NP directly dominated by S") must be +Animate. The intent of including such information in the grammar is to prevent it from generating unacceptable or ungrammatical sentences. It seems evident, though, that at least some of this information is really semantic; it concerns features or aspects of the perceived world that have been systematically encoded by linguistic forms. If some semantic information is necessary to satisfy the requirement of descriptive adequacy set by Chomsky, it may be that further modifications of deep structures along semantic lines would improve linguistic theory.

A number of linguists inspired by the transformational model have in fact worked out alternative semantic models of the base component of grammar. Charles Fillmore (1968), James McCawley (1968), Wallace Chafe (1970), and others have developed what is called generative semantic theory, which assigns a generative (descriptive) rather than interpretive function to semantic structures.[1] A grammar of this type would account for the possible utterances of a language (or for intuitions about the acceptability or unacceptability of utterances) in terms of a set of basic semantic rules. The proposal is that speakers interpret utterances and make other linguistic judgments on the basis of a knowledge of underlying semantic structures that have been mapped into surface structures through a set of syntactic/morphological conventions.

The generative semantic approach was motivated, in part, by a recognition that Chomsky's syntactic distinctions are "too shallow" to capture essential semantic differences among sentences.[2]

---

1. Chomsky (1970) has argued that generative semantic grammar is simply a notational variant of interpretive semantic grammar, since he does not assume any "direction of mapping" or "order of generation" in a C-model. I think, however, that there should be a major empirical difference between a theory that accounts for distributional structure (regularities in speech) by positing an autonomous, underlying system of syntactic structures and a theory that accounts for distributional structure by positing an underlying set of semantic structures. For example, Healy and Levitt (1978) have claimed experimental support for semantic versus syntactic deep structures.

2. Another reason for the shift to semantic grammar was a growing recognition among transformationalists that, contrary to Chomsky's claim that deep structures alone determined the meaning of a sentence, many types of transfor-

Again, a descriptively adequate grammar should capture semantic distinctions that are known intuitively by native speakers, and it is on this point that interpretive semantic grammar was found deficient. For example, consider the following three sentences:
1. "The door opened."
2. "The key opened the door."
3. "John opened the door."

In these sentences "door," "key," and "John" are simply, in a Chomskyan model, the respective subjects of the sentences. However, the semantic relations between subject and verb are very different in each sentence. Fillmore would explicate such differences through a set of semantic "cases." In Fillmore's system, "door" would be classed as a semantic object ("the pre-existent entity affected by an action"), "key" as an instrument ("a thing used [by an agent] to do something"), and "John" as an agent ("an animate, intentional thing that does something"). The point is that these semantic categories, not the abstract definition of deep structure subject-verb-object relations, enable one to interpret the three sentences and distinguish the role of the subject in each case.

Of course, semantic distinctions have syntactic consequences. For example, the sentence "What John did to the car was to hit it" is acceptable, but "What Mary did to the car was to build it" sounds "funny" or unacceptable, although both would be generated by an interpretive semantic grammar (unless more ad hoc semantic restrictions were incorporated into the syntactic base component). In purely syntactic (Chomskyan) terms, the relation between "John" and "car" is the same in "John hit the car" and "John built the car." In Fillmore's case grammar, "car" is classed as a semantic goal ("the object brought into existence by an action") in the second sentence, and as a semantic object ("a

---

mations (involving quantification, pronouns, reflexives, etc.) did change the meaning of a posited deep structure. The best way to maintain a general theory of structural relations seemed to many to involve positing semantic deep structures, a further move in the direction of including semantic information in context-sensitive deep structure rules. Chomsky's newer "trace" theory of surface structure interpretation may render this argument less significant.

pre-existent entity") in the first. Clearly, one cannot "do something" to a goal until it becomes an object.

Generative semantic theories were proposed initially by linguists who accepted Chomsky's claim that linguistic competence consists in a tacit knowledge of a descriptively adequate grammar. However, one could suspend the rationalistic requirements of descriptive adequacy and conformity with a theory of innate universal grammar (UG). An empiricist could treat semantic grammars as models of the cognitive structures encoded by surface structure syntactic and morphological patterns, without assuming that grammars must be generative. I shall summarize this position in Chapter 6.

Since Chomsky believes that the C-models developed by linguists should be evaluated in terms of formal conditions of adequacy, he has never acknowledged that experimental evidence could disconfirm a C-model which was consistent with linguistic intuitions. Though Chomsky (1978) has allowed that what he calls "performance data" might "in principle . . . have bearing on the investigation of rules of grammar . . . [or] 'linguistic competence'" (p. 209), this statement can mean only that performance data might tend indirectly to confirm a C-model that is a component of some P-model being experimentally tested. Thus, negative findings would be taken to disconfirm a theory of performance rather than competence. In general, a lack of experimental evidence that speakers know the rules postulated by a T-G grammar does not constitute an objection to the grammar whereas, on the other hand, linguistic arguments alone are held to be sufficient evidence of the psychological reality of the mental representations postulated by an adequate C-model.

Chomsky is able to insulate questions about competence from questions about performance because of the theoretical nature of the arguments he uses to establish his view of competence. The basic claim is that creativity in speech presupposes knowledge of a descriptively adequate grammar. It is the task of the linguist to describe this grammar, using as data the linguistic intuitions assumed to reflect such knowledge. Thus, it is actually assumed, rather than experimentally demonstrated, that speakers must possess an adequate generative grammar on the grounds that nothing else can account for creativity. From this claim it follows that speakers must possess innate linguistic knowledge (of universal grammar) as the only conceivable basis for the acquisition of such an abstract and complex system as a T-G grammar. Therefore, though experimental data may "have a bearing" on C-models by showing *how* postulated rules of grammar do or do not enter into processing mechanisms, linguistic theories are not directly evaluated in terms of or jeopardized by such data.

The task of the psychologist, in Chomsky's view, is to develop a P-model that explains how competence (as described in linguistic theory) is acquired on the basis of innate knowledge of UG (again, as described in linguistic theory) and how linguistic knowledge underlies performance. Thus the psychologist is asked to begin with assumptions that are not subject to experimental disconfirmation and to explain how speakers acquire and use a rather mysterious form of knowledge for which there may be no experimental evidence. The tacit knowledge of a descriptively adequate T-G grammar is mysterious because it seems to involve analytic knowledge of highly abstract syntactic categories and rules that are not derivable from the surface structures of utterances. Such an account of linguistic knowledge is very far removed from structuralist models of categorical judgments determined by linguistic structures that are readily accessible from paradigms. It is presumably because T-G grammars have such an abstract relation to surface structures that Chomsky posited a priori knowledge of essential linguistic concepts. Thus the hypothesis testing that the language learner is said to initiate on exposure to speech data is an innately determined process.

Thus far, Chomsky's theory that speakers know a T-G grammar has not produced a convincing empirical model of performance. Chomsky speaks of "input" into a syntactic or semantic or phonological "box," and of "tree diagrams" with their "abstract objects" entering a semantic box for interpretation, but all of this sounds suspiciously like a Cartesian "machine without a ghost." Since Chomsky insists that his theory is not a dynamic model (a flow chart) describing psychological processes and that his generative rules are not production rules, the theory has essentially nothing to say about how speakers might use "essential" grammatical knowledge. Thus the C-model Chomsky proposes does not itself explain performance.

Despite Chomsky's efforts to insulate theories of competence from performance data, the psychologists who have used T-G grammar as a model in psycholinguistic research have treated C-models as verifiable hypotheses about what speakers know. They have not simply assumed that the abstract structures posited by linguistic theory have a kind of psychological reality as objects of an unconscious and partly innate knowledge, but have tried to find experimental evidence supporting or disconfirming such a claim. Further, psychologists have taken Chomsky at his word: C-models should explain performance. Thus, there has been little interest in linguistic speculations that do not provide testable hypotheses about what speakers know, how such knowledge is acquired, and how it is used in the process of speaking and understanding. If there is no experimental evidence that speakers in any sense know or use the categories and rules posited by a T-G model of grammar, or if there is disconfirming experimental evidence, then that C-model will be rejected. Linguistic arguments alone may provide hypotheses, but they do not establish the truth of C-models.

During the early 1960s psycholinguists were primarily influenced by Chomsky's interpretive semantic version of T-G grammar. It was widely believed that Chomsky's C-model could be incorporated in P-models fairly directly. Thus, it was assumed that the structural descriptions generated by a grammar had psychological reality, that is, that such structural analysis of sentences was an essential part of the speech process. Accordingly, psychologists sought, and seemed to find, evidence that speakers analyzed sentences in terms of their surface constituent structure (Garrett, Bever and Fodor, 1965; Fodor and Bever, 1965) and in terms of their deep syntactic relations (Blumenthal, 1967; Blumenthal and Boakes, 1967). Other experiments tested the claim that in processing sentences speakers were obligated to perform a series of transformational or, in making inferences from surface structure to underlying structure, detransformational operations in a manner predicted by linguistic theory. The underlying methodological assumption was that there should be a one-to-one correspondence between the time needed to produce or in some way process a sentence and the number of transformational steps involved in its generation. Again, the overall results of these experiments (Savin and Perchonock, 1965; Miller and McKean, 1964; McMahon, 1963) seemed to support a transformational C-model.

The apparent early success of these experiments encouraged psychologists to apply the Chomskyan model to studies of child language. For example, David McNeill (1970) engaged in speculation about the complex, sometimes embedded and highly transformed deep structures underlying such child utterances as "dough" (for "drawer"). He suggested that this early one-word utterance was an embedded sentence with deleted deep structure subject and verb: "Thus, one child said, 'dough' . . . as he reached for a drawer in order to open it himself. The word is the object of the unstated verb 'open,' which in turn is embedded in an unstated sentence meaning roughly 'I want to. . .'" (pp. 131–32). David McNeill (1966) also suggested that children produce "base strings" without transformations. Lois Bloom (1970) spoke of children "processing" utterances by "chunking," which represented some formal model of deep constituent structure (S, NP, VP, etc.) and producing "reduction-transformations" with "dummy verbs" in a hypothetical tree diagram. Roger Brown (1973) criticized Chomsky's *formal* derivation of indirect objects from prepositional phrases by transformations (for example, "Adam gave a bone to the doggie" → "Adam gave the doggie a bone"), because of the *developmental* fact that in child speech, the allegedly "more complex" form comes first, which fact "calls this derivation into question. . ." (p. 233). Arguing in the same vein against Bloom's reduction transformation for child speech, Brown asserts: "The notion that development proceeds from the more complex to the less complex, that rules are dropped as the child develops, is not in accord with our expectations in these matters" (p. 239).

By the late 1960s, psycholinguists such as Lois Bloom, Melissa Bowerman, Dan Slobin, Roger Brown, and I. M. Schlesinger began looking to generative semantic models of T-G grammar, turning away from the earlier (Chomskyan) approach. They did so when it became evident that the experimental data did not unambiguously confirm a Chomskyan C-model. For example, the (1964) Miller and McKean study that (in a somewhat artificial way) asked subjects to perform transformations on sentences did not get the predicted result with expansions of the verb auxiliary. Moreover, they showed an unexpected time difference between negative and passive transformations (the former took less time). Again, the Savin and Perchonock (1965) study showed an unexplained difference in the opposite direction between negative and passive transformations, the former apparently requiring more "storage space" in memory than the latter. L. E. McMahon's study (1963), which forced subjects to interpret sentences to determine their truth-value, found that negative sentences took longer to evaluate than passives, contrary to Miller and McKean's findings and to the general theory. Further experiments (Slobin, 1963 and 1966; Wason, 1965; Gough, 1965 and 1966) suggested that when subjects are required to interpret sentences or determine truth-value, their reaction times will reflect the semantic functions of linguistic structures rather than a hypothetical level of transformational complexity. In general, negative sentences are more difficult to interpret than passive sentences in some contexts and as a function of their truth-value, and some but not all passives are more difficult to interpret than actives.[3]

These experimental results are inconsistent with the theory that T-G grammar corresponds directly with essential elements of speech performance. There is not, as was originally believed, a one-to-one correspondence between measurable aspects of performance and the degree of transformational complexity attributed to sentences by a grammar. In particular, semantic considerations seem to be critically important in predicting performance levels. This fact argued against the claim that semantic interpretation operates on syntactic deep structures and thus takes place only after detransformations have been completed.

It was thus clear by the mid-1960s that if C-models were to describe what speakers must know to produce and understand sentences, semantic factors would have to play a more central

---

3. For excellent summaries of the history of psychological experimentation with Chomsky's model during the 1960s, listing some of the disconfirming evidence, see Fodor and Garrett (1966), and Greene (1972).

role in models of grammar. In view of the experimental results bearing on interpretive semantics, Fodor and Garrett (1966) suggested that there must be an indirect or "abstract" relationship between Chomsky's C-model and what they call a psychological C-model (in Chomsky's terms, a P-model). They argue that a grammar may formalize a speaker's linguistic knowledge without being a component in whatever mechanisms are involved in producing and interpreting utterances. Thus, whereas structural descriptions would have psychological reality, grammatical operations (such as transformations) might not, so that one would not necessarily find a one-to-one correspondence between features of formal derivations and features of performance. (For example, Fodor and Garrett [1967] found further evidence that not every transformation leads to increases in psychological complexity.)

The idea of an abstract relation between competence and performance is a way of insulating linguistic theory from potentially disconfirming experimental findings. One can always explain any negative results as disconfirmation of a theory about how linguistic competence is used without discrediting the linguistic C-model itself. This strategy is not free of difficulties, however. The rationale for attributing to speakers knowledge of an adequate T-G grammar is the claim that structural analysis of sentences is a necessary condition for creativity and is, in general, the basis of linguistic intuitions. Thus, Chomsky (1957) claims:

> To understand a sentence it is necessary . . . to reconstruct its representation on each level, including the transformational level where the kernel sentences underlying a given sentence can be thought of, in a sense, as the "elementary content elements" out of which this sentence is constructed. In other words, one result of the formal study of grammatical structure is that a syntactic framework is brought to light which can support semantic analysis. [pp. 107–8]

The point has been restated repeatedly by Chomsky. Chomsky (1966a) asserted that a grammar provides an account of competence by discovering and exhibiting the "mechanisms" that make it possible for a speaker to produce and understand sentences

(p. 3), and he referred to a generative grammar as "a hypothesis as to how the speaker-hearer interprets utterances. . ." (1966b, p. 75n). Chomsky (1978) has reiterated the position that "the rules of grammar enter into the processing mechanisms" (p. 209), so that P-models must incorporate "representations of linguistic competence" in the form of "a system of rules of competence" (p. 210). Thus, "the goal of the investigator will be to determine the nature of the competence system that expresses what it is the mature speaker knows, and to develop process models that show how this knowledge is put to use" (p. 211). In light of this fundamental claim that grammars describe what speakers must know in order to carry out linguistic performances, denials that speakers in some manner analyze the grammatical structures of sentences make no sense.

A T-G grammar explicates possible linguistic structures in terms of specific generative sequences, including transformational operations. It should follow, then, that if a grammar provides an accurate C-model, it should predict that speakers will carry out the grammatical operations that are an essential part of a given structural description. Thus there should be some experimental evidence that speakers do in fact carry out the structural analyses that are said to be a precondition of performance.

Leaving aside the question of whether it is really meaningful for a T-G linguist to speak of structural analyses apart from specific grammatical operations, the suggestion of an abstract relationship between C-models and P-models does not eliminate the need for experimental confirmation of claims about linguistic knowledge. Linguistic arguments alone do not provide sufficient basis for a claim that speakers know the structures posited by a grammar, even with the reservation that the grammar does not stipulate how such knowledge is used. Even Fodor and Garrett (1966) agree that the structural descriptions of a grammar should mark the "psychologically real syntactic relations—the relations in terms of which sentences are understood" (p. 142). By this test, however, a given T-G grammar could be overturned if there were no evidence that it described the structural analyses speakers must make to produce or interpret sentences or make judgments about ambiguity, synonymy, and so on. Or rather, there would be two theoretical possibilities open to the researcher: (1) to save the theory (linguistic C-model) by arguing that speakers must be assumed to perform those structural analyses postulated by a grammar, attributing lack of experimental confirmation to a faulty P-model, or (2) to change the linguistic C-model. The first alternative might appeal to a convinced T-G linguist, but psychologists have tended, in the face of disconfirming evidence, to look for alternate C-models.

Models of semantic grammar have been of particular interest to psychologists because they are more consistent with available performance data than theories based on Chomsky's model of underlying syntactic structure. The experiments on transformations underlined the central role of semantic structures. These, rather than syntactic complexity, seem to correlate with levels of performance. Furthermore, the earlier studies of deep syntactic relations (Blumenthal, 1967; Blumenthal and Boakes, 1967) did not attempt to distinguish between deep structure syntactic and semantic roles. Thus, the results of these experiments are consistent with the hypothesis that recall is facilitated if prompted by the key *semantic,* rather than syntactic, structure used in processing sentences. Healy and Levitt (1978) tested this hypothesis by performing experiments on recognition memory and concept formation to determine the relative accessibilities of deep structure syntactic, deep structure semantic (Fillmore's 1971 categories of experiencer and goal), and surface structure syntactic concepts. They concluded that deep structure syntactic concepts are less accessible than deep structure semantic concepts. Healy (1978) noted that the experiment "casts doubt on the psychological reality of the syntactic level of deep structure ... [and] suggest[s] that the concept of deep-structure syntax should not be incorporated in a model of linguistic performance ... [or in] the most appropriate models of linguistic knowledge, or competence" (p. 484).

The semantic deep structures posited by linguists (and by some psychologists) have also been of interest because they seem to make a strong connection with theories of cognitive development, especially Piaget's model. Psychologists such as I. M. Schlesinger (1971), Dan Slobin (1970, 1971a), Melissa Bowerman (1973), and Lois Bloom (1970, 1973) have interpreted semantic categories as cognitive structures that have been mapped into specific lexical or grammatical forms or classes of forms. Thus, semantic deep structures correspond to linguistically encoded representations of types of states of affairs. (Speakers need not be explicitly conscious, however, of the nature of the categories or paradigms that have been linguistically encoded. They need not, that is, have a conscious knowledge of the semantic system of their language.) The aim of empirical research has been to establish that speakers actually do match certain cognitive categories with specific linguistic structures and to discover how they acquire a paradigmatic system adequate for their communicative needs. In the area of developmental psycholinguistics, Piaget's theory of cognitive development has seemed to predict the basic cognitive structures that serve as semantic paradigms at a given stage of development. That language acquisition is, in part, predicted by a cognitive theory of this type has lent considerable support to theories of semantic grammar

In Chapters 3 and 4 I shall present evidence that speakers acquire a semantic grammar on the basis of their experience, partly as a function of cognitive development, and that speakers possess language in the form of paradigmatic structures rather than generative rules.

CHAPTER 3

Acquisition of
Lexical Paradigms

Psychologists still do not agree on the process by which children acquire semantic categories, nor do they agree on the proper interpretation of early one- and two-word utterances. Still, a great deal of research has been done on these questions since the turn of the century, and at this point it is possible to make some very good estimates of the normal course of semantic development. As I shall use the term, a semantic category is a cognitive structure that underlies and regulates the use of linguistic signs in referential acts. Theories that posit the existence of such categories must describe them and explain both how they are acquired and in what ways they underlie and regulate speech. At this point, no complete theory has been developed, but the most plausible view is, I think, that the earliest semantic categories are experiential (perceptually derived) paradigms or "focusing instances" matched with linguistic forms. The precise form in which paradigms might be stored in memory is a subject on which I shall not speculate, although the Piagetian notion of experiential schemas may lead in a fruitful direction.[1]

1. Joseph Church (1961) provides a particularly clear definition of Piaget's concept of a schema: "Stated logically rather than psychologically, a schema is an implicit principle by which we organize experience. Psychologically, the schema has two faces. On the environmental side, we become sensitive to regularities in the way things are constituted and act, so that we perceive the environment as coherent and orderly.... On the organismic side, schemata exist in our mobilizations to act and react, which in turn reflect the environmental properties to which we are sensitive" (pp. 36–37).

It has been suggested that there are two sorts of early one-word utterances: those tied to children's perceptual schemas, such as 'doggie', and those tied to action schemas, such as 'walk' (getting out of a cart). See, for example, Hermina Sinclair (1970).

A few examples will illustrate common patterns that have been observed in the lexical usage of young children. The Russian psychologist Lev Vygotsky (1934) reported that over a period of 182 days a child used the word 'bow-wow' to refer to the following objects or situations: a china figurine of a girl, a dog barking in a yard, pictures of grandparents, a toy dog, a clock, a fur piece with an animal's head and glass eyes, a fur stole without a head, a rubber doll that squeaked, a father's cuff links, pearl buttons on a dress, and a bath thermometer. His interpretation of this pattern was that the child was primarily struck by an oblong shape or a shiny surface resembling eyes (an analysis that for some reason leaves out the furriness or noisiness of the stimulus). Roman Jakobson (1968) reports the following pattern in the speech of a one-year-old child, as observed by his father, Antoine Gregoire: "Edmund appeared to call back his mother, absent for the day, by saying 'mam-am-am', but it is 'papa' which he declared when he saw her return.... Edm. saw me prepare a slice of bread for him; he said 'mama', and not 'papa'."[2] Jakobson's analysis of this pattern is that 'papa' refers to a parent who is present, while 'mama' requests the fulfillment of a need or the presence of a parent who can fulfill a need. Heinz Werner (1948) described a child's use of 'afta' to refer to a drinking glass, a pane of glass, a window, and the contents of a glass. Jean Piaget (1946) observed this pattern in a (French-speaking) child's use of 'aplu': "T. at 1;5 [one year, five months] uses the term *aplu* to indicate a departure, then to indicate the throwing of an object onto the floor, then applied to an object that falls over (without disappearing), for instance, when he is playing with building blocks. A little later *aplu* means 'remoteness' (anything out of reach) and then the game of handing over an object for somebody to throw it back to him. Finally, at 1;7 *aplu* takes on the meaning of 'to start over again'."[3] M. M. Lewis (1951) made a detailed analysis of his child's developing animal names that illustrated a neat pattern of overgeneralizations gradually overcome as new terms were introduced. For example, between the ages of 21 months and 24 months, the child referred at some point to cats, cows, horses, and small dogs as 'tee', a contraction

2. Jakobson (1968) is reporting the findings of Antoine Gregoire (1937).
3. Quoted by Sinclair (1970), p. 125.

of "Timothy," their cat's name. As another example, Werner Leopold (1948) described in detail the semantic development of his daughter Hildegard, providing an analysis I find extremely persuasive. "Hildegard and her younger sister Karla both made excessive use of the word *pretty,* not because a strong power of abstraction allowed them to subsume a great number of impressions under one abstract concept, but because they lacked specific terms for many things.... Karla dropped, Hildegard reduced the use of *pretty* as soon as a more adequate vocabulary had been acquired" (p. 97). Similarly, for four months (age 17 months to age 21 months), Hildegard "called an older girl, who visited her occasionally, by her name, Rita, but used the same name for Rita's friend Helen. The latter never came without Rita..." (p. 99).

How might one account for such lexical patterns? First, one wants to know what function these words serve from the child's viewpoint. In particular, do these words simply accompany some action or behavior, or are they signs that the child intentionally uses to refer to something? Again, if the signs are intentionally used, are they simply the functional equivalent of a pointing gesture, or are they names matched with some particular paradigm? To say that the signs are names is to suggest that the child recognizes that certain words draw attention to certain things, or that things have names. These questions have arisen in developmental psycholinguistics, a field in which researchers are called upon to identify the point at which true language begins in infancy and to characterize the semantic deep structure of holophrastic and radically incomplete child utterances. To do this, psychologists are attempting to develop criteria, based on a child's behavior in concrete situations, for determining the form of a child's referring intention.

Investigators in this field generally agree that there is a difference between infantile cries that merely signal some internal state, such as hunger, pain, or comfort, and a combination of sounds and gestures that indicate an environmental entity or situation. In some cases it is difficult to tell if an infant is using a sign to refer or if a sign is simply a sort of reflex response to some internal or environmental stimulus. Yet it is clear that at some point an infant develops a referential pattern. As one would expect, there is disagreement about which utterances count as "first words." There is surprising agreement, however, that the language function *begins* (in a primitive form) with an intentional act of reference.

In characterizing infantile behavior as referential, one is, of course, interpreting the concept of referring very broadly. In fact, the earliest and most central aspect of reference seems to be simply focusing one's own (and later, another's) attention on some aspect of a situation. This broad referential function (as focusing attention or "framing" some aspect of the world) may be similar to what A. R. Luria (1959) called a "directive function" of speech. Early reference in a child is presumably "intentional" only in the sense that the child is paying conscious attention to the referent and the sign that carries the function is voluntary. It is only later in development that children become aware of the *act* of reference as having social effect (directing the attention of others) and, later still, of conventional verbal means for carrying out various referring intentions.

Most of the researchers in this area have taken the pointing gesture of young children as the first sign of reference. The psychologist Wilhelm Wundt, for example, believed that pointing gestures formed the first stage in the phylogenetic development of human speech. Vygotsky (1934), referring to William Stern's theory of an "intentionality function" as "directedness toward a certain content, or meaning," believed that the child's first words translate a pointing gesture, which already indicates intentionality or directed attention. As he put it, "The word, at first, is a conventional substitute for the gesture; it appears long before the child's crucial 'discovery of language' [the discovery at around age one and a half or two that things have names that can be used in referring].... The inescapable conclusion would be that pointing is, in fact, a precursor of the 'intentional tendency'" (p. 30). Once children learn that things have names, they show the new behavior of asking for the names of things, and their vocabulary increases rapidly.[4] More recently, Elizabeth Bates (1976) has restated the argument for this sort of

---

4. Jerome Bruner (1966) indicates another "turn" in linguistic development occurs when children ask what unfamiliar words mean, which, Bruner suggests,

referential interpretation of children's pointing gestures and suggested that words are later inserted into the referential schema first carried out by pointing (pp. 102–3).

Additional support for a referential (as opposed to a symptomatic) interpretation of pointing gestures comes from Roman Jakobson and Morris Halle's (1956) observations of aphasics suffering what they call "similarity disorder" (that is, a defect in performing linguistic acts of substitution—providing synonyms on demand). Jakobson and Halle claim:

> The aphasic with a defect in substitution will not supplement the pointing or handling gesture of the examiner with the name of the object pointed to. Instead of saying "This is [called] a pencil," he will merely add an elliptical note about its use: "To write." If one of the synonymic signs is present (as for instance the word *bachelor* or the pointing to the pencil) then the other sign (such as the phrase *unmarried man* or the word *pencil*) becomes redundant and consequently superfluous. For the aphasic, both signs are in complementary distribution; . . . "I understand everything" or "Ich weiss es schon" will be his typical reaction. Likewise, the picture of an object will cause suppression of its name: a verbal sign is supplanted by a pictorial sign. [p. 66]

This observation suggests, in the terms of Jakobson's model of the paradigmatic (vertical) and syntagmatic (horizontal) structure of language, that pointing gestures and words or expressions stand in a paradigmatic relation to one another: they may be substituted for one another in the same linguistic or situational "frame" because they serve the same referential function. The aphasic suffering an inability to make paradigmatic substitutions, on Jakobson's account, simply finds the use of one sign to perform the same function as another superfluous.

Not all observers agree that the pointing gesture marks the first referential function in child behavior. For example, Hans

---

indicates a realization that words have a categorical meaning. Of five-year-olds he said, "Their 'What's that?' is increasingly directed to unfamiliar words that are being used and to the unfamiliar senses in which familiar words are being used" (p. 32).

Hörmann (1971) gives as an example of early reference (which he calls "quasi-predication") the case of a baby reaching for a ball (grasping gesture) and whimpering. Hörmann says the coordination of the gesture and sound means something like "Mommie, give me the ball" (p. 286). Later on, Hörmann says, the child will reach for the ball and say something like "ball" or "want" thus producing something like a sentence or a contextually complete statement. Perhaps this example of semantic analysis points up the difficulty of evaluating claims about the referring intentions that might be attributed to early child speech and gesture. Despite the complexity of the problem, most researchers agree that criteria used to identify early language should mark the presence of a referring intention. The pointing gesture is usually taken as referential because of its developmental history (growing out of the orienting or attentional behavior of the child) and because it is a deliberate gesture.[5]

The same paradigm of referential function underlies the various criteria used by psychologists to identify a child's first words. For example, Bates (1976) infers an "intention to communicate" from, among other things, "the emission of some movement or sound in which eye contact is alternated between the object and the adult" (p. 51). The idea is that in genuine speech the child is attempting to use the sound or word to direct the listener's attention toward some object and checks the listener's gaze to make sure that the reference has carried through. Similarly, Lois Bloom (1974) takes a child's shift of gaze toward some object in response to an "acoustic event" (hearing the name of the object) as evidence of recognition of a link between word and object. Shift of gaze, gestural accompaniment, controlled intonation, persistence of behavior, and so on, are commonly taken as indi-

5. I find it illuminating to contrast the structure of the grasping and pointing gesture as follows: in a grasping gesture the eye serves as a tool guiding the hand, and the hand is used as a tool to reach some object; while in a pointing gesture the hand is used as a tool serving the eye, as it focuses on some object. In either case, the focus is not on the hand (the tool), but on the object of desire or attention that is the direct or indirect target of the gesture. At first, in the pointing gesture, the object stands simply as a focus of a child's own attention. When pointing takes on a communicative function, the gesture serves to focus the object for someone else.

ces of a communicative, referring intention, and therefore of genuine speech.

While it is generally agreed that first words must be referential in a broad sense, there is still disagreement about additional conditions such words must meet. Thus, Bates (1976) reports a discrepancy between her finding that the "first words with clear-cut referents are in fact declaratives or labels" and the findings of others (Piaget, for example) that "the first words by children are imperatives" (p. 77). The explanation she gives is that these discrepancies may result "from a failure to distinguish words with referents from wordlike signals without referents, used to serve performative functions" (p. 77). Bates appears to assume at least two things in making this judgment. First, she is claiming that genuine words must stand for some referent by way of some semantic representation or concept that captures the defining or central features of the object-class in question.[6] This assumption leads Bates to require, as strong evidence of genuinely referential speech, that a word be used to "depict an object or event in a variety of contexts" (p. 75). Using this criterion, Bates finds that the earliest instances of what Piaget called

6. See the discussion in Bates (1976), pp. 72–78. Bates notes, "It is difficult to specify the exact moment at which sounds are used to map an underlying symbol structure" (p. 77). By a "symbol" she means a sign related to the thing it stands for by an arbitrary bond agreed upon by those using the symbol (p. 2). In contrast to Bates, I would not define a symbol as "standing for" something else or require that symbols be mediated by some semantic paradigm. My disagreement with Bates on the characterization of referential symbols may be entirely "semantic," except I believe she confuses two questions: (1) whether a child using some sign *intends* to refer (point to or draw attention to some object) and (2) whether a child is aware that different words will draw attention to different referents, or that things have names. In her discussion, she does not consider the possibility that children might intend to refer (case 1) without using particular signs to "symbolize" particular referents (case 2). In my view, the use of the *same* sound to draw attention to *different* objects is parallel to the use of the same gesture (pointing) to draw attention to different objects. Both of these operations are intentional acts, yet Bates's schema does not permit a distinction between an intentional use of a sign that is not a name and a case in which some word-sound simply *accompanies* some act or gesture. Her only distinction is between these nonintentional ritualized components of acts and cases in which a *different* word is used consistently to draw attention to (or, she says, "stand for") *different* objects. It is possible, however, that children first use some verbal sign to refer to different things, with no underlying paradigm, and gradually learn to use different words to refer to different things.

imperatives, ranging from relatively natural sounds to more or less arbitrary signals, occur in a great variety of situations, having only the "subjective activities of the child" in common. For example, one of her subjects developed the sound 'na-na' in any situation of need, from wanting an object to calling an adult from another room. In Bates's words, "This *na-na* is similar in usage to the first word of Piaget's daughter Jacqueline, who used *Panama* ('grandpa') to express any desire or need regardless of the presence or absence of the grandfather himself" (Piaget, 1962, p. 73). Piaget interpreted this word as the child's first. The criterion Bates uses reveals her second assumption, which is that referential categories are necessarily "objective" rather than "subjective" (or functional). Against such a view, a Piagetian would certainly object that action schemas deriving from "the subjective activities of the child" provide categories that are as essential as those based on "objective" perceptual schemas.

Perhaps a clearer account of early varieties of speech can be found in M. M. Lewis (1937), who distinguished three functions in the earliest child utterances: (*a*) to accompany some action; (*b*) to declare something or, more accurately, to draw the attention of others to some object; and (*c*) to manipulate or draw attention to some object as a demand that some need in relation to that object be satisfied. The second case Lewis described sounds like Bates's "declaratives": the use of a word to draw attention to some object. I see no reason, however, to assume that the earliest declarative words are names guided by a "semantic representation" as Bates requires. It is plausible that very early sounds may be verbal equivalents of pointing gestures: intentional but not semantic. Lewis's third case, a manipulative use of words, sounds like Piaget's imperative. If one does not require that genuine words be guided by semantic paradigms, or by perceptual rather than functional schemas, then the only difficulty in deciding whether such utterances are referential in a broad sense lies in determining whether they serve an intentional function. To count as words, they must be used as tools to direct the attention of a listener toward something that concerns the child (for example, hunger or discomfort, or some object the child desires, wants taken away, etc.). Sounds that simply signal some internal state of the child do not serve a referential function.

Lewis's first case of speech that simply accompanies some action parallels Bates's discussion of wordlike sounds that accompany acts as part of a ritual. Both Lewis and Bates characterize such sounds as nonreferential performances. The interpretive difficulty, for observers, is distinguishing such ritualized sounds from sounds that, while accompanying an action or gesture (such as pointing) do serve an independent referential function.

Lewis (1937) emphasized the central role of a child's instrumental use of language in the development of referential categories. Early categories might be as relatively undifferentiated as, for example, "objects desired or requested" and "novel objects or events," which one child reported by Bates (1976) indicated through 'Mn' and 'Ay' respectively. However, sounds that start out as ritual accompaniments may also gradually become the names Bates says are "inserted into prepared performative structures" (p. 72). For example, Bates (1976) reports that one twelve-month-old child consistently said 'bam' when knocking over towers or messing up arrangements of toys and, at twelve months, six days, she "started approaching her toy piano, orienting for the position of banging on the keys. Before she reached the piano, she said *Bam* two or three times" (p. 74).

Sounds ritually accompanying activities might also be an important source of a child's comprehension and use of words serving a referential function.[7] For example, if the parents of the child Bates described (Carlotta) wanted to draw her attention to something that she could bang on, they could use her word ('bam') to express this intention. Similarly, if they wanted to draw her attention to her tricycle, or something else that could be ridden, they might say 'brr' (a sound Carlotta habitually produced while riding). Since parents are likely to give children such ritual sounds in the first place, they may well be predisposed to treat these sounds as names. (Bates notes that Carlotta picked up 'bam' and 'brr' from adults who used them when she

7. In this context, one thinks of Joseph Church's (1961) remark about the first words of a human child: "It is probable that the child's first speech occurs without any intention of speech, but it leads to a discovery in himself of a power of speech. . . ." (pp. 86–87).

knocked things down and rode her tricycle.) Moreover, since adults frequently point to things as they name them for children, the connection between the sounds and a pointing gesture might convey to children the referential potential of words (at least once children grasp the intentional function of pointing).

Once children learn that words can be used to focus attention, whether one's own (the directive function of speech) or a listener's (the communicative function of declarative and imperative speech), they are able to discover the important fact that *certain* words draw attention to *certain* things. As this is usually put, children learn that things have names. Once children recognize this, they must discover what these names are. They must also overcome errors in naming that result from faulty categorical judgments. In this task the child will receive much help from parents, who will assume that the child is attempting to name things and will correct usage that departs from the adult pattern. The child will also be passively assisted by hearing the patterns in adult speech.

I believe that one might account for early patterns in children's referential use of names in the following way. The child hears and understands the referential function of a word in some situation (as indicated by such signs of attention as appropriate shift of gaze) and attaches that word to the referent as a label or name. At this point, the referent is an unarticulated or global situation or event with aspects in which the child is especially interested and other aspects, of little importance, that remain in a sort of murky and undifferentiated background. For example, 'Mommie' might be the name of the warm and comforting presence that tends to the child's needs; 'Bow-wow' might be the label of a beady-eyed, noisy and furry apparition (or perhaps a warm and licking one); and Leopold's daughter Hildegard's 'Rita' might refer to anything that is part of visits by Rita, including Rita's not-very-significant friend Helen. Similarly, 'up' might refer to the event of things moving up; 'more' might name recurrence or another instance of something (that the child wants or simply notices); 'pretty' could label anything the child admires; and 'no' might name whatever the child dislikes or rejects ("That's a no-no"). Presumably, a number of factors determine those aspects of the world to which a child will pay particular attention and which will therefore have the greatest weight in categorical judgments. Among these aspects will be, certainly, those to which attention is frequently drawn by speakers around the child, events in a child's experience that are strikingly novel, unusual, or emotionally significant, and features of an environment or situation that are biologically or developmentally (cognitively) salient.

In naming things, a child must match a referent with a very restricted set of paradigms, that is, representations of an original focusing event, although there may be many experiences that are not particularly close to the focus of any category. The child must decide which paradigm is closest in type, or most similar to, a given referent.[8] However, since objects, events, and unanalyzed or global states of affairs are potentially similar to more than one sort of thing, the process of category formation underlying early naming is probably influenced by several factors. For example, human objects are undoubtedly preadapted to focus on or respond to certain environmental features or stimuli.[9] Such features might be common dimensions along which similarity is observed. Further, a number of studies in category formation have shown that such factors as cognitive (developmental) level, education, and a subject's experience with and interest in certain aspects or types of objects have a strong influence on

8. In addition to this "correct" approach to the categorical problem, Vygotsky (1934) described a number of associative patterns that he believed accounted for many aspects of early child language. Among these patterns, discovered through a nonverbal classification test, were syncretic "heaps" linking things together by chance, and "chain complexes" and "diffuse complexes." In chain complexes the basis of association might change several times so that there are no common properties, while in diffuse complexes there is an even more "fluid" or undefined associative link between any two parts. A simple chain might involve a switch from shape to color as a basis for classification; whereas a diffuse complex might lead from triangles to trapezoids to squares to hexagons to semicircles to circles.

9. Examples of such features or stimuli are the squares, lines, etc., that trigger individual neurons in the visual cortex of neonate kittens and monkeys (Hubel and Wiesel, 1962, 1963, 1965, 1968) or the lines and contours that are especially significant stimuli to the human brain (Hubel, 1963). Eleanor Rosch Heider (1972) has found evidence that there is a universal set of focal colors, which suggests a biological basis for the organization of color categories.

the sorts of perceptual classifications an individual will make.[10] Whereas one subject might group things together as most similar because they all serve the same function (as tools or clothing), another might group together all the red or blue things, and still another all the round or oblong (or fast, slow, noisy, or quiet) things. The child primarily concerned with subjective sensations of pleasure and pain is more apt to focus on the feature of "helpful or pleasing adults" as a dimension of similarity than on relatively uninteresting objective features that might be used to distinguish various adults.

Children's naming patterns become increasingly stable and consistent with an adult system as their original paradigms are modified and as they acquire more categories. As children hear a certain word used repeatedly to refer to some entities but not to others (and as their own usage is corrected), the linguistically significant features emerge as those possessed by members of a set, while other features are ruled out by objects not commonly possessing them. Thus, linguistic experience should modify the weight, or saliency of features, that determines a given categorical judgment.

The other important factor determining categorical judgment is the expansion of vocabulary and hence the acquisition of new paradigms. Many observers have noted a direct correlation between vocabulary expansion and the increasing predictability of children's naming patterns. For example, Lewis's (1951) study of his child's animal names revealed that the original category 'tee', which first included cats, cows, horses, large and small dogs, and a toy dog, was differentiated into several categories as the child was given new terms (which the child pronounced 'pushie', 'hosh', 'biggie-goggie', and so on). Once a new name is learned, the old name is dropped. Lenneberg (1971) commented on the same pattern in children's acquisition of sensory words, such as color terms: "As long as a child has just one or two words for

10. See Bruner, Olver, and Greenfield, eds. (1966) and Cole and Scribner (1974) for original studies and summaries of relevant data. See also the very interesting studies by David Olson (1970a, 1970b). Olson's work suggests that the aspects of an object or situation on which one focuses, or which will be salient, will depend on the type of action one is called on to perform with respect to that situation.

color, he uses them rather randomly. But when he has four or five color words, his usage suddenly becomes normalized; the relational system has been established, and now the only difference between his usage and that of the adult is that his individual color categories are still somewhat wider than those in the adult system" (pp. 8-9). A final example comes from Leopold (1948), who observed that once Hildegard developed a more adequate vocabulary for expressing emotional or admiring reactions to things, she reduced her use of 'pretty'. In general, he claims, in child language, "meanings become progressively sharper and closer to the standard" as vocabulary increases (pp. 97-98).

An obvious explanation of the correlation between vocabulary expansion and normal lexical patterns is that the new words provide new paradigms or foci against which similarity can be measured, and thus the boundaries of the original paradigms are limited. For example, a horse is more like a large dog than a cat, but it is most like a 'hosh'; that is, it has more salient features in common with one paradigm than with others. Thus, the acquisition of additional paradigms and the modification of paradigms through reference should produce increasingly predictable or normal patterns of naming. This is merely to say that the child's pattern of naming will conform increasingly to a standard adult pattern as a function of the gradually elaborated paradigm system the child has acquired.

It should be emphasized that, since objects or events may be similar in a number of ways, the aspects that are significant for comparison in a given language can vary in a number of seemingly arbitrary ways. Thus, features that mark a significant difference in one categorical system may be overlooked in another. For example, Leopold noticed that Hildegard, who spoke both English and German, referred to a painter's brush as 'Bürste' rather than 'Pinsel', a usage incorrect in German, which has a special word for painters' brushes, but quite correct in English, which classes painters' brushes along with hairbrushes, clothes brushes, toothbrushes, and so on, because of their common brushing function. The speaker who has acquired a specific paradigmatic system unconsciously focuses on those aspects of objects that represent a significant basis for comparison within the system or that are the common distinctive features of members of some referent class that has been introduced and narrowed down during the naming period. I shall have more to say about the distinctive features of elaborated semantic paradigms under "The Formation of Classes" in Chapter 8.

Of course, an adult system of categories does not embody an absolute standard of consistency since it contains homonyms and idioms that must be quite confusing to a child. Furthermore, semantic interpretation depends in part on the grammatical function assigned to a given form. Thus, English-speaking children must learn that 'glass' names both a substance and things made from it, that one can both 'train' a dog and ride a 'train,' that a 'chicken' both lays eggs and is a coward, and that a 'yellow' dress can 'yellow' from mildew. The acquisition of a semantic system is further complicated by the fact that semantic categories are ordinarily not defined in explicit logical terms but are, rather, understood through paradigms in a way that leaves room for borderline cases.

Paradigmatic categorizing involves two very different judgments about category membership. One is about the degree of similarity between some instance and a paradigm along specific criterial dimensions. For example, if a system of color terms distinguishes colors according to saturation or intensity, some color of medium intensity, standing somewhere between an intense and a faint variant of the same hue, might be a borderline case. Speakers might hesitate in classifying the color as, for example, light red or deep pink. The second judgment is about categorical criteria rather than about the properties of some referent. For example, speakers may disagree about whether some edible object is a vegetable or a fruit, whether some piece of furniture is a chair or a stool, or whether some doctrine or practice is religious. This kind of judgment is necessary whenever a referent possesses some but not all of the features of a certain paradigm for which there is no logical definition. One must either decide on a definition or assign the troublesome case to the category to which it bears the greatest resemblance without attempting to produce explicit criteria of category membership.

Doubts about categorical criteria reflect the original process of category formation. I have suggested that children learn to disregard highly variable features of items within a category and that they make categorical judgments by matching an item with the paradigm with which it shares the greatest number of significant features. There is, then, no guarantee that all members of a given category will possess an identical set of features, though some adult categories may be more consistent than others. As children acquire categories, they are, in a sense, receiving information about linguistic (social) decisions that have already been made with respect to a range of common experiences and in terms of a given set of paradigms. Once children's categories have stabilized and after they have developed a feeling for the invariant or at least highly predictable features significant for classifying referents, they must continue the social process of making judgments for novel and possibly difficult cases. They must, in short, contribute to a general consensus, or an ongoing dispute, about category membership or, on an analytic level, the "proper" definition of some category.

If it should happen that the significant features of one category (such as, animal) are also invariant features of some other categories (such as horses or dogs), one can formalize such categorical relations in a hierarchical system expressed by such logical statements as "All horses are animals." The set of significant features that distinguish one category from other categories (for example, animals from vegetables and horses from dogs) may be called distinctive features. Of course, only some of the significant features of a category will distinguish that category from all others. For example, Lewis's child discovered, in effect, that although dogs and cats and horses were similar in various ways, there were also specific differences that counted in distinguishing a 'pushie' (reduced category including the cat 'tee') from a 'hosh' or a 'biggie-goggie'. An elaborated paradigm should provide a schema of features that are critical in distinguishing objects of one type from objects of another type. Though one may be able to determine category membership easily if a referent possesses all of the relevant critical features of a category, there still will be, as I noted, unclear cases whenever an object lacks one or more features. A new animal species, for example, that is very close to an existing one but that could also create a new category, or a world view which is neither clearly religious nor secular might be unclear cases.

Eve Clark's (1975) theory of "partially overextended terms" in children's speech (between the ages of one year and two years, six months) is similar in some respects to a model of focusing paradigms. Clark has recently shifted from her position (1971, 1973a) that children's categories are fully overextended to the theory of partial overextensions. Originally she believed that children initially attribute an incomplete set of criterial attributes to terms that are then overextended to include all entities possessing those features. For example, the child who refers to dogs, horses, cows, and sheep as 'doggie' has defined the class perhaps in terms of "having four legs" along with other features of movement and texture. These features constitute the sole meaning of the term for the child. Clark (1975) proposes that children may attribute a complete set of features to a term, but pick out only some of those criterial properties in overextending the word to a new case. Thus a child may recognize all the properties of a dog that define 'doggie', while referring to horses and cows also by this term because they have at least some of the criterial attributes of the class.

The theory of partially overextended terms, based on studies indicating fewer overextensions in comprehension tests than in productions (Huttenlocher, 1974), is consistent with an empiricist model of elaborated paradigms, although the language Clark uses conjures up a pupil in the school of Thomas Gradgrind. (Gradgrind's students learned, for example, that a 'horse' is "Quadruped. Graminivorous. Forty teeth, namely 24 grinders, 4 eye-teeth, and 12 incisive. Sheds coat in the spring; in marshy countries, sheds hoofs too. Hoofs hard, but requiring to be shod with iron. Age known by marks in mouth"—Charles Dickens, *Hard Times*). Without taking literally the view that children are engaged in the activity of constructing a dictionary, one may interpret Clark's new theory as saying that children begin with a concrete paradigm that may include all of the criterial features determining a category and, in the absence of closer matches, they may, often hesitantly, overextend terms to cases possessing at least some of the requisite features.

I should note that the model of paradigm formation I have outlined is oversimplified in a number of ways. In particular, adults possess a great deal of purely verbal knowledge, frequently using terms that have, for them, merely a formal or nominal meaning. One speaks of quasars and atoms and so on without necessarily having formed any experiential paradigms. Again, speakers class together things like whales and cows, or Saint Bernards and poodles, not because they judge them similar in relation to a given schema, but simply because they have learned that cows and whales are mammals, and poodles and Saint Bernards are dogs. They need not be able to define 'mammal' or 'dog' or 'canine' to class things in this way.

A number of psychologists have made tentative proposals about the referential basis of early semantic categories, but more empirical work is necessary to discover exactly how such categories might be stored in memory, retrieved when necessary, and modified through the course of time. I have suggested that the first paradigms are representations of focusing events matched with names, but it remains for psychologists to work out the details of this approach and to subject hypotheses to empirical testing. For example, it is not clear what role associations play in the elaboration of initial paradigms. Successive acts of reference might have the effect of strengthening an associative bond between some name and those aspects or features that are predictably found in a referent. Repetition might have a sievelike effect, causing those features that do not often recur to be dropped from memory and those that do recur to be retained in a schema. Thus, such accidental features of, say, dogs and cats and horses as their space-time location, color, or stance should be, in effect, set aside as features that do not count in identifying objects of that type. At the same time, as speakers are introduced to new terms in new focusing situations, these new paradigms might modify the original set by filtering out those significant features that are common to several categories and are thus not distinctive. Whatever the nature of the mechanisms involved in acquiring a semantic system, it is clear that a speaker must intend a categorical use of terms. Associations may be involved in an unconscious process of forming paradigms, but in selecting a term one doesn't simply associate from some perceptual schema to a name. Rather, one intends to classify an object in a specific way and to refer to that object in terms that will identify it in some context.

Several recent studies of category formation have a particular bearing on the model of lexical paradigms I have proposed. Eleanor Rosch and her associates have developed an influential theory of "natural categories" based on a number of studies concerned with the psychological reality of so-called fuzzy sets[11] (Rosch, 1975; Rosch and Mervis, 1975; Rosch, Mervis, Gray, Johnson, and Boyes-Braem, 1976). The major argument is that the first categories children learn will be "basic object categories," which are founded in physical reality as the "most discriminable" kinds of objects. Moreover, such "natural" categories will evolve with fuzzy (indeterminate) boundaries and degrees of prototypicality measured in relation to some prototype that might be a kind of generic or composite object having superior "imageability."

Rosch's theory has been interpreted as evidence against Benjamin Whorf's hypothesis that language determines or strongly influences thought. (see Brown, 1978; Bowerman, 1976.) From a somewhat different angle, Whorfian theory has been opposed to the "cognition hypothesis" (Cromer, 1974), which is the broad view held by Piagetians and other developmental psychologists that independent cognitive categories or structures (sensorimotor schemas, for example) are the original basic categories mapped into lexical and grammatical forms. Thus, language is structured by thought, which reflects a genetically based developmental pattern.

Finally, a number of studies of early lexical patterns (especially overextensions and occasional underextensions of terms) have tried to isolate features that might be highly salient to children and that thus would strongly influence their categorical judgments. Eve Clark (1973a, 1974, 1975) claims that shape, espe-

11. Rosch's "fuzzy sets" are similar to my "focus categories" or "paradigms" in allowing degrees of prototypicality and uncertain ("fuzzy") boundaries, unlike "logical" categories. My explanation of these properties of nonlogical categories differs from Rosch's, however. My own ideas on the subject were first expressed in 1973 (*"A Descriptive Approach to Linguistic Meaning,"* unpublished manuscript) in response to Vygotsky's discussion of children's lexical categories.

cially roundness and length, seems to "provide the primary basis for overextension" (Clark, 1975, p. 82). Movement, size, sound, and texture also seem to be important features, while a few overextensions are based on taste. Color was not a significant factor for the children Clark studied, who were between the ages of one year and two years, six months. In addition to these perceptual factors, Clark isolated salient functional features determining action categories (such as 'open' and 'allgone'). In general, Clark's view is that perceptual rather than functional features are most salient in the case of object (versus action) categories. In contrast, Katherine Nelson (1973a, 1974) found that even in the case of object categories, children between 12 and 15 months were influenced more by functional than perceptual features in choosing members of some class. (The 1974 study explicitly tested this claim in the way Clark [1975] had suggested in criticism of Nelson's earlier study.) Nelson (1973b) also found evidence of a difference in "cognitive style" between children who saw language primarily as a referential tool, for whom "objective" properties of objects were most salient, and children who tended to use language to express feelings and achieve social contact, for whom "subjective" emotional or social factors were most significant. (see Bowerman, 1976, pp. 120–23.)

I think the model of paradigm formation I have outlined provides the most plausible interpretation of the actual data on early categorical judgments. First, the language Rosch uses in characterizing some categories as "natural" if they represent some "most discriminable, basic objects" suggests a type of naive realism. I am not certain whether Rosch would consider herself a realist, but it is difficult to avoid such an interpretation. If she is claiming that perception is essentially a passive process of recording objects, events, and states of affairs that exist in their own right exactly as we perceive them and to which our ideas correspond whenever they provide a kind of picture of this independent reality, then she is subject to a host of philosophical objections. Such objections need not be decisive, but as a scientist she ought to provide at least some indication of how one might verify claims that are ultimately philosophical. On the other hand, Rosch may be saying simply that human beings are biologically predisposed to notice or record certain kinds of perceptual features. Such a claim would be consistent with her discovery (Heider, 1972) of a universal set of color foci and with other research establishing biologically based priorities in category formation and need not imply any metaphysical claims about "natural kinds" as (Kantian) noumenal entities.

However, if Rosch is actually saying that the first categories learned by children will be those reflecting biologically determined saliency, the claim seems in part true and in part rather doubtful. It seems obvious that children's first lexical categories will reflect what is in broad terms salient to the child. This view is implied by the cognition hypothesis (that early speech encodes sensorimotor schemas that become salient in experience at a given developmental point), and one might even take the fact that a given linguistic category has been acquired by a young child as evidence for the saliency of the cognitive structure it expresses. On the other hand, though the exact meaning of a "natural category" is vague, there is reason to doubt that the earliest lexical categories are determined solely or even primarily by a perceptual "feature detection system." As I have indicated, there is evidence that early categories are influenced by several factors, including, but not limited to, perceptually salient features. Children may be influenced by functional features reflecting either emerging "action schemas" or their own individual (and variable) functional interests. Brown (1958) discovered that parents in a given society tend to select the same kinds of words in speaking to children and suggested that they anticipate the "functional structure" of a child's world. For example, mothers choose such labels as 'dog' or 'cat' rather than 'animal' because they express categorical distinctions that will be useful to the child. Brown understands the usefulness of categories in behavioral terms: a child must respond in different ways to different types of animals; therefore it is useful to the child to distinguish among these types. Since these functional distinctions are not "objectively" or biologically determined, one expects to find some individual as well as social variation in the saliency of potentially significant features. Even Rosch tacitly admits this point in assuming that subordinate categories in a standard semantic system, which may have more features than their superordinate "basic object" terms (for example, beagle versus dog) will not be the first categories acquired by children because such distinctions have no functional significance at that point.

Rosch's model of categories may also be subject to the traditional arguments against John Locke's theory of a "generic image," which are summarized under "The Arguments against Classical Empiricism" in Chapter 8. As I understand her position, basic object categories are determined by a prototype that is a highly discriminable "composite image" formed by repeated exposure to objects in a way determined either biologically or by the nature of physical reality. Presumably, more abstract categories (animal, fruit) are acquired later, as an image having fewer attributes (a more abstract generic image) is formed. Thus, objects that are very similar to these composite images will be judged to belong to a given category, and those that are not very similar will be borderline cases or will be excluded from a category. The problem is that any particular "image" or representation will have its own individual, nongeneric properties, while a truly generic object cannot be any individual (and thus imaginable) representation. An adequate theory of category formation must face the philosophical problem of universals if it is to account for paradigmatic or conceptual intentional objects. (I shall present a theory of intentional objects in Chapter 8.)

According to the model I have presented, terms are initially matched with some paradigmatic focusing event, and this paradigm is gradually elaborated (in terms of significant and distinctive features) as a term is used in a number of referential contexts and as other paradigms are acquired. As a child searches for the right word for distinguishing some intended referent, these categorical judgments are undoubtedly influenced by the saliency as well as the number of significant features a paradigm and some referent have in common. Thus, for example, if asked to decide between a rigidly mounted sphere and a cylindrical object that can be rolled and bounced as an instance of a 'ball' (Nelson, 1974), a twelve-month-old child might be strongly predisposed to organize the world in terms of action schemas and for this reason might select the cylindrical object, finding its functional features especially salient in deciding degrees of similarity. In general, one expects some features to carry more "weight" than others as a function of biological factors (including the level of cognitive development) as well as cultural and linguistic influences and stylistic and individual differences that might affect the saliency of features for some subject. If so, children should be more hesitant in making categorical judgments whenever a referent has relatively few significant or salient features, and linguistic categories that are consistent with the predispositions of some child (that is, categories distinguished by developmentally salient features) should be the easiest to acquire.

The Whorf hypothesis probably does not provide the clearest framework for discussing the relationship between thought and language during the early acquisition period. Linguistic determinism is a theory notoriously difficult to formulate in precise empirical terms (see Kates, 1977). In any case, neither the cognition hypothesis nor the evidence for biological or other cognitive predispositions in category formation shows that language itself has no influence in structuring these categories. Some of the recent discussions of this issue (for example, Bowerman, 1976) suffer from an unclear notion of a prelinguistic "concept." In Chapter 8 I shall present an account of concepts as intentional objects that, on the level of perception, are apperceptive structures. Perception is structured whenever some sense-contents are treated as irrelevant (are, as it were, "placed in brackets": sensed but not counted) in recognizing or classifying some object. All perception is structured. If it were not, there would be no order in experience. Further, both the fact of structure and, to an extent, the kinds of structures found in human perception have a biological foundation. It is in this context that I would interpret the cognition hypothesis and other research on prelinguistic categories.

To attribute prelinguistic (for example, sensorimotor) concepts or schemas to children is to say that their experience is structured in specific ways. Thus, if children are predisposed to form action schemas, they will tend to bracket out irrelevant perceptual differences or variations among situations or objects that are functionally the same, or indiscriminable, in some respect. It is this functional invariant that the child will recognize as the salient feature. Similarly, children may be predisposed to recognize similarities or identities in shape, in emotional impact, or in such relational structures as possession or action-affecting-something. Just as we automatically hear speakers with very different accents say the same thing, or read the same letters represented in different scripts, so one must assume that children "read" their experiences in terms of the salient structures they are able to identify.

Although prelinguistic experience is structured, it does not follow that language does not also impose its own structure on apperception. One may say that a linguistic structure has been acquired when its use reflects a categorical intention. Thus, a child may in fact apperceive objects or events in a certain way without realizing that certain linguistic forms express and can be used to refer to those structures. Once a child deliberately selects some form to classify a referent, one can say that the child is able to say what she means: that the cognitive structure has become a semantic structure. It is certainly plausible that there may be linguistic universals that reflect biologically based predispositions toward certain cognitive structures. If a linguistic category encodes a salient cognitive structure (a claim that has been made about sensorimotor schemas), that category should be relatively easy to acquire. However, there is no logical requirement that all prelinguistically salient structures be mapped into linguistic categories, nor are linguistic structures restricted to this narrow cognitive domain. Just as a phonological system can use rather subtle, nonsalient aspects of sound as distinctive features, so semantic categories can *create* linguistically salient features that, presumably, are culturally or aesthetically significant. For this reason, the child who in fact follows her prelinguistic dispositions in naming the objects to which her attention is directed will make mistakes before discovering exactly how a given language makes categorical distinctions.

The theory of lexical development that I have been presenting rests on the empiricist premise that perceptual experience is the ultimate source of the cognitive structures mapped into language. As I noted in Chapter 1, an alternative, rationalistic model of language acquisition has been proposed by Chomsky. The semantic implications of this theory have been elaborated by Fodor and Katz (1963, 1964), Katz and Postal (1964), and

Katz (1972). In general, Katz follows Chomsky's lead in proposing that competent speakers have an unconscious knowledge of a descriptively adequate grammar, the semantic component of which can generate the meaning of any possible sentence. The original semantic theory (Fodor and Katz, 1963, 1964) was designed to supplement Chomsky's interpretive semantic theory by providing "dictionary entries" for each lexical item in the language (an "indexed lexicon") and a set of "projection rules" that would provide interpretations of the deep structure "output" of the syntactic component.[12] In theory, an adequate semantic component should provide semantic interpretations of the set of all and only sentences of a language.

Katz (1972) restated this view of the goal of semantic theory in the following terms:

> Semantic theory must also contain a model of the semantic component of a grammar which must describe the manner in which semantic interpretations are mapped onto underlying phrase markers. . . . It must also explain the semantic competence underlying the speaker's ability to understand the meaning of new sentences chosen arbitrarily from the infinite range of sentences. This explanation must assume that the speaker possesses, as part of his system of internalized rules, semantic rules that enable him to obtain the meaning of any new sentence as a compositional function of the meanings of its parts and their syntactic organization." [p. 33]

For example, Katz (1972) gives the following example of the sort of "dictionary entry" that might be included in a semantic component of grammar:

kill; [+N, +Det____, +Count, . . .] (Cause) (Become) (Not) (Alive)

He adds that he does not endorse this particular analysis of 'kill' because it does not make a distinction between causing someone's death and being the ultimate (efficient) cause of a death but not

12. Jerrold Katz (1972) notes that so-called type-2 projection rules, operating on sentences that have undergone transformation, have been eliminated from the theory because Chomsky eliminated "generalized transformations" from the syntactic component of grammar. "In the theory as it now stands, there is one projection rule . . . and it is stated in semantic theory, not in any semantic component" (p. 116).

the agent doing the killing. He does, however, endorse this type of analysis. A complete or descriptively adequate entry for 'kill' would enable one to make all the necessary distinctions.

In Katz's system, lexical interpretations are made through what he calls "semantic markers" (such as Cause, Become, Not, and Alive), which are semantic representations of the "concepts" that combine to form the "sense" of a lexical item. Some of the semantic markers found in existing statements of semantic theory may be found to be derived from more primitive markers. "In the final statement of semantic theory, the theoretical vocabulary of semantic markers will consist of each and every primitive semantic marker that is required in the formulation of dictionary entries" (Katz, 1972, p. 38).

Like Chomsky, Katz assumes that the acquisition of a descriptively adequate T-G grammar can be accounted for only on the assumption of innate, a priori linguistic knowledge. Accordingly, he argues that all speakers have an innate knowledge of a set of ultimate or primitive semantic "concepts" that are to be represented through semantic markers. These concepts are substantive semantic universals that provide the "theoretical vocabulary from which semantic constructs required in the formulation of particular semantic interpretations [of grammatical sentences] can be drawn" (p. 33). Along with semantic formal and organizational universals, these substantive universals provide constraints on the structure and content of any natural language. Further, though the universal concepts that provide the "vocabulary" of semantic theory may combine to form different lexical senses in various languages, they specify, in themselves, the set of humanly possible concepts and thus of possible senses.[13]

On the rationalistic account of lexical development, then, perceptual experience is not the ultimate source of semantic competence. In Chomsky's words (1971a), "it is at best misleading to claim that words that I understand derive their meaning from

13. For example, Katz (1972) asserts that a complete grammar must include a "semantic theory to provide a representation scheme for meanings, that is, a universal theory of concepts in which the notion 'possible (cognitive) meaning in a language' is defined by a recursive enumeration of the set of possible senses" (p. 32).

my experience. . ." (p. 17). Though experience is necessary to elicit or activate semantic concepts, concepts that are mapped into language as semantic structures (senses) are "abstract" objects of innate a priori knowledge. This rationalistic view contrasts sharply with the empiricist account of category formation I have outlined. The view that language acquisition is facilitated by prelinguistic cognitive development is consistent with the possibility of linguistic universals that might have, in a broad sense, a biological foundation, but it does not limit the range of possible concepts or senses to those that are biologically determined. At the same time, the cognition hypothesis is consistent with an empiricist perspective that is testable and for which there is already experimental support.

Linguistic rationalism attributes to the language learner a genetically based language acquisition system that allows speakers to proceed systematically in (1) performing linguistic inductions and (2) constructing a correctly indexed lexicon or dictionary. Thus, Jerry Fodor, Jerrold Katz, and others who begin with this assumption treat children as, in effect, computers "wired up" with certain linguistic concepts, "scanning" utterances to extract the critical attributes or features (represented in semantic theory by semantic markers) of referent classes that define the senses of terms. A sense will, in turn, be stored in memory as something analogous to a dictionary entry. For example, Fodor (1972) rejects Vygotsky's theory that lexical development reflects a cognitive developmental process in children, arguing that since "the mathematics required to characterize the structure of faces or the syntax of a language" is so difficult, and beyond the "general problem solving" abilities of a child, it must follow that the "computational procedures that are most central to the child's [linguistic] concept attainment" have an innate basis (p. 86).

If an innate linguistic system, rather than general cognitive development and "problem solving abilities," operates in the construction of an adequate dictionary, one would expect to find that all children follow an identical "logical" path in language acquisition, beginning with an initial set of a priori concepts and ending with identical semantic categories built from those concepts. Evidence that this is not the case—for example, evidence of the essential role of general cognitive processes (rather than specialized, prior linguistic knowledge) and of the referential history of a word in the experience of an individual in determining categorical judgments—should, then, constitute evidence against rationalistic semantics.

A number of psychologists have used something like Katz's model of systematic dictionary entries to study the acquisition of semantic categories. Eve Clark (1971) originally claimed that children learn new terms by acquiring superordinate and then subordinate semantic features in a certain order. For example, she claimed that when three- to five-year-old children first begin to interpret 'before' and 'after', both terms are initially understood through the features −Simultaneous +Prior, until 'after' is finally grasped as −Simultaneous −Prior. Herbert Clark (1970b) also proposed that children acquire the semantic features of polar terms in a fixed order: first learning a nominal, noncontrastive meaning for *both* terms in each pair, then a positive meaning for both terms, and finally a contrastive, negative meaning for each marked term. For example, both 'old' and 'young' might initially be used to mean something like "having age," then to mean "having much age," and finally be distinguished by the feature ± quantity of age. Clark proposed that this analysis of antonyms or implicitly relational terms (involving comparisons with respect to some implicit norm) would account for acquisition of such explicitly relational terms as 'more'/'less', 'before'/'after', 'better'/'worse', 'bigger'/'smaller', 'darker'/'lighter', and so on. For example, children might begin by treating both 'more' and 'less' as meaning "some" (+Quantity), then treat both as meaning "much" (+Quantity +Number (?)), then distinguish them as meaning "much" and "little" (+Quantity ± Number). (See Donaldson and Balfour, 1968; Donaldson and Wales, 1970; and Palermo, 1973, for supporting data. For conflicting results, see Weiner, 1973.)

Since this logical "computer" model of feature acquisition was first proposed, further research on the question has tended to undermine the original neat picture of uniform semantic development. Stanley Kuczaj (1975) found individual differences in the lexical categories formed by children which seemed to reflect differences in the individual experience of each child. He tested subjects between the ages of three years, four months and five years, one month for comprehension of 'always' and 'never', and 'always', 'never', 'usually', 'seldom', and 'sometimes'. He was especially interested in discovering if there were individual variations in the "acquisition strategies" used by the children and if the acquisition patterns reflected the logical relations among the terms. Kuczaj discovered that some children treated both 'always' and 'never' as simple positives, while others treated them both as simple negatives. His explanation for this difference was that the children had heard the terms used in various contexts, which led to different interpretations (or different initial paradigms). For example, one child who interpreted 'always' as meaning 'never' had heard her mother tell her very firmly, after she had spilled her food, "You always make a big mess when you play in your food." Since the intonation pattern suggested an imperative, it is quite likely that the child understood 'always' to mark a simple negative imperative, something like "You should never make a mess with your food." Presumably, contextual variations of this sort might also account for the conflicting results obtained by Susan Weiner (1974) and others for 'more' and 'less' and 'before' and 'after'. For example, Lorraine Harner (1976) found that two-, three-, and four-year-old children understood 'after' better than 'before' when both served as adverbs (contrary to Eve Clark's [1971] prediction) and that both terms were better understood when used to relate the present to future events rather than to past events. She suggested the children may have been used to hearing these terms in relation to future (but not past) events, as in "After lunch you may play outside," and "Eat your lunch before you go out to play." 'Before' may also have been less well understood as an adverb when used to refer to past events.

Some evidence seems to show that a general tendency in children to treat 'less' as 'more', 'after' as 'before', 'different' as 'same', 'on' as 'in', 'under' as 'in' or 'on', and so on, might simply reflect "nonlinguistic strategies." These are "natural" preferences for responses to questions or commands that are not fully understood. For example, children may be predisposed to place objects on or in things rather than under them (E. Clark, 1973b; Wilcox and Palermo, 1974/1975; Grieve, Hoogenraad, and Murray, 1977), to treat order of mention as temporal order (E. Clark, 1970), or to notice larger objects before smaller ones, or similarities rather than differences among stimulus objects. As Kuczaj (1975) put it, "the child's task strategies may lead an investigator to conclude that the child believes that word X means Y when the child actually knows nothing about word X" (p. 341).

The data on individual and contextual variations in word comprehension led Eve Clark (1975) to modify her original proposal about "dictionary entries." She now suggests that children acquire only a partial meaning for pairs of relational terms, and these partial meanings, in combination with various preferred nonlinguistic strategies, account for the responses that seemed to confirm the original theory of logically ordered feature acquisition. For example, three- and four-year-olds might understand both 'more' and 'less' as meaning something like "an amount." If they were then asked to point to an instance of something that had either more or less of something, they might follow the nonlinguistic strategy of always choosing the greater of two amounts (along some salient dimension). Under these circumstances, the experimenter might falsely conclude that the child understood the full meaning of the positive term ('more') and attributed that same meaning to the negative or marked term ('less'). Similarly, children might understand 'in', 'on', and 'under' as having a common locative meaning without knowing the distinguishing features of any of them. They might respond to these terms by following the nonlinguistic strategy of placing objects inside containers whenever possible, or placing them on top of a supporting surface. Clark suggests that such strategies, which may at first be substituted for semantic interpretation, can later, in effect, be mapped into language as the "procedures" that carry out certain linguistic instructions.

The fact that acquisition of relational terms does not reveal the sort of uniform logical pattern that a rationalistic theory seems to predict argues against an innate language acquisition system. How, then, do children acquire the meanings of relational terms? If Eve Clark's suggestion is correct, children face an initial difficulty in discovering the specific variable aspect of an object or event to which such terms refer. They may understand that 'more' and 'less' indicate properties of quantity or that 'before' and 'after' refer to temporal properties without having formed paradigms that provide contrastive meanings or recognizing a purely relational use of descriptive terms.

Herbert Clark (1970a) has proposed that relational terms form pairs of marked and unmarked terms. The unmarked, or "positive" term has both a "nominal" and "contrastive" meaning, while the marked term has only a contrastive sense. The unmarked term, accordingly, can be "neutralized" to cover an entire dimension of a superordinate category, (that is, "nominal use"), or it may be used "contrastively" in opposition to the marked term. For example, 'good'/'bad' might be understood in terms of the features +Value ±Evaluation. In some contexts (for example, "How good is it?"), 'good' may be neutralized to mean only +Value (nominal use). One can answer a question of this sort with either "It was good" (+Evaluation), or "It was bad" (−Evaluation): a contrastive use of 'good' and 'bad'. One cannot, however, neutralize the marked term 'bad'. If one says, for example, "How bad was it?" one is assuming that it *was* bad, and to reply "It was good" is to reject the evaluation implicit in the question. The same is true of *long* and short, *big* and little, *deep* and shallow, *happy* and sad, *intelligent* and stupid, *high* and low, *far* and near, *distant* and close, and so on. In all cases, the unmarked term (in italics) can serve a purely nominal function, while the negative term cannot.[14]

A paradigmatic account of relational terms would propose that children must first acquire semantic structures providing the distinctive features that contrast such categories as 'more' and 'less', 'before' and 'after', 'fast' and 'slow', 'good' and 'bad', and so on. As such terms are focused for children through their application to appropriate referents, what Herbert Clark calls nominal meanings emerge as significant features of a category. Even after contrastive meanings are understood, though, children may treat relational terms in an absolute or nominal way. For example, a child might understand 'more' as a term distin-

14. See E. Tory Higgins (1977) for a major study that casts doubt on some of Herbert Clark's assertions. In particular, there seem to be contexts (for example, "A jet plane is slower than a rocket ship") in which a marked term can be used in a neutral sense.

guishing something like a lot of or a large number of some unit in contrast to something that is 'less' by virtue of possessing only a little or a small number of something. (Of course, in a purely relational use of terms, such positional features are bracketed out, and only a relative contrast along some dimension is criterial.) Certainly there is abundant evidence that adults, as well as children, treat antonyms such as 'good' and 'bad', 'big' and 'little', 'dark' and 'light', 'high' and 'low', and so on, in this nominal way. Though these terms are all implicitly relational, involving comparison with some implicit norm, it is frequently quite difficult to keep this in mind; one is always tempted to believe that things simply "are" good or bad, intelligent or stupid, big or little, and so forth.

An empiricist would expect individual variations in the nominal paradigms formed by children as a function of the contexts in which terms are introduced. For example, children who do not understand relational judgments would naturally be confused by statements describing the same thing as, in one context, 'more' or 'before' and, in another context, as 'less' or 'after'. Such confusion might lead a child to assume that contrastive terms have the same meaning. Or some children might understand one term in a pair in a nominally contrastive sense (for example, 'more' as "a lot") without fully understanding the nominal meaning of the related term. In that case, they might be able to choose correctly examples of things that have 'more' of something (on the basis of semantic knowledge), while relying on nonlinguistic strategies to select things that have 'less'.

Once children have acquired the contrastive (nominal) meanings of relational terms, they must come to recognize their purely relational function. Specifically, they must recognize that such terms are used to describe variable, relational aspects of things rather than to name absolute properties. It is not clear at what age such a change might occur. Piaget has given nine- and ten-year-old children certain reasoning problems which may require this sort of comprehension and which he says they are unable to solve. The problem is of this type: Edith is fairer than Susan; Edith is darker than Lili. Which of the three has the darkest hair? According to Piaget, most of the children answer "Lili." He says they seem to substitute a judgment of membership for a judgment of relation, reasoning that Edith and Susan are both fair, Edith and Lili are both dark (suggesting that both marked and unmarked terms are taken as giving positional information), and therefore Susan is fair, Lili is dark, and Edith is between the two. Whether or not Piaget's analysis of children's reasoning in this case is accurate, it is clear that to solve this sort of problem one must understand that these terms are changing descriptions of one thing in comparison with another, rather than names of features which things absolutely possess.

It is not yet clear how marked and unmarked terms function in various linguistic contexts to provide either positional or purely relational information. Ordinarily, a marked term cannot be used in a nonpositional (neutral) sense. If one says "How long is it?" one means what is the degree of length, long or short, without an assumption that the thing in question is itself either long or short. Similarly, if one says X is longer than Y, there is no presupposition that either X or Y is long. On the other hand, if one says "How short is it?," the marked term carries the presupposition that the referent is in fact short; in the same way "X is shorter than Y" presupposes that both X and Y are short. Some contexts seem to block or neutralize these presuppositions, however. For example, "A jet plane is slower than a rocket" has a purely relational meaning, and does not "position" either jet or rocket at the slow end of a continuum. Higgins (1977) has discovered a number of effects of this kind that seem to be a function of distinctions between positive and negative comparative statements; adjectives involving a ratio scale (such as 'tall' and 'short') and ordinal adjectives without a metric or zero point (such as 'agile' and 'clumsy'); and extreme and regular comparatives (such as 'saintly' and 'good'). It may be that positional information presupposed by marked terms reflects a level of what I called nominal contrast, which is not modified (as it is for unmarked terms) by their relational use, unless the context explicitly cancels a positional interpretation. (For example, one knows very well that neither rockets nor jets are slow.) However, since the linguistic structures involved have not yet been fully sorted out, it would be premature to draw conclusions about how the full system of relational terms is acquired.

Despite the questions that remain about the nature of lexical development, the empiricist model I have presented represents a plausible account that is consistent with the empirical data presently available. In particular, it accords well with recently developed pragmatic models of speech, which explain the acquisition of a linguistic system in terms of a child's use of verbal signs to perform various communicative functions. Speakers may be said to understand the sense of a word when they grasp its referential function, as pointing to or framing a specific structure of experience. The speaker who understands a word automatically focuses on those structural features of objects that are selected by the relevant schema and thus count in determining category membership. I have suggested that schematic paradigms or structures emerge gradually from exposure to speech, as initial focusing events are elaborated until a stable system is formed. The precise nature of this acquisition process must be established through further research.

CHAPTER 4

Acquisition of
Grammatical Paradigms

In Chapter 3, I described a process through which speakers might acquire a lexicon. But most recent psycholinguistic research has concentrated on the questions, How do speakers acquire a grammatical system, and What is the nature of the system that is acquired? I believe the most fruitful approach to this subject derives from the empirical study of semantic grammars, more recently supplemented by pragmatic models of speech.

It is difficult to distinguish between lexicon and grammar, but a distinction can be made, and I think the best and clearest approach was taken by Leonard Bloomfield (1933) and the structural linguists who developed and refined the theory of distributional grammar. Bloomfield divided linguistic forms into "free" and "bound" forms. (He defined a linguistic form as "a phonetic form with its constant meaning.") Bound forms are linguistic forms that are never spoken alone (such as the plural suffix '-s'), and free forms include all other linguistic forms. He then defined morphological constructions as those in which bound forms play a part and syntactic constructions as those in which none of the immediate constituents is a bound form. Grammar is understood to include syntax and morphology. In a broad sense, then, morphology has to do with the internal structure of free forms, while syntax deals with their external relations. In Bloomfield's system of distributional grammar, linguistic forms were classified in terms of the "form-classes" to which they belonged. A form-class was defined in purely "formal" terms: items having similar "privileges of occurrence"—that is, being acceptable substitutes for some other item in the same linguistic frames—belong to the same form-class. In Charles F. Hockett's system, relations between linguistic forms, called "constructions," were classified in terms of "construction-types." A construction is a way of putting forms together to form larger forms, and a construction-type is a group of constructions that are similar in some respect. Accordingly, distributional analysis of a language involves listing the free and bound forms, form-classes, constructions, and construction-types of a language: in short, describing the recurrent patterns in the admissible combinations of forms, or the "distribution" of those forms in certain frames. For example, in English, such free forms as 'Marj', 'Joseph', 'my friend', and 'the lady of the lake', but not 'her', 'him', 'find her', and 'no', belong to the same form-class and may be put together with other forms (belonging to another form-class) in such "predicative" constructions as "Marj likes carrots" and "the lady of the lake studied calculus."[1]

Bloomfield defined a word as a "minimum free form," admitting the difficulty of deciding in some cases if a form is bound or free.[2] In Bloomfield's view, the boundary between lexicon and grammar is not entirely clear because, as he pointed out, (1) many lexical forms have some morphological structure (for example, 'strawberry', 'slower', or 'calls'), and (2) every lexical form appears in speech as serving some grammatical function. On the other hand, one can distinguish between a list of linguistic forms (free and bound) that are not produced analogically, and a list of productive patterns (constructions). Thus, Bloomfield (1933) called a lexicon "an appendix of the grammar: a list of basic irregularities" (p. 274). The suggestion is that speakers are able to form novel utterances by analogy, using the regular patterns or constructions of a language, whereas they cannot utter a form in the lexicon without having heard it. For example, one cannot produce 'Ophelia' or 'fly' or 'moon' unless one is

1. Some of my examples are taken from Hockett's (1958) discussion of distributional grammar. Bloomfield's working principle for discovering the forms and productive patterns of a language was to "go from form to meaning." Thus a regular variation in form is assumed to be correlated with a variation in meaning. However, as I noted in Chapter 1, Bloomfield did not believe that linguistic theory could provide an adequate model of semantic structure.

2. See Yen Ren Chao (1968), pp. 181 ff., for a discussion of the problems involved in identifying a word.

already familiar with these terms, but with an adequate vocabulary and without having previously heard the utterance, one could produce "Ophelia flies to the moon" on the basis of analogy from a predicative or actor-action construction. Of course, it is not always possible to tell whether a particular form belongs to the lexicon of a given speaker as a minimum free form or whether it is an utterance produced on the basis of analogy. An instance of such a borderline case would be 'slower', which might be a simple lexical item for one speaker, and, for another, an utterance produced from 'slow':'fast'::'slower':'faster'.

Perhaps because of this sort of potential variation among speakers in the production of free forms by analogy, Hockett (1973) defines a lexicon as "a speaker's stored stock of linguistic forms" and characterizes grammar as "the analogies which are ready to function, singly or in blending, in a speaker's production of new linguistic forms..." (pp. 8, 25). The distributional structure exhibited within speech reflects the analogical use of certain patterns to produce novel combinations of linguistic forms.

Hockett's approach is useful because it points up the difference between a formal (distributional) model of language—which attempts to list all of the free and bound forms of a language at some point in time and all of the major constructions that can be isolated in a given language—and an empirically accurate description of the forms and constructions that are actually used by a given speaker at a given point in time. A speaker may store whole phrases or sentences in memory as part of a "stored stock" of forms potentially available to serve a grammatical function, and these stored forms in turn may have been learned directly or produced by analogy. On the other hand, a complete grammatical description of a language attempts to abstract from a speech corpus as many forms and patterns of forms as are potentially available to speakers, whether or not they are actually realized in all cases.

In the discussion that follows I shall use the term "grammatical categories" to mean those semantic paradigms that regulate the use of productive patterns (constructions involving items in various form-classes) in a given language.

Experimental study of semantic models of grammar has actually reversed the relationship that existed between linguists and psychologists working with Chomsky's theory in the early 1960s, although linguists have not yet fully recognized this reversal. During the earlier period, linguists developed models of grammatical rules designed to satisfy formal criteria of descriptive or explanatory adequacy, and psychologists attempted to test the "psychological reality" of these rules. But semantic grammars propose that linguistic deep structure is *semantic*, and psychologists such as Lois Bloom, Dan Slobin, Roger Brown, Melissa Bowerman, Hermina Sinclair, and others have interpreted semantic structure as cognitive structure that has been mapped into linguistic forms and patterns. The aim of these psychologists is not to verify a performance model incorporating the most economical or mathematically elegant theory of grammar that can be devised by linguists, but rather to discover the actual cognitive structures encoded in speech forms and the essential psychological operations that occur as speakers produce and interpret utterances. Many psycholinguists have turned to the theories of Jean Piaget as a source of evidence for hypotheses about the semantic intentions of child speakers. If semantic structure is linguistically encoded cognitive structure, then nonlinguistic evidence of the cognitive abilities of speakers at various developmental levels is obviously relevant to a semantic description of the speech produced at that stage. Presumably speakers notice, and talk about, those aspects of the world they are interested in and that they are cognitively equipped to recognize. It follows, then, that hypotheses about the basic semantic categories encoded in grammatical patterns might very well come from psychologists (as was the case with I. M. Schlesinger, 1971), rather than from linguists. If the theory of semantic deep structures is correct, linguists and psychologists together should continue to try to develop an adequate model of speaking and understanding, linguists describing the recurrent formal patterns or distributional structure of a language and both jointly investigating the nature of the semantic structures governing the use of productive patterns by speakers.

Although the volume of research bearing on the acquisition of semantic categories is enormous, psychologists and linguists are still very far from working out a complete account of the semantic structure of a single language. Since some of the most intensive and fruitful studies in this area have focused on very early child speech (especially from age one to age three), and since the semantic structure of early speech ought to be simpler than that of later speech, I shall illustrate a semantic model of deep structure with data from these studies.

Roger Brown (1973) has reported findings from the first phase of his longitudinal study of language acquisition in three children. The study is particularly useful because Brown considered a number of linguistic and psycholinguistic positions, testing each against his own data and that reported by other researchers and finally opting for a semantic model of grammar. Brown's specific proposal about the semantic structure of what he called stage I speech (defined by an MLU—mean length of utterance—of 1.75 and a maximum utterance length of 5 morphemes) was that it encoded three operations and eight semantic relations. The three operations Brown discovered were nomination, recurrence, and nonexistence. He defines nominations as "the presence of the referent made manifest by some action calling attention to it for the members of the communicating group, usually a dyad" (p. 189). Recurrence "may mean the reappearance of the same referent already seen, it may mean the appearance of a new instance of a referent class of which one instance has already been seen, and it may mean an additional quantity . . . of some mass of which a first quantity has already been seen" (p. 190). Of nonexistence Brown says, "What is essential is an expectation of existence which the nonexistence sentence disappoints" (p. 192). Perhaps it would be better to say the nonexistence sentence is a sign of disappointed expectation or that it refers to the absence of something the speaker had expected to find.

The eight semantic relations Brown described were: (1) agent + action; (2) action + object; (3) agent + object; (4) action + locative; (5) entity + locative; (6) possessor + possession; (7) entity + attribute; and (8) demonstrative + entity. Most of the categories Brown claimed to discover in early speech can be found in the generative semantic models developed by such linguists as Wallace Chafe and Charles Fillmore. For example, an agent is the (usually animate) someone or something that causes or instigates an action or process. It must be perceived as having its own animating force (for example, "wind" in "the wind ripped the curtains"). An object (or patient) is the someone or something either suffering a change of state or receiving the force of an action. A locative refers to the place or locus of an action or entity. An entity is any thing or person having a distinct separate existence. An attribute is some contingent feature of an entity; and, Brown says, possessor and possession express a primitive notion of property and territoriality. Finally, a demonstrative is used to specify a particular entity or to perform the operation of nomination.

Brown believes that knowledge of these operations and relations is probably not innate. He suggests that they may be representations of sensorimotor intelligence developed during the first 18 to 24 months of life. The theory of sensorimotor intelligence originally proposed by Piaget (1937) says that during this first developmental period children gradually learn certain things about the world through the action schemas that develop as they manipulate and adapt themselves to things in the environment. Without at first symbolizing or knowing figuratively how the world is structured, the child learns through action that objects exist, disappear, belong to or are consistently used by certain people, and so on. Presumably, early child speech will somehow encode or refer to these primitive perceptions.[3] The relation that Brown sees between cognitive development and early semantic structures may be summarized as follows. Expressions of nomination and recurrence require the ability to recognize objects and actions. Expressions of nonexistence require the ability to connect objects and actions with their natural signs and to notice when predictions or anticipations of the appearance of objects and actions are not confirmed. One type of nonexistence expression, a question about the location of an

3. For a discussion of the Piagetian view of the relation between language and cognition (and an experimental refutation [in 1969] of one of Jerome Bruner's claims about this relation), see Hermina Sinclair (1969, 1970, 1978). See also Bärbel Inhelder (1962, 1978) and Ruth Tremaine (1975). For a critique of Piaget's methodology, see Martin Braine (1962).

absent object, requires a representation of a world of enduring objects that do not cease to exist when they are no longer within sight. According to Piaget, the intellectual abilities Brown lists as prerequisites for the acquisition of these semantic structures all develop in the period of sensorimotor intelligence.

Brown's theory is that linguistic development is a gradual mapping of structural meanings (operations and relations) into grammatical devices, both syntactic and morphological, and thus that the development of semantic categories reflects and is limited by cognitive development. According to Brown, the earliest speech encodes only the basic semantic relations previously listed, and once these are acquired, the child gradually develops more elaborate linguistic means for expressing "fine tunings" or modulations of these basic structures. A few examples of stage I speech, as Brown interprets it, should give the flavor of early productive patterns:

I. Operations of Reference
    A. Nominations: that (or it or there) + book, cat, hot, etc.
    B. Notice (a type of nomination): hi! + cat, Mommy, belt, etc.
    C. Recurrence: more (or 'nother) + milk, cereal, read, green, etc.
    D. Nonexistence: allgone (or no-more) + rattle, juice, green, etc.

II. Relations
    A. Attributive (entity + attribute): Adj. + N (big train, red book, etc.)
    B. Possessive: N + N (Adam checker, Mommy lunch, etc.)
    C. Locative: N + N (sweater chair, book table, etc.)
    D. Agent-Action: N + V (Adam put, Eve read, etc.)
    E. Agent-Object: N + N (Mommy sock, Mommy lunch, etc.)
    F. Action-Object: V + N (put book, hit ball, etc.)

Brown argues that the earliest constructions are used to perform one of the three basic operations (referring to the presence, recurrence, and nonexistence of entities), or to refer to a basic set of relations among entities. Thus, in early speech, a closed set of forms ('hi', 'that', 'allgone', 'more', etc.) is combined with a very large set of forms ('Mommy', 'cat', 'sweater', etc.); or forms belonging to the latter set are combined in utterances expressing one of the (eight) semantic relations.

Brown claims that after children have learned to express basic semantic operations and relations, they acquire a set of grammatical morphemes that represent, in semantic terms, a "fine tuning" or modulation of the basic structures. Specifically, Brown traced the acquisition of 14 morphemes, in rank order: (1) present progressive (temporary duration, possibly also a process-state distinction), (2) in (containment), (3) on (support), (4) plural (number), (5) past irregular (earlierness), (6) possessive (possession), (7) uncontractible copula (number, earlierness), (8) articles (specific-nonspecific reference), (9) past regular, (10) third person regular (number, earlierness), (11) third person irregular, (12) uncontractible auxiliary (earlierness, possibly also a process-state distinction), (13) contractible copula, and (14) contractible auxiliary.[4] These markers modify or modulate basic semantic relations in various ways. Brown summarizes their semantic roles as follows:

> 1. The progressive, past, and plural inflections . . . seem to modulate the references made, in Stage I, by nouns and verbs in the sense that the modulations are inconceivable in isolation. 2. The locative prepositions seem to modulate, in the sense of specifying more exactly the locative relation expressed by word order. 3. The present-tense copula and the possessive inflection seem to add redundant markers to relations of attribution, location, and possession expressed by word order in Stage I. 4. The present-tense auxiliary *be* seems to add a redundant marker to the progressive modulation. 5. The past-tense copula and auxiliary *be* . . . seem to modulate further the meanings in question. [p. 254]

Brown notes that the fourteen morphemes "may not constitute a single class semantically" except in the sense of being less essential than names of entities and actions or terms coding basic semantic relations, "either because they are inconceivable in isolation or because they render a meaning more precise or because

4. The average rank (in parentheses) and mean order of acquisition for these morphemes was: (1) present progressive—2.33; (2) *in*—2.50; (3) *on*—2.50; (4) plural—3; (5) past irregular—6; (6) possessive—6.33; (7) uncontractible copula—6.50; (8) articles—7; (9) past regular—9; (10) third person regular—9.66; (11) third person irregular—10.83; (12) uncontractible auxiliary—11.66; (13) contractible copula—12.66; (14) contractible auxiliary—14.00. See Kuczaj (1977) for evidence against Brown's claim that the irregular past tense form is acquired before the regular past tense form.

they are usually redundant" (p. 254). He suggests a parallel between basic meanings/modulations and substance/attribute in
that terms coding basic meanings can be used as free forms
without inflections (and are so used by children), while other
morphemes take on significance only in combination with terms
belonging to the former category. As Brown emphasizes, however, it is difficult to specify precisely the semantic role of the
individual morphemes as they appear in adult speech. It may be,
as he suggests, that grammatical morphemes, like many content
words, "have in the course of time come to stand for a chain
complex of related but distinguishable meanings. . ." (p. 315).

On the other hand, for children to acquire morphological
structures, it is probably necessary that they initially recognize a
consistent semantic distinction which such structures express. As
Slobin (1971a) put it in describing "Universal Operating Principles" in language acquisition, "The use of grammatical markers
should make semantic sense." For this reason, "when selection of
an appropriate inflection among a group of inflections performing the same semantic function is determined by arbitrary formal criteria (e.g. phonological shape of stem, number of syllables
in stem, arbitrary gender of stem), the child initially tends to use
a single form in all environments, ignoring formal selection restrictions" (pp. 365–66). On this account, children first recognize
or select forms that encode a categorical distinction and only
gradually respond to formal linguistic contingencies, such as
phonemic environments, which alter the formal patterns in
speech.[5] Children may also develop alternative semantic
paradigms that are cued in in some way by the referential context. Moreover, grammatical morphemes in children's speech
probably play semantic roles that are much more consistent than
the roles played by those same morphemes in adult speech.[6]

5. For example, English-speaking children typically go through this pattern
in the acquisition of past tense forms, presumably *after* they have acquired the
basic paradigm of a past situation: (1) break, drop; (2) broke, drop; (3) breaked,
dropped; (4) breakted, dropted; (5) broke, dropped. This pattern follows the
general outline of stages in the linguistic marking of a semantic category given by
Slobin: (1) no marking; (2) appropriate marking in limited cases; (3) overgeneralization of marking (often accompanied by (4) redundant marking); (5)
full adult system. See Kuczaj (1977) for experimental findings on the acquisition
of regular and irregular past tense forms.

6. Brown (1957) reported finding that children as young as two and three

As Brown notes, it is not easy to decide what a child knows about language, especially about grammatical morphemes. Brown attributes a specific semantic intention to a child only if the child is capable of selecting an alternative form that expresses a relevant contrasting meaning. Thus, "Whether the child intends temporary duration must depend not only on his referential consistency but on whether he has the possibility of expressing anything other than temporary duration. Whether the child intends a reference to the 'present' must depend on whether he has the possibility of referring to anything other than the present" (p. 317). This is a fairly stiff criterion that might be relaxed a bit if one could find evidence that a child comprehends references that require a semantic interpretation of some morpheme or perhaps indications that a child has acquired several linguistic forms that express the same semantic structure during the same time period.

Brown's comments about the semantic structure of definite and indefinite articles are of particular interest. He uses the metaphor of a filing cabinet with "cards" including "specific referent cards" and "nonspecific referent cards" to account for the use of the alternative article forms. A speaker referring to a specific referent, that is, selecting a card listing a particular thing or event, will use the definite article. A speaker referring to a nonspecific referent, that is, selecting a card listing a type of thing or event, will use an indefinite article, subject to selection restrictions on mass-count, proper-common, and singular-plural nouns, and assuming the selection would be appropriate given the social situation. Brown says, "Speaking in a purely impressionistic way I would say . . . the definite and indefinite articles seem to involve the greatest semantic complexity of the [fourteen grammatical morphemes]" (p. 356). I would add to this

---

years old had some "notional" or semantic paradigm of nouns and verbs, as names of things and actions, that were much more semantically consistent than an "adult" category would be if it were based on an analysis of what all things referred to by nouns or verbs had in common. Similarly, an attempt to find a consistent semantic meaning of certain morphemes, such as prepositions and suffixes, would be difficult because of various idioms and semantically empty cases in adult speech.

account of articles only that I suspect Brown has underestimated the role of pragmatic considerations such as whether a listener can be assumed to follow one's reference to some particular object, either because a specific, identifying reference has already been made in the course of a conversation or because the listener shares some nonverbal context that would lead to immediate identification of an intended referent. Since this sort of understanding requires an ability to take on the role of a particular or hypothetical listener to which one's own speech must be adapted, I would suspect that full competence in the use of definite and indefinite articles takes many years. (In fact, many adults make egocentric mistakes in this area.)

In his interpretations of children's utterances, Brown uses the method of "rich interpretation" developed by Lois Bloom (1970). Bloom (1975) suggests that semantic relations between two words be identified on the basis of how the words are used. Thus, the observer must rely on both verbal and nonverbal (contextual) clues to infer the referring intentions of child speakers. For example, the child utterance 'Mommy sock' (to use Bloom's famous example), may use the same word order to express two very different relations between the two entities named: agent-object (Mommy in the act of putting on the sock) and possessive (the sock as belonging to Mommy). A description of the utterance that used purely syntactic categories would simply list 'Mommy sock' as an N + N construction.

The method of rich interpretation is supported by two observations. First, the speech of young children is usually not displaced (that is, about entities which are not physically present). Thus, children's speech has a particularly close relationship to the immediate context so that one seems well advised to take context into account in interpreting early utterances. Second, inferences about the sorts of structural relations among entities children might be aware of become more plausible when they conform to theories of cognitive development, which predict which aspects of the world will become salient to speakers at various developmental stages. Bloom's interpretations have been influenced by Piaget's theory, which predicts that at the stage at which children typically produce two-word utterances they will be aware of and capable of referring to such things as agents acting on or possessing things, objects disappearing and reappearing, and so on. Thus, if a child at this developmental stage is able to recognize a certain sock lying on a table as belonging to Mommy, and has also seen Mommy putting on a sock, and says 'Mommy sock' on both occasions, it is plausible to assume that the child is referring to a different relation between Mommy and her sock in each case. Further, if a child consistently uses some syntactic or morphological structure in referring to such structural aspects of situations, there is reason to attribute grammatical knowledge to the child, that is, to assume that the child is selecting grammatical structures (such as word order) that classify an object or event in a specific way. Grammatical structures that express some categorical intention encode a semantic deep structure.

Brown's model of the earliest constructions in child speech fits in well with Bloom's (1975) finding (on the basis of data from five children—Gia, Kathryn, Allison, Eric, and Peter) that there are two strategies used by children to express semantic relations:

> One strategy depends upon the child learning to use certain words with constant form and constant meaning (such as the inherently relational terms "more," "this," "no," "my") in two-word utterances, where such words determine the semantic-syntactic relationship. The second strategy involves a linguistic categorization, where different words (such as "Mommy," "Daddy," "Baby") form a class for the child because they can have the same meaning (for example, agent) relative to other words. In this case, the semantic-syntactic relationship between the words is independent of the lexical meaning of either of the words. [p. 260]

Bloom agrees with Brown that certain words are used more than others by children between the ages of one and three years, because, as she says, they "happen to code important cognitive distinctions" (Bloom, 1975, p. 258) which seems to constitute "virtually a closed set" (p. 259). For example,

> "more" or "another" signaled another instance or *recurrence* of an object or an event after its previous existence; negative words like "no," "no more," or "all gone" signaled the *disappearance* or *nonexistence* of an object or action in situations where existence was somehow expected; and words like "this," "that," "Hi," or simply "uh"

(/ə/) served to point out the *existence* of an object or action. (This last function was referred to as "ostension" by Schlesinger and "nomination" by Brown.) In two-word utterances of this type, the meaning of the relation between the words was derived from the meaning of one of the words, such as "more," "all gone," or "this." [Bloom, 1975, p. 259]

Bloom goes on to say that in the case of the remaining semantic relations (possession, location, agent-object, etc.), the meaning of expressions must usually be read off from the meanings of the component words and the nature of the situation in which they are used (second strategy). Bloom notes that there are individual differences among children in the use of one or the other strategy to express semantic relations. For example, Kathryn, Gia, and Allison represented possession by two substantive words ('Daddy coat') and later used a possessive marker ('my' or 'your'). They represented location at first by two substantives ('sweater chair') and later by locative markers such as 'up,' 'there,' 'on,' and 'right there'. In contrast, Eric and Peter always indicated agent, object, possessor, and location "by a function form ('I,' 'it,' 'my,' and 'there') that determined the relational meaning between the two words in an utterance" (p. 260).

If two-word utterances express structural relations, the acquisition of grammar must involve a mapping of these relations into conventional syntactic and morphological devices for expressing them. Such a process would be consistent with a general pattern of linguistic development that Slobin (1971a) has summarized as follows: "New forms first express old functions, and new functions are first expressed by old forms" (p. 317). Once children have discriminated such structural aspects of situations as agents acting on objects, possessors and their possessions, locations of objects and events, recurrence of objects and events, and so on, and have begun to refer to these salient features within their experience, they are able to acquire new grammatical forms that express such categorical judgments.

Bloom (1975) agrees that cognitive development will be a major factor determining which syntactic markers are learned first. Summarizing her own data, she concludes, "The order in which children learn syntactic structures apparently reflects the order in which they learn to distinguish and organize aspects of their environment" (p. 260). On the basis of a number of developmental studies conducted with speakers of various languages, Slobin (1971a) notes that both the inherent difficulty ("formal linguistic complexity") of a grammatical device and a child's level of cognitive development, which limits what the child can grasp and also directs the child's attention to certain aspects of the world, will determine the order in which grammatical markers will be acquired. Within the limits of formal complexity, "the earliest grammatical markers to appear in child speech seem to express the most basic notions available to the child mind" (Slobin, 1971a, p. 305).[7] Brown (1973) concurs that (1) some grammatical devices are more complex than others, and in general the less complex devices will be the earliest learned, and (2) grammatical devices that encode basic semantic relations will be learned before those that encode modulations of meaning.

There is some evidence that one of the earliest formal structures to be acquired is word order. Word order may be a device that children universally pay attention to at an early age, and it has been argued (Slobin, 1971a) that such a strategy may be innate. Slobin suggests that word order may be "a more basic device than inflection. It is also probably the case that all languages make use of word order as a basic linguistic means of signalling underlying relations, while the use of inflections is not universal" (p. 376n). One would expect, then, that word order would emerge early as a device expressing semantic relations. That is, if children are predisposed to interpret word order in a certain way, they should find it easier to acquire semantic structures when they are consistent with such initial expectations.

Brown (1973) summarizes data suggesting that if word order in a given language is highly consistent with respect to particular semantic relations, most children will use appropriate word order at an early age. If a language is not highly consistent, children will either select one order from those heard or vary

7. Slobin (1971a) notes the value of data from bilingual children in determining measures of grammatical as distinct from semantic complexity (for example, when two languages use different grammatical devices to mark the same semantic notion). The article gives ample illustration of the kinds of grammatical devices marking semantic relations in a number of languages and lists what may be universal principles determining the acquisition of those devices.

word order, depending on such variables as frequency, attention, reinforcement, and spacing and array of instances. In English, there is evidence that children as young as 5 years old use word order to decode semantic relations and that their use of standard word order (in English, subject-verb-object) is highly consistent, though it has not been conclusively demonstrated that they intentionally use word order in their own utterances to express semantic relations.

Most of the comprehension tests investigating word order have concentrated on a connection between surface structure subject and object (the first noun, or "entity" word, before or after the verb, or action word) and the semantic role of agent and object or patient. For example Janellen Huttenlocher and Susan Strauss (1968) and Huttenlocher, Karen Eisenberg and Strauss (1968) investigated sentence comprehension in five-, seven-, and nine-year-olds, and in fourth graders, to see if they showed a preference for marking an agent-object structure with a particular word order. They found that the children made more errors and required more time for their responses when the semantic agent was named by the first noun after the verb in a passive construction. In both experiments they concluded that the role of agent (or actor) is ordinarily ascribed to the grammatical (surface structure) subject of a sentence. This finding is consistent with the conclusions of Colin Fraser, Ursula Bellugi, and Roger Brown (1963) that English-speaking preschoolers interpreted passive sentences as though they were active constructions.

If children do go through an initial phase of matching word order with an agent-action-object relation, it is likely that they first overgeneralize this structure and misinterpret passive constructions. Lila and Henry Gleitman's (1972) interview with their seven-year-old daughter Claire provides an amusing example of this sort of error. Claire was asked whether the sentence "Golf plays my sister" was well formed in her dialect. She replied, "I think that sounds terrible, you know why?" "Why?" she was asked. "Poor girl!" "Well, what does it mean?" "It means the golf stands up and picks up the thing and hits the girl at the goal" (p. 149). Such overgeneralization fits Slobin's (1971a) claim about an allegedly universal feature of language acquisition: "Sentences deviating from standard word order will be interpreted at early stages of development as if they were examples of standard word order" (p. 350).

The psycholinguistic evidence supports the theory that children acquire semantic deep structures after they have distinguished various structural relations among things in the world. Next, they begin to refer to structures that are salient. Finally, they acquire the linguistic structures that express specific categorical judgments.[8] Some children may adopt the strategy of naming structural features (for example, marking recurrence with 'more' or nonexistence with 'no'). Others may, as Slobin says, at first use old forms (names of entities and actions) to refer both to those entities and to serve the new function of indicating structural features or relations. Next, they acquire new forms, such as word order, to mark the old function of referring to those features and relations (Bloom's second strategy). Through this process, syntactic and morphological structures acquire a semantic deep structure that motivates (that is, regulates) their productive use.

The claim that deep structures are semantic rather than syntactic does not, of course, deny that speakers acquire syntactic and morphological structures. On the contrary, if children did not at some point recognize that such linguistic structures as word order and inflections express certain categorical judgments, there could be no semantic grammar. There is controversy, however, first, about whether children (or adults) form representations of deep syntactic structures (Chomsky's "logical" subject and object of a sentence), and, second, about the sense in which children represent sentences as having a predicative structure.

The first point of controversy concerns Chomsky's claim that speakers have knowledge of "basic grammatical relations," defined in terms of the underlying phrase structure of sentences. Thus, if a sentence consists of an NP (noun phrase) and a VP

8. Of course, beyond the very basic categories connected with what may be universal patterns of cognitive development (which, moreover, need not be expressed through grammatical structures), children's structural (as well as lexical) categories will also be formed through exposure to a language that systematically marks certain categorical distinctions.

(verb phrase), the NP is the *subject of the sentence,* and VP is the *predicate;* if a VP consists of a V and an NP, the V is the *main verb of the verb phrase* and the NP is the *object;* and if an NP consists of an N and a determiner, the N is the *head of the noun phrase* (or the head noun), and the determiner is the *modifier*.

What Chomsky calls the logical subject of a sentence is defined in terms of initial phrase markers generating a kernel sentence which may be subject to transformations. Thus, a deep structure object may be expressed as a surface structure subject, as in "John is easy to please." To say, then, that children or adults have a knowledge of syntactic deep structures is presumably to say that they are able to distinguish underlying and surface structure relations and to analyze the subject-verb-object (s-v-o) structure of a kernel sentence. I have already suggested my basic disagreement with the Chomskyan model of grammatical competence. There is, at this point, no conclusive evidence that children or adults have any knowledge of such syntactic deep structures, and there is data (Huttenlocher and Strauss, 1968; Huttenlocher, Eisenberg, and Strauss, 1968) suggesting that children use the surface structure feature of word order (rather than any model of syntactic deep structure relations) to make semantic interpretations. Bloom (1976) has concluded that children "do not know the distinctions between underlying structure and surface structure subject/predicate relations . . . [and] do not know the transformational rules that operate on subject and predicate constituents in adult grammar . . ." (p. 21). Alice Healy and A. G. Levitt (1978) also doubt the "psychological reality" of syntactic deep structures in models of adult as well as child competence.

The second point of controversy concerns the stage at which children acquire a representation of a linguistic subject-verb-object structure that defines an obligatory predicative structure for sentences. Bowerman (1973) has proposed that children do not possess such grammatical categories as subject, predicate, and object. Rather, children's linguistic knowledge is semantic; that is, it consists of such basic structures as agent-object, possessor-possession, and location. Both Bowerman (1973) and Schlesinger (1971) argue that children's two- and three-word utterances express structural semantic relations that are marked

97

(in English) by word order. Thus, to acquire grammar is to acquire markers for semantic categories and relations.

Lois Bloom has objected to this account of grammatical knowledge because it does not clarify "the nature of the child's linguistic knowledge that underlies his being able to use syntactic patterns of word order with consistent semantic functions, that is, the form of predicative sentences" (Bloom, Miller, and Hood, 1975, p. 35). Bloom's argument is that children are able to use such devices as word order in a systematic way because they map semantic structures into surface (syntactic and morphological) structures which are represented in categorical terms. Thus, the child who says 'Mommy sock' to refer to an agent in the act of putting on a sock has not simply acquired a word-order rule—agent before object—for agent-object structures. Rather, the consistent word order reflects an awareness of a more complete paradigm mapping an agent-action-object structure into a subject-verb-object (surface) structure. "Subjects" are categorically defined syntactically as nouns ("entity" words), playing a number of semantic roles, that occur before the verb; "objects," which may also play several semantic roles, occur after the verb (Bloom, 1976); and verbs may be distinguished in terms of a number of semantic "molar" categories such as action/state, locative/nonlocative, activity, etc. (Bloom, 1978). Presumably, then, there is in such two-word utterances "a fuller constituent structure than is actually realized" (Bloom, 1976). The child knows that agent-action-object structures are expressed through subject-verb-object constituents, and thus the word-order regularity exhibited reflects grammatical knowledge that agents occur, not simply first, but before the (action) verb, while semantic objects occur after the verb.

Bloom (1976, and Bloom et al., 1975) cites evidence that children acquire categories of verbs that are consistently related to categories of nouns through semantic-syntactic (word-order) structures. These structural regularities would not be possible without an awareness of the s-v-o structure as a categorical feature that conveys semantic information in relation to a specific, semantic category of verbs. However, although children may be aware of a full semantic-syntactic structure, they may nonetheless be unable to produce a full sentence, such as "Mommy puts on the sock." In this sense, performance may not fully represent the extent of a child's linguistic knowledge.

Bloom and her associates (Bloom et al., 1975) have proposed a "variation" model of competence to account for the gap between the constituent structure, which is said to form part of a child's representation of an intended utterance meaning, and the constituents, which are actually expressed at the two-word stage. The model is also intended to explain the gradual transition from two- to three-word utterances. According to the variation model, there is a variable influence of lexical, grammatical, and discourse factors on the length of an utterance. If a word has been acquired recently or is not very well understood in its referential or syntactic function, or if an utterance contains internal semantic distinctions such as negation, two-part verbs, or possession in addition to those semantic relations marked by the s-v-o structure, these added lexical and grammatical complexities will tend to reduce the length of utterances. In addition, utterance length will vary as a function of such discourse factors (in order of increasing complexity) as whether an utterance is an expansion of a previous utterance (by the child or an adult "prompter"), a spontaneous utterance, or a response to an adult topic.

Bloom's proposal is that a child at the two-word stage may already have made a linguistic induction about the obligatory syntactic structure of sentences, before the child is fully competent to produce utterances exhibiting a complete s-v-o structure. As competence increases, the child will gradually produce longer and structurally more complete utterances. In sum, "It appears that the increase in utterance length reflects increased access to the fuller constituent structure that is represented in long term memory—through lexical and discourse factors as well as other possible mnemonics that result from cognitive development" (Bloom et al., 1975, p. 51).

Bloom notes that the variation model clarifies her controversial (1970) proposal that two-word utterances had undergone a "reduction transformation." Her intention in using a Chomskyan model of grammar to represent such utterances was not to attribute some obligatory linguistic rule to the system of child grammar, but rather to suggest that children at that stage may represent a full, and obligatory, constituent structure which they are, for various reasons, not always competent to express. Thus,

> reduction is a grammatical process that changes, with respect to the conditioning factors under which it operates, in relation to other developments in the child's linguistic system. The reduction transformation (Bloom, 1970) was one linguistic scheme for representing these phenomena; the variation paradigm ... appears to offer a more informative scheme for representing the same phenomena. [Bloom et al., 1975, p. 46]

Brown (1973) proposed that children's utterances grow longer and more complex as they acquire an increasing number of semantic structures. As a child gradually becomes aware of salient structural features of situations and attempts to refer to such structures, both one- and two-word utterances should gain referential complexity. As a child acquires the linguistic structures that express these categorical intentions, utterances should gain semantic complexity and utterance length should increase. Thus, as Brown says, three-word utterances represent "unfoldings" of the cognitive intentions expressed earlier in two-word utterances.

At the same time that children's linguistic competence is increasing, their performance as measured by utterance length is probably limited by the cognitive difficulty of representing more than a small number of semantic relations simultaneously. As evidence for such a cognitive "complexity limit" Brown (1973) cites the fact that the earliest three-word utterances express the same number of semantic relations (three) as the preceding, and still occurring, two-word utterances. For example, children might produce the following utterances around the same time period: 'Adam hit ball' (agent-action-object), 'sweater chair' (entity-locative, with the phrase as semantic object), and 'Adam ball' (possessor-possessed, with the phrase as a semantic object). Brown's proposal about a limit on the semantic relations expressed in early speech is similar to Bloom's claim about the influence of grammatical factors on utterance length, except that Bloom considers such constraints a matter of competence rather than performance. Evidently Bloom, unlike Brown, thinks of linguistic knowledge as a matter of context and degree.

The difference between the two positions can, to some extent, be empirically decided. If utterances seem to express a fixed number of semantic relations regardless of lexical and discourse factors, this would support Brown's position. Bloom (1976, and Bloom et al., 1975) has claimed that systematic variations in the length of utterances support her model of variable competence, although she has analyzed her data in terms of the number of syntactic constituents present, rather than the number of semantic relations expressed.

There is a major difference between Brown's model of early grammar and Bloom's account with respect to syntactic structure. Whereas Bloom claims that children know an s-v-o structure is obligatory for all sentences, Brown (1973) proposes that children at the two-word stage treat s-v-o constituents as optional rather than obligatory. In his view, "The facts ... suggest ... that the child does not understand how much it is necessary to say to make well-formed sentences" (p. 239). In response, Bloom and her associates (1975) point to regularities in children's speech that seem to argue for a knowledge of constituent structure. In particular, she notes that lexical, grammatical, and discourse factors that increased the complexity of an utterance "occurred more often with two-constituent utterances than with three-constituent utterances" (p. 52). Moreover, the evidence she cites of systematic use of word order at the two-word stage (which she says presupposes knowledge of a complete s-v-o structure), provides support for the claim that children intend a full predicative structure even when they are unable to produce one in some contexts.

I find Bloom's argument that children use or represent constituent structures to express semantic intentions persuasive in some cases. If nouns (or pronouns) and verbs are classified in semantic terms, and syntactic subjects and objects distinguished by the surface structure feature of word order in relation to the verb, it would follow that word-order mappings of such semantic structures as agent-action-object must involve these syntactic categories. An agent, expressed by the pre-verb noun or pronoun, is, by that word-order structure, a subject, just as an object or patient, expressed by the post-verb noun or pronoun, is for that reason a syntactic object. Thus, if a child says 'Mommy sock' with the intention of expressing an agent-action-object semantic structure, the word order of the utterance does, as Bloom says, reflect the syntactic structure of the more complete paradigm. There may be a number of semantic structures mapped into an s-v-o structure as Bloom has defined it, and I do not think that any proponents of semantic grammar would deny that the relative position of categories of words (such as nouns and verbs, or modifiers and nouns) is an important structure marking semantic relations. The initial controversy about Bloom's (1970) model of reduction transformations in early speech concerned the issue of whether children had knowledge of deep structure, or "logical," subject and object categories, and not whether children used surface constituent structures to make semantic interpretations.

Although some semantic structures may be mapped into an s-v-o structure, others, such as possessor-possession, are not. Thus, a child who says 'Mommy sock' to express possessor-possession may exhibit a consistent use of word order that reflects a modifier-noun construction rather than a predicative (s-v-o) construction. It is quite possible, as Brown suggests, that children at this stage are not aware that the s-v-o structure is obligatory for all sentences. The fact that utterance length may vary as a function of lexical, grammatical, or discourse factors does not demonstrate an obligatory s-v-o rule for all sentences. As Bloom notes, verbs are the most frequently expressed constituents in early speech, followed by constituents naming an object affected by movement. Thus, the semantic relations that children most often intend are those mapped into an s-v-o structure. For this reason, one may agree that children frequently intend to produce utterances which, to be semantically complete, must contain three constituents, without assuming that children always intend such (predicative) structures or assuming that they recognize the obligatory nature of the s-v-o structure (in English) for all sentences, regardless of their semantic content.

Bloom might object to this account of semantic-syntactic structures because it does not characterize an essential unit of discourse. Her claim is that children are aware of the obligatory predicative structure of sentences, which Bloom defines in terms of a complete s-v-o constituent structure. From this syntactic point of view, 'Mommy sock' is not a complete and acceptable utterance, even if it expresses a relation of possession intended by a child. Thus, the issue is not simply whether children map such semantic paradigms as agent-action-object into an s-v-o structure, but how children know that certain forms *complete* the meanings of other forms, or that "sentences are regularly occurring events." In short, how is one to define the structure of a basic unit of discourse (the "complete" sentence), and in what sense do children (and adults) have a knowledge of this hierarchical grammatical structure? Bloom's answer, I take it, is that speech is essentially predicative, and that predication is defined by a constituent, subject-predicate structure. In the following chapter I shall argue that predication should be understood in pragmatic terms as a topic-comment structure which may, but need not, be expressed (in English) by the conventional s-v-o pattern.

CHAPTER 5

Pragmatic Structures

The definition of pragmatics most often given by linguists and psychologists is taken from the semiotic theory of Charles Morris (1938) based on the earlier work of the philosopher Charles Peirce. Morris distinguished syntactics, semantics, and pragmatics, respectively, as the study of relations (1) among signs, (2) between signs and their referents, and (3) between signs and their human users. Elizabeth Bates (1976) notes that Morris's definition of pragmatics has been criticized because it does not recognize Peirce's distinction between signs (or things denoting something for someone) that can be interpreted independently of a referring situation (symbols and icons) and those that must be understood through the actual situation in which they occur (indices). A symbol is related to its referent through an arbitrary conventional bond, and an icon is related to its referent through a direct physical resemblance. In contrast, Peirce (1897) defined an index as a "sign which refers to the Object that it denotes by virtue of being really affected by that Object" (p. 102). Concurring with this criticism, Bates (1976) redefines pragmatics as "the study of linguistic indices" (p. 3).

Despite this criticism, I shall continue to use Morris's definition and treat pragmatics very generally as the study of the ways in which people use signs to perform various communicative functions. I would hold that something becomes a sign only insofar as it is used or interpreted by a subject to express information. A sign is anything whatsoever that serves a semantic function— whether arbitrarily, iconically, or indexically. Thus things are not signs "in themselves." Whether or not something is a sign will depend on its use or its function in relation to a subject. In this sense the pragmatic level would seem to provide a foundation for syntactic and semantic relationships.[1]

As I shall use the terms, a "symbol" is a sign used or interpreted to refer to something. By "reference" I mean an intentional act of indicating, "framing," or (in a sense) pointing to something. In the act of referring, one is presenting or showing an intended object to an observer, and the act serves the function of directing or focusing the attention of the observer on the referent. As Peirce noted, one may distinguish between iconic signs that are physically similar to their referents and arbitrary symbols. An index becomes a symbol when it is understood as indicating or pointing to some (referent) situation.

If one accepts the definition of a sign as something necessarily constituted by a subject it is clear that all signs stand in an essential pragmatic relation to those who use or interpret them. The syntactic and semantic structures of a language provide a system that enables speakers to transcend the private and contingent aspects of their experience and, using signs, to express specific referring intentions. As I shall argue, to interpret an utterance as a symbolic expression of an intention one must have information about the context of use.

Recently, linguists and psychologists have been investigating pragmatic structures, or regularities in the use of signs in certain situations.[2] This research complements earlier descriptive studies of grammatical (distributional) regularities, and ongoing investigation of cognitive (semantic) deep structures and may be viewed as a contribution to the empirical study of communicative competence. As I noted in Chapter 1, the empirical study of semantic and pragmatic as well as syntactic (and morphological) structures involves cooperative investigation by linguists, psychologists, and anthropologists, a development foreseen in 1936 by Malinowski, arguing for a truly empirical approach to the study of language:

Language cannot remain an independent and self-contained object of study, once we recognize that it is only the general norm of

1. Bates (1976) seems to hold essentially the same view, as she concludes that "semantics is derived from efforts to do things with words" (p. 354).

2. See, for example, *Papers from the Regional Meetings of the Chicago Linguistics Society* during the 1970s; the *LACUS Forum* series beginning in 1974; and the 1973 *Papers from the Texas Conference of Performatives, Conversational Implicature, and Presuppositions.*

human speech activities. . . . The dilemma of contemporary linguistics has important implications. It really means the decision as to whether the science of language will become an empirical study, carried out with living human beings within the context of their practical activities, or whether it will remain largely confined to deductive arguments, consisting of speculation based on written or printed evidence along. [p. 63][3]

The empirical study of pragmatic paradigms, as productive structures of a language, includes a number of areas. Philosophical analyses of "speech acts" (performatives), linguistic descriptions of "presuppositions," topic-comment structure, and deixis (indexical terms), anthropological models of ritualized speech, and psychological investigations of communication strategies explicate the prerequisites for communicative competence. In all of these areas one finds, again, a theoretical conflict between those who hold a rationalistic view of linguistic competence and those who hold an empiricist position. In general, the rationalistic claim is that the competent speaker possesses a tacit knowledge of a descriptively adequate (T-G) grammar. Knowledge of grammar accounts for the creativity of the speaker by providing a structural (phonological, syntactic, and semantic) description of all and only possible sentences of a language. Recently, rationalists have attempted to incorporate a pragmatic dimension in models of grammar by proposing "contextual rules" that will generate utterances as tokens of sentence types. The assumption is, again, that speakers are able to interpret novel utterances in context because of a knowledge of such rules.

In what follows, I shall first present an account of predication in terms of the pragmatic, topic-comment structure of utterances and second, argue against the rationalistic view of pragmatics by showing that linguistic judgments (of meaning and acceptability) are necessarily directed toward utterances rather than sentences, and that it is in principle impossible to generate the set of all and only possible utterance types. Thus, linguistic competence cannot involve knowledge of a descriptively adequate (T-G) grammar.

3. Hockett (personal communication) pointed out that in this passage Malinowski was inveighing against "arm-chair antiquarian philology." However, the remark has a contemporary application.

The Pragmatic Structure of Predicative Acts: Topic and Comment

Psychologists generally assume that the basic unit of discourse is the sentence, a linguistic structure that expresses a complete thought. It is not clear, however, how to characterize the specific, complex cognitive structure that counts as a complete thought: the predicative structure that is generally thought to be an essential feature of human speech. I shall consider a syntactic, semantic (logical), and pragmatic approach to this question, and argue for a pragmatic, topic-comment analysis of predication as the hierarchical structure determining the unit of discourse.

Leonard Bloomfield (1933) attempted to give a purely formal description of the "favorite sentence-types" of a language, commenting that they are "typically predicative." He defined a sentence as follows: "When a linguistic form occurs as part of a larger form, it is said to be in *included position:* otherwise it is said to be in *absolute position* and to constitute a *sentence*" (p. 170).[4] He distinguished full and minor sentences on the basis of whether or not they conformed to "favorite sentence-forms," or forms that enter into many types of constructions other than simple parataxis (conjunction). Sentences that contain favorite sentence-types, such as (in English) actor-action, goal-action, place-action, and so on, are full sentences, and those that do not are minor sentences. According to Bloomfield, minor sentences are either exclamatory ("Hello!," "This way, please!," "Mary!," etc.) or completive (forms that answer questions or supplement a situation, as, for example, "This one," "Gladly," and "When?"). Most, though not all, full sentences are predicative. Bloomfield defined a predicative form as a "bipartite favorite sentence-form" in which "the more object-like component is called the *subject,* the other part the *predicate*" (p. 173). Predication is understood formally as a construction combining members of the "subject" and "predicate" form classes.

Bloomfield gave the following informal, notional characterization of a sentence: "the meaning of the full sentence-type is

---

4. Hockett (1958) gives what he takes to be essentially the same definition of a sentence, only stated more clearly: "A *sentence* is a grammatical form which is not in construction with any other grammatical form: a constitute which is not a constituent" (p. 199).

something like "complete and novel utterance"—that is, the speaker implies that what he says is a full-sized occurrence or instruction, and that it somehow alters the hearer's situation" (p. 172). He went on to say, however, that it is a mistake to try to provide an exact definition of the "episememe" (meaning) of full sentences because such a task "lies beyond the domain of linguistics" (p. 172). And yet a purely syntactic analysis of predicative structures, and of sentences generally, fails to answer the question of just what makes a novel utterance "count" or be accepted as "complete." Why is it that some forms, in some situations, can be used as sentences, that is, spoken alone? What sort of cognitive structure underlies the use and interpretation of forms as predicative structures or as sentences? Bloomfieldian or distributional linguistics does not try to answer such questions because of the methodological requirement that linguists should limit themselves to describing formal structures in a language, simply using semantic information as a clue to the privileges of occurrence of a particular form.

Psychologists, on the other hand, are concerned about the type of thought or mental representation that linguistic structures express. Thus, psychologists are interested in describing the structure of predication in its cognitive dimension. For example, Bates (1976) thinks that predicative structures express a proposition, which she defines as "an internal activity of speakers rather than an object located in sentences" (p. 12). She claims that "when we provide formal representations for propositions, each predicate or argument node should stand for a corresponding mental operation or recurring complex of operations" (p. 12). Of course, in attributing semantic intentions to speakers, psychologists are undoubtedly influenced by presuppositions about the nature of human cognition. Rulon Wells (1971) summarized the matter very nicely:

> One basic logical truth that many human beings understand is that every sentence must have at least two components in its expression, the logical subject and the logical predicate. . . . All human beings who understand this truth will, when they turn their attention to facts of natural language, apply it by interpreting every language in such a way that this truth is conformed to. Any sentence that appears to have only one functional part will either (a) be treated

as elliptical, or (b) be viewed (like the 'one-word sentences' of child language) as not really a sentence after all, but only a signal, or (c) be broken up into functional parts even if the expression as such cannot be broken up into expressional parts.... The proposition, "Every sentence of every language has at least a subject and a predicate," is not an ... inductive generalization; it is a stipulation, true *a priori*, and stipulated on the basis of an understanding of logic. [p. 107]

Wells is saying that sentences, or "complete" utterances, express a basic logical structure of human thought, which he calls predicative. Thus (contrary to Bloomfield) all sentences are fundamentally predicative, and to interpret an utterance as a sentence is to attribute a predicative (semantic) structure to it.

But what, precisely, is the nature of the cognitive structure that provides the underlying semantic structure of sentences as composed of a subject and predicate. Wells suggests that predication is, in some sense, a logical structure, involving the attribution of a logical predicate to a logical subject.[5] According to this interpretation, predication would seem to be the logical operation of stating or asserting a proposition. Propositions might be characterized as the vehicles carrying truth-values (Bertrand Russell's [1919] account of propositions as "what we believe when we believe truly or falsely"), the "complete thought" expressed by sentences (Katz's [1972] position that "concepts and propositions are senses of expressions and sentences"), or the "common content" of various speech acts (John Searle's [1965] "propositional components" of illocutionary acts).

If predication is to be understood in terms of a "logical" model of propositions, of the sort worked out by Russell, then predicative structures are attempts to characterize matters of fact. If they are accurate characterizations, that is, if they correspond to a certain matter of fact, or state of affairs, then they are true. To give the meaning of a proposition is to specify its truth-conditions, that is, the conditions that must be met for the proposition to be true. On this account, to say that speakers produce sentential utterances that express or contain propositions is to say that speakers entertain or assert claims about matters of fact.

5. See Tsu-Lin Mei (1961) on frequent confusion between logical and grammatical criteria of a "sentence."

If propositions are the meanings of sentences, or at least components of the meanings of various sorts of utterances, and to explicate the meaning of a proposition is to specify truth-conditions, then the "logical" account of predication implies that speakers intend to consider and assert or deny a categorical description of some type. It implies that ordinary speakers are concerned about correspondence between propositions and fact: about whether or not sets of truth-conditions are met. When speakers believe something, what they believe is that some proposition is true or that some set of truth-conditions has been met or is met. For example, if one says, "Close the window," one is entertaining the proposition: some X that belongs to the class of persons one is addressing (at some time) and that is the only member of that class also belongs to the class of persons closing a particular window (which would be true if the person in question closed the window in question); and also expressing a desire (or command) that the action that would make the propositional content of the utterance true be carried out. If one says, "I found a shell on the beach," one is asserting the proposition: the one and only one member of the class of speakers at some point of space and time is also the only member of the class of persons who at some time found a shell on a particular beach. That is, one is saying that a representation of events corresponds to some matter of fact.

As is now well known, there are a number of difficulties resulting from a view of propositions as both the meanings (or "primary conceptual content") of utterances and the bearers of truth-value.[6] To the extent that propositions are introduced as the semantic structure underlying ordinary utterances and intended by speakers, my view is that such semantic descriptions should be subject to the same sort of empirical test as any other semantic model of natural language. From this perspective, one would treat the alleged propositions contemplated or asserted by speakers as logical statements. In the act of stating, a speaker contemplates the possible category membership of some logical subject, and in the act of asserting, a speaker makes a claim

6. For discussions of the issues see George Pitcher (1964), E. J. Lemmon (1966), Alonzo Church (1956), Bertrand Russell (1919), and Willard Quine (1969), pp. 139–160.

about the truth of a categorical judgment. The meaning of a logical statement is specified by truth-conditions that make explicit the conditions of category membership intended (stated or asserted) by a given speaker. A statement is thus a type of utterance meaning that takes into account the referring intention of a speaker.

There is an obvious difficulty in taking a theory of logical statements as a *general* account of the essential predicative structure of all complete utterances. The empirical question is, do speakers typically intend to express and assert logical statements when they speak? Do they understand that an utterance must assert a logical statement to be complete? Can they ordinarily specify truth-conditions for their utterances? Do they even have the notion of truth as correspondence between some statement and a state of affairs (assuming that is a clear concept), and are they contemplating sets of truth-conditions, or asserting that truth-conditions are met, when they say "Close the window" or "I am tired"? If the logical account of predication is a semantic theory, and not simply an attempt to "clarify" ordinary language by fitting it into the conventions of some logical system or making it scientifically accurate, then these are all empirical questions. I take it that the most plausible answer to such questions is no, ordinary language is not like that at all.

At least one recent controversy in philosophy of language suggests the difference between ordinary speech and "logical" models of statements. That is the controversy between Bertrand Russell and P. F. Strawson, or between Russell's Theory of Description and Strawson's Truth-Value Gap theory. Russell analyzed the sentence "The present king of France is bald" as meaning: there is one and only one king of France, and that person is bald. He claimed that to utter this sentence is to assert both parts of the proposition. Such an analysis gave him a statement having existential import, which would be false in case there were no king of France. Strawson objected that in this sentence, "There is a king of France" is only presupposed but not asserted. Thus, in case there is no king of France, a kind of felicity-condition for the aptness or appropriateness of the utterance is not met, and there is a truth-value gap. The sentence is neither true nor false. Strawson (1971) has decided that it is not important in any absolute way which analysis of the sentence is *the* correct one since (and here he seems to revert to the view that his analysis is correct after all) "it is still a decisive objection to the [Theory of Description]... that the existence of something answering to a definite description used for the purpose of identifying reference is *presupposed* and not *asserted* in an utterance..." (p. 92). Strawson goes on to point out that this Truth-Value Gap theory should probably appeal to people interested in describing actual speech situations, while the Theory of Description is likely to appeal to those concerned with the logical structure of impersonal statements. But the case of definite descriptions, interesting as it is, is simply the tip of the iceberg. Once one begins to take an interest in what speakers mean, or how they use language, one can never rest content with general assumptions about the logical meaning of any sentence. Semantic analysis is an empirical field. Therefore, hypotheses or intuitions about whether proper names have meaning or whether speakers must be able to provide identifying descriptions to use proper names, or whether speech acts have a conceptual content, or what the truth-conditions for a given sentence might be should be clearly labeled with respect to their empirical basis. The question for philosophers of language to answer first is, in what sense are descriptions of the meanings of utterances said to be true?

The question remains, how should predication be described as an essential linguistic structure, intended by speakers, which determines the basic unit of discourse? When speakers select certain linguistic structures to express a referring intention, the choice of those structures reflects a specific categorical judgment. Speakers who understand that certain linguistic forms express certain kinds of categories may be said to have linguistic knowledge. To claim, then, that speakers understand how much they must say in a complete utterance is to attribute to speakers a knowledge of an essential, predicative function that utterances must serve. If, then, utterances do not ordinarily express logical statements or intentions (though they presuppose categorical judgments that can be made explicit), a logical model of predication fails as a description of the more general linguistic function.

In my view, the predicative function of speech is most plausibly described in terms of topic-comment constructions. Hockett (1958) describes topics and comments as the immediate constituents of predicative constructions: "The speaker announces a topic and then says something about it. Thus *John/ran away; That new book by Thomas Guernsey/I haven't read yet.* In English and the familiar languages of Europe, topics are usually also subjects, and comments are predicates: so in *John/ran away.* But this identification fails sometimes in colloquial English, regularly in certain special situations in formal English, and more generally in some non-European languages" (p. 201). Clauses as well as sentences may be analyzed in terms of a topic-comment structure, for example, "In formal [English, in] *the man whom you visited here yesterday,* the relative clause *whom you visited here yesterday* has *whom* as topic, the remainder as comment" (Hockett, 1958, p. 201).

Though Hockett does not say so, it seems clear that the topic-comment structure of utterances is pragmatic. That is, the structure is defined neither by the grammatical relations of the terms (in discourse, for example, grammatical subjects or objects, clauses, sentences, or even several sentences may present either a topic or a comment) nor by their semantic structure (as, again, there are no restrictions on the semantic categories that can provide constituents for the topic or comment roles.) In general, something is treated as a topic, whether it is linguistically expressed or not, when it is taken as an intentional object or structure (invariant) of some type. A comment refers to some way in which that object can or should or will or does, etc., appear or manifest itself. Thus, a comment characterizes some structure in terms of one of its possible variations: it presents something (X) as something (Y). Though one can analyze such a predicative utterance, making the criteria underlying its categorical judgments explicit and converting it into the logical statement that (some) X is Y, the topic-comment structure does not itself ordinarily express this logical judgment. Thus, speakers who do not intend to make logical statements understand that an utterance is complete when it conveys, in context, a comment about some topic: presenting some X as Y.

It should be emphasized that a pragmatic model of predication does not, by itself, describe the deep structure of child (or adult) utterances. If children are in fact attempting to make predicative utterances in the sense of commenting on some probably contextual topic, they must pay attention to the formal devices available to express semantic intentions and thus to identify a topic and characterize it in a way that others can understand. A purely pragmatic account of holophrastic and two- and three-word utterances, such as Martin Braine's (1974) theory, leaves out this essential process of acquiring semantic-syntactic structures. Thus, Lois Bloom, Peggy Miller, and Lois Hood (1975) criticize Braine's pragmatic theory on the grounds that his formulation, "and pragmatic explanations in general, establish a serious discontinuity with later development. Such claims fail to contribute to explaining either (1) how the child eventually learns grammatical structure, or (2) the systematic (semantic-syntactic) regularities that are manifest among the earliest multi-word utterances" (p. 33).

Braine's proposal was that one-, two-, and three-word utterances have no more than a probabilistic distribution in child speech, based on the probability that a child will use one or more expansion rules in any utterance. "The small number of three- and four-word combinations in early corpora is probably due to the fact that when there are many one-word utterances, the probability of a child using any combinatorial rule in making an utterance is not great, and the probability of two or more rules being used in the same utterance is therefore very small" (p. 453). Braine argues that a child simply seizes "on some salient feature of the action [or situation] for which he has a word readily available.... His choice is pragmatic, and not determined by syntactic or semantic structure" (p. 455). This pragmatic selection of words continues for a while, even after children learn rules, because it takes more effort to use a rule than to select a word or words that single out the pragmatically salient feature to be communicated.

The problem with Braine's theory, as Bloom points out, is that it does not explain how children finally acquire "rules," or the syntactic-semantic patterns that are productive in a given language. I would add that it does not really characterize the meaning of one-word or multi-word utterances. Are they nothing more than verbal pointing gestures, or do they somehow encode semantic paradigms which then underlie the referring intention? Braine has nothing to say about this question. Bloom also criticizes Braine's hypothesis for being theoretically untestable (since the model would predict only that action events would call forth action utterances or no utterance at all, without specifying the form or length of the utterance). There is no way of demonstrating that the production of any given utterance is either "rule-governed" or "pragmatic." Further, the idea that words single out what is pragmatically salient rests on a circular argument, if pragmatic saliency is established from the fact that something is referred to or talked about. One needs a nonlinguistic measure of saliency. Moreover, it is unlikely that saliency alone determines what children talk about since there are at least two actions or occurrences that children perform or demand that they notably do *not* talk about: "dative" structures (giving or showing something to someone) and "instrumental" forms (using some means to achieve some end). As Bloom, Miller, and Hood (1975) point out: "However pragmatic such aspects of events may be (trivially, when a child wants to draw, crayons will be more salient than other objects) the children studied so far in this investigation and others use the corresponding linguistic forms only rarely (in this case the structural relations between such words as 'crayon' or 'fork' and action verbs)" (p. 34). Bloom et al. conclude from this point that linguistic complexity must be a factor in determining which forms children are able to use.

In the discussion of grammatical deep structure in Chapter 4, I concluded that the most plausible view of early utterances is that they express increasing semantic complexity as the child gradually becomes aware of and refers to salient structural features of things and events in the world and acquires the linguistic structures that express these intentional structures. But this semantic account does not fully explain what the unit of discourse is in child (or adult) language. The question is, what motivates children to select certain terms or expressions in certain situations? How do they know when they have said enough, or is there an obligatory predicative structure in child speech? A pragmatic theory of predication as the function of expressing comments about topics answers these questions and completes the earlier account of essential linguistic structures.

A number of empirical studies support the view that the earliest utterances express an explicit comment on an implicit topic and that children gradually learn to produce full topic-comment structures, probably both as a function of acquiring paradigms of "normal" (surface structure) subject-verb-object patterns (in English), and as a result of understanding how much information must be provided to communicate with others. Children at the earliest stage of speech have a knowledge of the predicative, topic-comment structure of utterances only in the sense that they are motivated to learn the forms that can be used to make or communicate comments. At a later stage, they learn to identify and articulate a topic within increasingly abstract or sophisticated contexts, and to express or identify comments in relation to such topics.

A number of psychologists have argued that holophrastic and early multi-word utterances have a comment or topic-comment structure. Lev Vygotsky (1934) argued that "egocentric" speech consisted of comments on a contextually implicit topic that was obvious to the child and therefore in no need of expression. Such comments enabled a child to focus or concentrate on those aspects of the world, or her own activity, that were of primary concern, as a kind of salient "figure" against an implicit situational "ground." More recently, Hermina Sinclair (1970), speaking from a Piagetian framework, noted that "present opinion has swung towards the idea that ... holophrases are first instances of the topic-comment combination with the topic deleted" (p. 125). Adopting Piaget's distinction between "action-judgments" (judgments about regularities in action patterns or schemas) and "observation judgments" (judgments about regularities in properties of objects, or perceptual schemas), Sinclair agrees with Piaget that the child's first utterances represent translations of action patterns and suggests that they are more like fused topic and comment than a topic and comment *construction*. For example, when a French child says 'ate' (for "par terre"—on the floor—when something has fallen down), it seems counter to common sense to say the child is *commenting* ("it falls") on a topic ("the book"). "Such expressions seem much nearer to an adult exclamation like "There!," which reflects a whole event without any analysis" (Sinclair, 1970, p. 125). I take this comment to mean that the child is probably not explicitly *representing* a full semantic or linguistic structure such as "The book falls on the floor" and then expressing only the "comment" portion, 'ate', for "falls on the floor." However, the expression is a comment in the sense that it refers to some new or salient aspect of a given entity.

Elizabeth Bates (1976) reported a number of studies, carried out by herself and by other researchers, that bear directly on the topic-comment structure of speech. Bates's work represents one of the most sophisticated and complete studies of pragmatic structures yet to appear in print, so I shall cite a number of her observations and conclusions. Bates essentially concurs with the conclusions reached by Patricia Greenfield and Joshua Smith (1976) in a study of holophrastic speech that specifically considered speech in relation to dialogue and situation. As Bates (1976) points out, "the child builds his comments onto externally supplied topics" (p. 98). The first topics are immediately physically present in the situation, then adults provide verbal frames that indicate topics, and finally children learn to construct their own verbal contexts that present topics within an imaginative "discourse space."

Bates accepts Piaget's theory of cognitive development from implicit schemas to explicit figurative and operative knowledge and argues on this basis that early speech occurs on two "symbolic" levels. "Due to limits in the capacity for symbolic representation, the child must select only one element from a structured sensorimotor scheme for encoding into speech" (pp. 104–5). That is, the *topic* of early utterances exists within the environment that has been "organized" or structured at the perceptual-motor level, but is not expressed or "symbolized" because the child has not completed the process of converting all of the implicit schemas into figurative knowledge. "Later, when the child has a larger capacity for symbolic processing, he may incorporate both the topic and comment into his utterance. But the original topic-comment distinction in speech is based on a distinction between what is said and what is not said" (p. 105).

Once the child has converted implicit knowledge of the world into figurative knowledge, both topics and comments may be expressed in a single utterance, and the child is ready to acquire those grammatical conventions imposed by a given language which govern the function of expressing topics and comments. In English, one of these conventions is that the subject of a sentence will ordinarily be interpreted as the topic, and the predicate as the comment, though this is not necessarily the case. Bates cites N. S. Trubetzkoy's (1939) markedness theory in support of the claim that the active declarative form in English is unmarked with respect to topic and comment structure. "A man drank beer" may suggest that "a man" is the topic and "drank a beer" is the comment, but if all the information presented by the utterance is new, it is possible that it might present some beer as drunk by a man. "A beer was drunk by a man," however, marks "a beer" as topic, and "was drunk by a man" as comment, as would such other devices as emphasis or intonation ("A *man* drank a beer" or "A man *drank* a beer"), use of definite articles ("A man drank the beer"), and clefting ("It was a man that drank the beer"). These grammatical devices are indices of a speaker's recognition that some aspect of a situation should be taken for granted as already understood or structured in a specific way, while the "point" or interest of a remark lies in some variation or contingent aspect of the given structure. (See MacWhinney and Bates, 1978, for experimental data.)

In one respect, then, the topic-comment distinction can be identified with a "given-new" distinction, since a topic is taken as structured in a given way, while the comment presents new information about that structure. Furthermore, if some structure is treated as contextually given, it will serve as the topic of further relevant comments. On the other hand, a topic may also introduce new information, just as a comment may express old information about some structure. Thus, a topic-comment structure represents "givenness" in relation to the intentional framework established by a speaker, who distinguishes an intended referent in a specific way. In discourse, the focus of interest is on the comment, which typically presents new information about some, usually variable, aspect of a given structure.

It is generally assumed that children's first comments will express perceptually salient aspects of the child's experience. Saliency might be a function of biological predispositions, novelty or "information content," or some other factor. This assumption is plausible (keeping in mind the possibility that something might be salient in one respect but not in another), as long as it is not assumed that, in general, topics can never express salient dimensions of experience while comments must always do so.

Bloom, Miller, and Hood (1975) have objected to the idea that children's comments reflect the saliency of features because, they say, this claim seems to rest on a circular argument. The claim that children talk about what is salient (that is, that if something is talked about it is salient) is supported by evidence that presupposes the truth of that claim, since the evidence that something is salient is that it is talked about. (Being salient is not a sufficient condition for being talked about, though, since, as Bloom and her associates note, dative and instrumental situations are clearly salient—children constantly give and show things and use instruments to accomplish ends—but children use dative and instrumental forms infrequently.) Bates is aware of this dilemma and says that the solution is to find an independent method of determining what is salient to a child in an experimental situation and observe the child's language. For example, in the Greenfield and Smith (1976) study, the informative aspect of a situation, which was expected to elicit comment from a child, was defined in terms of its variability or uncertainty. For example, if a child did a number of things to the same object (putting it in her mouth, throwing it in the air, etc.), each action would be the salient feature likely to be referred to or commented on; whereas if a child did the same thing to a number of objects (putting various toys in a box), the salient point would be the identity of the object. Similarly, if there were a dispute about who owned or who could play with a toy, the identity of the owner was likely to be salient. When such situations do occur, Greenfield and Smith reported, children comment on the salient or informative element.

The idea that the salient feature eliciting comment in some situation will be that subject to the greatest change or uncertainty might account for the low frequency of dative and instrumental forms reported by Bloom et al. (1975) as evidence against the claim that children talk about what is salient. Though dative and instrumental forms would express salient structures in children's experience, children would be unlikely to refer to the instrumental function of something, or to a person who is to take or receive something, unless there were some uncertainty about these points. The object of attention is more likely to be *what* should be given or taken or what is being or should be done with some instrument. Thus, something becomes a focus of linguistic comment not simply because one is aware of it or because it is a salient structure in a general sense, but because one needs to focus attention on it in some situation.

Bates and her associates took advantage of a grammatical feature of casual Italian speech to see if children first produced comment-topic (or, new information-old information) utterances, before switching to the more standard topic-comment order of adult speech. Although the standard word order in active declarative sentences in Italian is subject-verb-object (s-v-o) as in English, with the grammatical (surface structure) subject ordinarily encoding the (pragmatic) topic, word order is fairly flexible in casual speech, and it is possible to produce the subject at the end of a sentence. Bates theorized that children who were already encoding both topics and comments would, at first, produce a comment-topic structure as a result of spontaneously referring to new or salient information, adding on a topic as an afterthought; and then switch to a topic-comment (or s-v-o) format, perhaps as a result both of becoming aware of a standard s-v-o pattern and of the need to identify a topic in communicating with others. The results supported the hypothesis:

> The longitudinal records for Claudia and Francesco yield an unusual developmental pattern for standard versus optional SVO ordering. In the first transcripts, there is a tendency to preserve subject-final orders, although subject-first order do occasionally occur. This is followed by a long period of session by session alternation between subject-final and subject-first preference. Around MLU [mean length of utterance] 4.0, both children pass through a brief "conservative" period in which they strongly prefer SVO ordering, and express the subject under conditions in which an adult would delete it. Finally, both children display patterns indistinguishable from those of adults. [Bates, 1976, p. 208]

Bates concludes that the subject-final word order is an extension of the child's first strategy of expressing only comments, or salient new information, leaving the context to provide an implicit topic. Gradually, the child adds on the topic, still referring first to the element of a situation that seizes attention. Finally, the child becomes aware of standard word order for a syntactic subject (usually also the topic): the term that comes before the verb and agrees with it in person and number.

Bates's study of early speech patterns suggests that children treat utterances as "complete" when they express or communicate an intended comment in some context. One assumes that they treat utterances that do not express a topic or a comment as elliptical forms that may be understood within the immediate context if that provides the missing information. Children gradually learn to supply their listeners with information about an intended topic in response to communication pressures, and it is only at a later stage that they acquire a standard word order as a formal structure of sentences rather than as, perhaps, an occasional effect of other pragmatic-semantic intentions. If this view is correct, then the obligatory predicative structure discussed by Bloom should be described in pragmatic rather than syntactic terms.

The pragmatic model of predication I have been considering is intended to describe adult as well as child utterances. If there is a difference between the predicative structures of child and adult speech, I think it is likely to be found in the range of comments that can be communicated. Adults have a better command of the semantic structure of a language, a better understanding of the information requirements of others, and, perhaps, a greater capacity to represent and remember a number of complex aspects of the communicative context in which they are producing and interpreting comments. In general, one would expect adults to communicate better than children when the topics were not easily discoverable from a discourse context.

Adults are also aware of a number of rhetorical possibilities. They recognize a number of mental attitudes and social conventions on which they are able to comment and about which children know little or nothing. For example, if a woman were discussing a situation that angered her with someone who believes it is wrong for people, especially women, to express anger, she might say, "Of course, I would never want to seem angry." The statement is ironic because it seems to be making one comment (anger is something that shouldn't be expressed) when it is actually making another (that people should be allowed to show anger). Irony is a rhetorical mode that "frames" one position or attitude held by a speaker that is the very opposite of the (usually conventional) view or sentiment expressed by the sentence. One must be familiar with the use of irony and aware of the attitude of the speaker to grasp that a sentence is being used in a way that undermines its ordinary meaning. (If a speaker who didn't ordinarily use prim expressions said something like, "Of course it would never do to be angry," the phrase "it would never do" might be a clue to the ironic intention.)

Another rhetorical form that suggests the range of comments that can be framed by language is what Ann Weiser (1974) called "deliberate ambiguity." Weiser argues against a pragmatic model that would try to define rules assigning a definite, unambiguous meaning to utterance types used in certain situations. Her point is not that one can't describe rules, but that there must be a rule allowing some utterances to be deliberately ambiguous. She says that in socially tricky situations this sort of ambiguity is essential. For example, suppose one has a friend on a committee conducting a secret investigation of some subject in which one is very interested. One wants to see if one's friend will say what is going on, but does not want to suggest that one's friend is unethical. What does one say? One could say, "I'm curious about what went on at the hearing." If the friend is willing to talk, the sentence will be treated as a request for information; if not, as a simple statement that one is curious. To interpret this utterance, one must be aware of the considerations that might have passed through a speaker's mind in framing it. One might simply take it as a declarative statement or as a request. Or one might realize that it is a deliberately ambiguous utterance and respond (humorously or disapprovingly) with, "But of course you wouldn't want to ask!" Obviously, the most interesting conversationalists are those who respond not simply to the straightforward level of what is conventionally said, but also, when appropriate, to the *person* who decided to say, or not to say, certain things in certain situations. A conversation in which the participants seem to understand the motives for saying certain things in certain ways is apt to seem particularly interesting or intimate to them, while it may appear utterly incomprehensible or boring to some observer.

Weiser seems to think that deliberately ambiguous sentences have two definite meanings and that only one of the meanings will be conveyed to a listener, without the speaker's being able to predict which one. But it seems to me that the utterance that is *understood* as intentionally ambiguous is more interesting and occurs more frequently. For example, suppose that I am a health fanatic, faithfully taking vitamins and exercising and eating organic food every day, and that I have a friend who is not terribly concerned about these things. I say to my friend, "*I* exercise every day," stressing the "I." What does the utterance mean? My friend knows that I wouldn't simply refer to or describe my practice because she knows that I know that she already knows about it. Perhaps, then, I am covertly advising my friend to start exercising, or gloating about my superior virtue. On the face of it, the stress on "I" might suggest this interpretation (perhaps marking "my doing it" as the comment, leading to some further comment such as "Why don't you do it" or "Isn't that great?"). But suppose my friend knows that I wouldn't gloat about that and that I think she should exercise and knows that I know repetition of the advice would be futile. What interpretation is left? I am, of course, being humorous—using an utterance that *might* be intended and interpreted as deliberately ambiguous to frame my own lack of serious intention to give her deliberately ambiguous advice. The topic-comment structure presents the ambiguous utterance (the covert advice) as a comment that I am not in fact making seriously, but that I nonetheless present as a comment that is amusing for all the reasons leading my interlocutor to reject the possibility that I am serious.

I hope that my example will not be thought unduly complicated. My purpose is to show the flexibility of topic-comment analysis in dealing with the sorts of conversational exchanges and shifting levels of seriousness common in speech. In the next section, I shall consider the limitations that the open possibilities of utterance meanings place on the goal of descriptive adequacy as formulated within rationalistic linguistics.

Rationalistic Pragmatics: Contextual Rules

Linguistic competence accounts for the ability to produce and interpret novel utterances. From the rationalistic perspective, competent speakers know a set of rules that, in Katz's (1972) words, "enable [the speaker] to obtain the meaning of any new sentence as a compositional function of the meanings of its parts and their syntactic organization" (p. 33). One cannot interpret an utterance, however, without some knowledge of context, and for this reason, linguists who have accepted Chomsky's model of a descriptively adequate linguistic theory are attempting to supplement syntactic semantic theory with pragmatic rules of contextual construal.

Katz (1972) has acknowledged that in many cases a "sentence means one thing while its utterance (in context) means another" (p. 443). He sees the sentence-utterance distinction as one of type and token, claiming that syntactic rules generate the set of all and only grammatical sentence types and semantic rules provide sentence meanings for this set, while, in principle, pragmatic rules complete the interpretation of an utterance (sentence token) by generating its meaning as a function of contextual features. He concludes that "a theory of linguistic communication involves principles of contextual interpretation that go well beyond the scope of semantic theory [although] . . . these principles require antecedently specified semantic representations of the sentences of the language" (p. 443). Thus, a complete or adequate theory of competence would include a "theory of contextual construal," or a set of pragmatic rules of the sort proposed by Grice, which would determine the utterance meaning of all sentence tokens, given a prior semantic interpretation of their sentence type. Essentially, such rules would, in my view, represent an expansion of semantic theory necessary to accomplish the rationalistic goal of providing a structural (syntactic and semantic) description of all possible utterances as exemplars of sentences of a language: reducing possible utterance meanings to a set of possible sentence meanings determined by a finite number of grammatical rules. On this account, the competent speaker would interpret an utterance as a token of a sentence type by selecting one interpretation from a set of possible senses, as a function of the meaning of the sentence type generated by semantic and pragmatic rules.

Katz believes that a "significant advance" in the formulation of pragmatic rules has been made by Grice, who presented a theory of "conversational implicature" in the 1967–68 William James lecture series at Harvard. Grice proposed that speakers informally agree to be "cooperative," and hence to be informative enough (but not too informative), clear, succinct, relevant, and truthful. Thus, if someone asks if one has the time, one doesn't simply say yes, but interprets the question as a polite request for relevant information ("what time is it?"). According to Grice, this interpretation is based on knowledge of the rule "Be relevant!" One can thus reason that a simple statement that one knows the time must be irrelevant to the questioner, and that therefore the question must be relevant to the questioner's desire that one share one's knowledge of the time. Again, if someone states publicly that "Richard Nixon steals candy from babies," knowing that whoever hears this utterance does not know that Richard Nixon is the name of the speaker's grocer (who steals candy from babies), then the "cooperative principle" justifies the interpretation that the speaker is referring to a former United States president, and the speaker is responsible (and may be held liable) for this interpretation. The cooperative principle requires speakers to provide as much information as is necessary for listeners to identify an intended referent, and since all speakers are held to know this principle, the speaker may properly be taken to intend a reference to the former president.

From an empirical standpoint, Grice's proposal is subject to experimental confirmation insofar as it purports to describe an aspect of linguistic knowledge that enters into the production and interpretation of utterances. I do not find it convincing as a description of linguistic rules. For example, though it might be true that speakers use a conversational postulate to interpret expressions such as "Do you know what time it is?," it is more plausible that such expressions are taken as requests for information simply because they are conventional formulas. One is familiar with a number of questions such as "Do you have the salt?," "Would you mind moving a bit?," "Do you have a program?," etc., which are immediately recognized as polite requests, just as "My name is Mary Doe" is taken as a conventional way of introducing oneself. The idea that speakers somehow agree to cooperate by being clear, succinct, truthful, informative, and so on, strikes me as a bit utopian. There may be speakers who do this (perhaps Grice does it), but I suspect that most speakers not only do not follow this rule but are not, in any verifiable sense, aware of it.

What is true, of course, is that if speakers are to communicate, they must provide sufficient information *in context* for a listener to identify an intended referent. (Speakers may also, at times, choose to deceive or mislead listeners on this score.) Grice's rule, however, does not provide a means of determining *the* intended referent and thus *the* meaning of a given utterance. At best, it suggests assumptions most listeners may take for granted—that a speaker is telling the truth and is aware of the need to consider the listener's informational needs in the context of the utterance. But even if these assumptions are usually correct, the meaning of a given utterance will still vary as a function of the speaker's referring intention, and that may be determinable only by a listener who has nonlinguistic information about the context, and thus for whom the utterance "makes sense."

Gordon and Lakoff (1971) have expanded Grice's proposal into a set of rules for interpreting utterances. For example, suppose someone says, "Why do you paint your house purple?" This question is said to be intuitively ambiguous. (The authors do not raise the question of intonation.) It might be a simple request for reasons, or it might be a negative judgment about the color of the paint. On the other hand, if someone says, "Why paint your house purple?" it is intuitively clear, according to Gordon and Lakoff, that the utterance means, "Unless you have a good reason for painting your house purple, you shouldn't do so." According to Gordon and Lakoff, one is able to make this judgment because of tacit knowledge of a rule that there can be "*you* + tense" deletion only if a negative judgment is intended.

With this sort of analysis, Gordon and Lakoff have expanded Chomsky's theory of descriptive adequacy by providing rules that account for pragmatic ambiguity and that, in theory, describe systematic relationships between linguistic structures and specific (pragmatic) referring intentions. The problem with this notion of pragmatic ambiguity is that it opens the door to a potentially unbounded set of referring intentions that would render all sentences ambiguous in an indeterminate number of ways. For example, if I happen to love the color purple, and know that my neighbor knows that, and I see my neighbor has chosen purple to paint her house, I might think she has done so because I like purple. Thus I might ask, "Why do you paint your house purple?" as a request for reasons, as an expression of positive judgment about the color, and perhaps to indicate tacit understanding of the act as a gesture in my direction. To say the sentence is ambiguous, then, is simply to acknowledge that it is an utterance that might be used in many situations, and that might be accompanied by various feelings in the speaker (curiosity, disapproval, hilarity, approval, etc.). Either it is a mistake to call such a question ambiguous, or the question, along with all other sentences, is ambiguous in many more ways than Gordon and Lakoff allow. And surely one does not interpret the feelings behind such utterances by means of a linguistic rule. This sort of pragmatic ambiguity points to the irreducibility of utterance meaning. At some point listeners must base interpretations of utterances on their knowledge of the context and the speaker, and such knowledge is not a part of linguistic theory.

But what about the alleged nonambiguity of "Why paint your house purple?" (This might have been a linguistically "purer" example if the color had been white.) *Must* it imply a negative judgment? Is there a "*you* + tense" deletion rule that describes this case and accounts for one's intuition? Another possibility is that the "deleted" (or elliptical) question involves a linguistic pattern that sets up an expectation that it will be followed by a clause such as "when you could paint it yellow" or "when you could use weathered shingles" or "when you know I hate the color." This need not involve a knowledge of any abstract rule, but simply the operation of a certain structural analogy. A formula one often hears and uses is "Why do X when you could do

Y? This formula suggests some measure of disapproval of the choice of *X*. The form "Why do *X*?" might also suggest such disapproval because it is similar (analogous) to that formula. On the other hand, "Why are you doing *X*?" might be the first part of the formula "Why are you doing *X* when you might be doing *Y*?" (thus indicating disapproval), or it might simply stand as the neutral question formula, "Why are you *X*-ing?" If there is some reason to think that a questioner using this formula disapproves of one's "*X*-ing," one might very well interpret a question of this form as ambiguous because it is not clear whether the speaker disapproves. (Of course, there is reason to think that people might disapprove of purple house paint.)

The interpretation that "Why paint your house purple?" expresses a negative judgment might be informally tested as follows. If the intuition is based on an analogy, then it should be possible to provide a context that blocks out that interpretation (or which inhibits the operation of that analogy), and in that context the question should cease to imply a negative judgment. On the other hand, if the intuition is based on a rule that stipulates a negative interpretation in all contexts, the negative connotation should remain. Suppose, then, that I am arguing with someone about whether or not people have rational reasons for doing things or simply do things because of irrational preferences or tastes. My friend insists that she has reasons for everything. I think not, and so I say, "Well, why live in the country? Why grow daffodils? Why paint your house purple?" I am simply asking for reasons.

My intention is not to evaluate a list of pragmatic rules, some of which are more vulnerable and absurd than others. I am not denying that there are pragmatic structures in language, in the sense of regularities in the use of linguistic signs in certain types of situations, and I agree that the description of such regularities, as paradigms that inform linguistic competence, is a legitimate empirical goal. I would argue, however, that there can be no descriptively adequate grammar, even one supplemented by pragmatic structures, that enables speakers to determine either the grammatical acceptability or the meaning of all possible utterances.

To use language effectively means to succeed in directing the attention of the person one is addressing to one's intended referent. This involves providing sufficient information in a context so that the intended listener can identify the topic and comment presented in an utterance. The syntactic, semantic, and pragmatic structures of a language are tools that are used, more or less effectively, to perform this referential and communicative function. However, the interpretation of a given utterance requires, in addition to a knowledge of linguistic structures, knowledge of context and of a speaker's intention that cannot be included in linguistic theory. For this reason, no grammar can generate all and only acceptable utterances of a language.

Once one approaches language as a communicative system, or a set of tools that convey a referring intention, it becomes clear that intuitions about the grammatical acceptability or meaning of an utterance reflect the judgment that it does (or might) successfully convey a particular intention in some situation. To decide that some utterance is acceptable is to find a context in which it could be used in this way. An utterance for which one can find no context (and which is thus "meaningless") is, to that extent, unacceptable or "ungrammatical"; and utterances that make sense in some contexts but not in others are, in relation to those contexts, acceptable or unacceptable. Thus, intuitive linguistic judgments of acceptability are directed toward utterances in possible contexts rather than sentences considered apart from any context or communicative function.

For example, consider the sentence "She thinks soup." Is it grammatical or ungrammatical? That depends. It is quite acceptable as a response to "Ask Mary if Bill would prefer soup or salad with dinner." On the other hand, one can't find a context in which "soup" might stand as the direct (semantic) object of "thinks," so on this interpretation it is unacceptable. What about "He throws," which, on Chomsky's account, is ungrammatical because it violates the rule that transitive verbs must take objects? There are, in fact, a number of contexts in which such an utterance might be used, for example, in response to the question "Does a pitcher throw or hit the ball?" Conversely, a sentence that, in general, sounds all right, such as "He went to town," would be judged unacceptable if it were used (for example, by a child, or someone just learning English) to refer to a present or future state of affairs. That is, one accepts the sentence as a possible utterance because one can think of contexts in which its use would be appropriate, but in some possible contexts uttering the sentence would be unacceptable.

Ordinarily, one would assume that utterances such as "He throws" or "She thinks soup" are elliptical expressions, but this assumption requires clarification. Chomsky's claim is that such an interpretation reflects the judgment that such sentences violate certain syntactic rules, for example, a rule of strict subcategorization governing transitive verbs, or a selection restriction on the kinds of nouns that can function as a direct object of a verb such as "thinks." From this perspective, one possible interpretation of the sentences is that they are deleted versions of kernel sentences that do not violate the rules of grammar. If a C-model describes what speakers know about language, and what speakers know enters into the processing of utterances, then Chomsky's theory says that in some sense speakers are aware of the more abstract syntactic structures from which the surface structure is derived. However, this theory (which, as I indicated, may be doubted for more general reasons) does not really account for the acceptability or unacceptability of sentences as utterances. For example, if "She thinks soup" is "derived" from "She thinks that she would like soup" or "She thinks that her preference would be soup," it would be grammatical in Chomsky's sense, but unacceptable as a response to a question about Bill's preference. In that context it would fail to communicate an intended referential meaning.

A pragmatic model of language offers an alternative explanation for the intuition that in some sense sentences such as "He throws" are ungrammatical or incomplete. The problem with "He throws" is that "throwing" is an action that is cognitively tied to an object or patient that is acted on: in traditional terms, the direct object that "receives" the action. Semantically, then, the verb indicates a relation between some agent ('he'), as acting, and some object acted on. Thus, to say merely that an agent stands in some active relationship, without specifying the object to which it is related, leaves the comment unfinished or incomplete. For this reason, it can be interpreted as a communicative utterance (and thus as grammatical) only on condition that one is able to supply a referential context that completes the semantic schema indicated by the sentence by supplying an object as an element of an unstated topic. By contrast, sentences such as "He dies" or "The plot thickens" do not require a context to fill in terms of a semantic relationship. So-called intransitive verbs attribute a sort of absolute, or nonrelational, property to a subject and thus convey a complete comment. Thus one can interpret such sentences as communicative and therefore grammatical utterances simply by providing a context in which such a referring intention would be appropriate. Such sentences are complete in the sense that one does not require a context of use to supply an unstated topic or comment.

In the case of verbs that can be interpreted as transitive or intransitive, the deciding factor seems to be context, which determines whether the verb expresses a comment (intransitive), or requires an object that will express or complete a comment (transitive). For example, "He dances" expresses a complete topic-comment structure if one views it as presenting some male as dancing. Questions such as "What does he do on weekends?" or "Is he a singer or dancer in the show?" provide a context for this interpretation. But other contexts might produce a different interpretation of topic-comment structure. For example, if someone is asked what kind of dancing someone does, the topic becomes that person's dancing, and the response "He dances" would be inappropriate since it repeats the topic but fails to comment on it by characterizing the dancing in some way. "He dances the waltz" makes a comment in this context, and under that interpretation the verb is transitive.

In general, a pragmatic model of elliptical sentences differs from Chomsky's formal model of sentence derivation by focusing on such sentences as utterances in possible contexts. On this approach, what is said may be viewed as a comment on an unsaid topic, which is supplied by the verbal or situational context of the utterance. Thus, one possible context for "He throws" might be the question "Does a pitcher throw or hit the ball?," which supplies a topic—what a pitcher does with a ball (as object)—for the spoken comment "He throws." Alternatively, a sportscaster might be describing a baseball game play by play and about a crucial pitch comment, "He throws," followed by, "and it's hit out of the field." Similarly, one can imagine a verbal context— "What does Mary think Bill would prefer with dinner?"—that would supply an unspoken topic for the spoken comment "She thinks soup." Accordingly, "full" or nonelliptical versions of these utterances would express the implicit or unsaid topic: "A pitcher throws the ball," and "Mary thinks Bill would prefer soup with dinner." These utterances would be acceptable insofar as they use the syntactic-semantic conventions of the language to communicate a given referring intention in some situation.

If the judgment that a sentence is grammatical turns on the recognition that it may serve a communicative function as an utterance, the judgment that a sentence is ungrammatical turns on a recognition that it does not serve a communicative function in any obvious context. Thus, for example, on the face of it, "He went to town tomorrow" suggests a semantic structure that can never find a proper referential context. "The pitcher threw one balls" suggests both that only one ball and more than one ball was thrown, a state of affairs that is presumably impossible. Such sentences, of course, would not be produced as utterances by anyone familiar with the language. In both cases, the ultimate judgment of grammatical acceptability turns on the communicative function or potential of the utterance. On the other hand, a science fiction writer might be able to invent a context in which "He went to town tomorrow" would be a perfectly acceptable utterance. In the same way, there might be contexts (for example, a Disney cartoon) in which one would accept "My frying pan thinks I'm crazy." Again, a poet might refer to jealous ideas as "colorlessly green" and "furiously sleeping," and a painter might express a desire to "paint a circular square." If the painter spoke sincerely and literally we would, perhaps, take his utterance as a symptom of insanity, but if the tone were wistful, we would interpret it as a perfectly acceptable statement about the impossibility of some task. I conclude that judgments about grammatical acceptability are directed at utterances rather than sentences, and that such judgments are dependent on context rather than determined by rules that generate the set of all and only grammatical sentences of a language. A knowledge of linguistic structures is necessary but not sufficient to judge the grammatical acceptability of utterances.

The pragmatic basis of interpretation is still more obvious in determining the meaning of a given utterance as it is used in some context. So-called deictic terms, such as pronouns, demonstratives, and adverbs of time and place, have a sort of general, structural meaning in that they signal information about the individual who uses them. Thus, 'I' is always the speaker, 'you' the listener or set of listeners, and 'they' others who are not being addressed. Similarly, 'now' indicates the moment at which the utterances occurs, and 'then' some other time. 'This' refers to an object spatially close at hand or to a topic of conversation that has already been identified in some way. A knowledge of these structures is necessary to use such terms properly to provide accurate information about one's referring intention in some context. A listener who hears someone say, "I am getting tired" will know that it is the speaker who is tired; similarly "I must go now" indicates that the speaker plans to leave immediately. However, unless one knows who the speaker is, or at what time the utterance occurred, one cannot fully determine the meaning of the utterance.

In general, speakers use context to minimize the amount of information that must be provided in an utterance. Failure to do so would lead to intolerable verbosity. Given the communicative function of speech, one is required only to provide sufficient information so that one's interlocutor can follow one's reference in context. If a listener cannot identify a particular referent (or interpret some comment), she is free to ask questions, to demand clarification, or to test an interpretation in some way. But no conceivable set of grammatical rules and lexical entries can provide *the* utterance meaning of what I shall call an indicative utterance—one that indicates or points to a particular individual object (or set of objects) known to the speaker and about which some comment is made. Thus, "The book on the table is yours" or "These problems are enormous" may mean one thing (and have one truth-value) in one situation and something else in another.

When such sentences are "mentioned" to illustrate a point

about language rather than "used" to make a comment about a particular referent, the terms or expressions under discussion are signs that express or frame a specific paradigmatic (semantic) structure, and the ordinary communicative or indicative use of such signs is suspended. For example, "These problems are enormous" above expresses a certain semantic structure but does not refer to any particular "problems." However, this sentence-meaning, abstracting from a referential context, is incomplete, since no particular referent is intended or specified, and thus the utterance has no truth-value.

Information that is essential for the interpretation of an utterance may also be provided by a discourse context. Thus, to follow the referring intention of the speaker who says, "The type of person you described last night is sure to be unhappy," one must search one's memory of previous discourse to identify the speaker's topic. (See Bransford and Johnson, 1972; Schallert, 1976; Thorndyke, 1976; and Swinney and Hakes, 1976 for studies of discourse factors in comprehension.) In fact, the contextual factor is of such fundamental importance that some utterances are virtually unintelligible when taken out of context. Bransford and Johnson (1973) conducted some interesting experimental tests of language comprehension in what I would call a referential vacuum (that is, without providing a topic) that bears out this claim. They asked subjects to rate a set of instructions in terms of their intelligibility. The following paragraph was generally rated incomprehensible.

> The procedure is actually quite simple. First you arrange things into different groups depending on their makeup. Of course, one pile may be sufficient depending on how much there is to do. If you have to go somewhere else due to lack of facilities that is the next step, otherwise you are pretty well set. It is important not to overdo any particular endeavor. That is, it is better to do too few things at once than too many. . . .

This "incomprehensible" paragraph becomes quite clear if one interprets it in relation to the topic of washing clothes; in fact, these are the kinds of instructions people habitually give when it is already clear what one is talking about.

Thus far, I have observed that one may require contextual

information to identify a speaker's intended referent or topic. One may also require information about context or about a speaker to determine the nature of the comment which a speaker intends. For example, suppose one hears someone say, "The window is open." Is this utterance a simple declarative sentence or a command or request of some kind? To decide, one must know something about the situation and make inferences about the situation or the rhetorical style of the speaker. If the speaker is cold, or one thinks she might be, it could be (depending on the authority of the speaker) a command or a request. Similarly, if someone asks me if I've read Plato, I may interpret the utterance as a simple question, an insult, or a humorous remark, depending on the context, and what I take to be the speaker's referring intention. If I've just criticized some interpretation of the *Ion,* it's probably an insult. If someone has just said that to be fully civilized one must read Plato, it may be humorous. But if someone asks me such a question in response to my criticism of a mutual friend, the remark might be an abrupt, and disapproving, change of topic.

In the interpretation of rhetorical modes one is, of course, aided by the conventional markers provided by a language. There are special intonation patterns or linguistic formulas that convey intentions to question or make polite requests, promises, and so on. An indefinite number of intentions, however, are not marked in any particular way, and it is often quite a difficult matter to decide whether some utterance is, for example, friendly or condescending, critical or complimentary, and so on. Yet, the utterance meaning of such classic formulations as "You are quite remarkable" hangs in the balance.

Moreover, the interpretation of a speaker's referring intention is not confined to questions about the "use" to which a given speaker might put some independently meaningful "proposition." In fact, it is the speaker's intention that determines the comment that is expressed by a sentence. John Austin's (1962) example "France is hexagonal" makes this point nicely. As Austin pointed out, the truth or falsity of this claim depends on the "speech act" that a speaker performs in uttering the sentence. If one means to make a mathematically precise statement, it is false; but if one intends to speak only very roughly, then it is true. One cannot decide this question on the basis of linguistic knowledge.

One can think of many examples of utterances that clearly call on a listener to make inferences about the referring intention of a speaker. In general, one must determine the "logical" or paradigmatic criteria that underlie the categorical judgments made by some speaker. One may need both contextual information and some understanding of a speaker's paradigms to discover the utterance meaning of such sentences as "The theatre is very far away," "I never waste time," and "My neighbor is crazy." Indeed, if one is dealing with poetic metaphors or with an utterance of some profundity (Shakespeare's "Life . . . is a tale told by an idiot"), one may spend a lifetime discovering a deepening set of possible utterance meanings as one's context shifts and one's categories grow more subtle.

I have been arguing that the reality of a language is to be found in the utterances that express the referring intentions of speakers in context. In producing and interpreting utterances, speakers must of course use grammatical and lexical structures. These structures place constraints on the interpretation of utterances and on the contexts in which some utterance is acceptable. Neither the acceptability nor the meaning of an utterance, however, is determined solely on the basis of linguistic knowledge.

Judgments about the acceptability of a sentence cannot be made apart from some referential context. A sentence may be generated by a syntactic rule (of some T-G grammar) yet be quite unacceptable as an utterance in some context, while a sentence that is not generated by any such rule (or that violates the rules) may be perfectly acceptable as an utterance in context. If intuitions about grammatical acceptability rests on judgments about the possible communicative function of an utterance in context, then any descriptively adequate grammar proposed to account for those intuitions would have to generate all and only acceptable utterances (utterance-types) of a language.

Katz has accepted this challenge to generative grammar by proposing, in essence, a reduction of utterance meanings to sentence meanings generated by syntactic, semantic, and pragmatic rules. On this account, utterances are tokens of such sentence types. Thus, the syntactic and semantic components of a T-G grammar should, in principle, provide a structural interpretation and sentence meaning for all and only grammatical sentences of a language, while pragmatic rules should assign contextual meanings to utterance tokens of the set of sentence types. In short, a complete (descriptively adequate) grammar should provide rules for determining the acceptability and utterance meaning of all possible sentences in all possible contexts. Such a grammar would, in theory, provide a causal basis for speakers' intuitions about the acceptability, ambiguity, synonymy, and, in general, meaning of the set of possible utterances of a language by treating such intuitions as an effect of knowledge of generative rules.

I have rejected Katz's attempt to treat utterances as tokens of sentence types generated by rules. In fact, utterance meanings are determined by the referring intention of a speaker. One may certainly apply a token-type distinction to utterances, since there can be a number of individual utterances (tokens) that express the same referring intention. To interpret an utterance type, however, and to determine the grammatical acceptability of an utterance type, one requires information about context and about a speaker's intention that cannot be reduced to rules. One may speak of a sentence meaning (that is, of sentence types) as a kind of abstraction from utterance meaning. That is, for any utterance type, one may set aside the nonlinguistic (contextual) information that affects the interpretation of the utterance and consider only those constraints on interpretation that are a function of syntactic-semantic and pragmatic structures. These structures offer certain possibilities of interpretation based on the conventions of a system that all competent speakers have acquired. But to carry out an interpretation or other linguistic judgment for an utterance type as an expression of a specific referring intention one must also consider the referential and discourse context of the utterance, as well as the nature of the person who is speaking. Such information goes well beyond what can properly be included in a grammar or reduced to rules, and it is this fact that ensures the genuine novelty of utterance meanings: they are not reducible to sentence meanings as a "compositional function" of a system of elements and rules. Ultimately, the interpretation of utterance types involves all aspects of knowledge in the ordinary sense: of other people, of the world in general; and this is what one should expect, given the fact that all human knowledge is expressed through language (or through symbolic systems which depend on language for their interpretation).

If competent speakers do not possess a language in the form of a descriptively adequate grammar, or a set of generative rules, they do require a knowledge of linguistic structures to express their communicative intentions and to interpret novel utterance types in context. In the next chapter I shall summarize the role of such structures in grammatical judgments and in analogical constructions.

CHAPTER 6

Linguistic Creativity

Saussure (1916) distinguished between individual speech (*la parole*) and the public system of a language (*la langue*), which in some way regulates speech. Today, of course, the precise nature of *langue* is a subject of much dispute among linguists. There is general agreement, however, that a grammar is a description of *langue* and that in some sense the speech of competent speakers reflects a system of *langue*. Chomsky's claim that competent speakers have a tacit knowledge of *langue* in the form of a transformational-generative grammar has led to the search for a set of descriptively adequate syntactic, semantic, and, more recently, contextual rules. The basic assumption is, again, that without knowing such rules speakers would be unable to produce, interpret, or judge the acceptability of novel sentences or utterances of a language. In Chomsky's view, the possibility of creative speech rests on the fact that novel utterances are tokens of sentence types in *langue,* that is, of the theoretically infinite set of grammatical sentences generated by rules of which speakers have an unconscious knowledge.

I have argued against the view that competent speakers possess *langue* in the form of a generative grammar. Given the pragmatic-semantic account of language I have presented, it seems clear that judgments about the grammatical acceptability of sentences depend on their communicative function as utterances. It seems equally clear that no set of rules can distinguish between the set of acceptable and unacceptable utterances, or generate the set of all and only acceptable utterance types. Thus one cannot account for linguistic intuitions in Chomsky's causal terms, claiming that whenever a sentence is described by a rule of *langue,* its utterance token will be intuitively acceptable, whereas any sentence not described by (or in violation of) rules will seem ungrammatical.

The alternative, empiricist model of competence I have advocated would treat langue as a system of structures mapped into sound, structures that are in principle accessible to consciousness and that provide an intentional as well as a causal foundation for linguistic intuition. From this perspective, competent speakers are those who have acquired the phonological, syntactic-morphological-semantic and pragmatic structures of a language at a given stage of history, and who understand the referential and communicative function of speech. Such speakers are then able to produce and interpret appropriate novel utterances that, in some context, express specific referring intentions.

The precise nature of any system of structures is, of course, an empirical question. Jakobson's work in phonology provides an example of this sort of structuralist model of *langue.* Speakers who have acquired a phonemic system have learned to unconsciously classify acoustically different sounds (phonetic shapes) in terms of the distinctive features that count in that system. There is considerable evidence that speakers acquire other levels of linguistic structure in essentially the way they acquire phonology. The semantic categories mapped into lexical and grammatical forms seem to represent specific cognitive structures that are acquired through an unconscious process, but that can be made explicit. There are also pragmatic structures regulating the use of certain forms in particular contexts. For example, speakers must acquire some conventions governing the use of the definite versus the indefinite article, the provision of identifying descriptions or other specifications of a topic, expression in a specific style, or, generally, performance of a given speech function.

Speakers who have acquired linguistic structures are then able, in context, to select the forms and constructions that best express a specific categorical intention. Of course, speakers vary in their ability to express themselves. Some are more aware than others of the need to provide a context for remarks to some interlocutor, or are more skillful in finding formulas or building contexts that give a precise expression to the specific cognitive or apperceptive structure intended.

In principle, it is possible to match a new referring intention to the semantic structures encoded in a system of *langue*. If a speaker intends to refer to a structure that has not already been linguistically expressed, it is possible to combine existing categories to provide definitions of new concepts, to modify existing categories through analogy, or to express new ones through metaphor. One can also coin a term to direct the attention of others to some specific perceptual feature in context (for example, a "brillig" quality invariably present in certain lighting effects). In general, one should be able to express any categorical intention in language, or at least to use language in context to show others an intended perceptual or cognitive structure.

Hockett's widely accepted statement that languages vary not in what can or cannot be said in them but in the relative difficulty of saying something suggests this creative role of speech. For example, Malinowski claimed that when Christian missionaries first arrived in the Trobriand Islands, the natives had no conception of biological paternity, and their system of matrilineal descent created a sociological definition of the paternal role that was quite removed from the Judeo-Christian image of "God the Father." Thus the missionaries were hard pressed to explain this concept. To do so, they had to teach the islanders a bit of biology and then develop the theological concept through analogy.

If language presents speakers with a specific mapping of cognitive structures, there is no mystery in the fact that language provides a means of expressing new referring intentions. Speakers have only to select those features or invariants that are of interest in any novel situation, and, having framed the intended object in that way, to choose the speech forms that express that categorical judgment. An interlocutor, in turn, is justified in attributing a specific semantic intention to the speaker who has selected those forms. On the other hand, as I have emphasized, the interpretation of an utterance is not fully determined by linguistic structures. The structures chosen by a speaker to express an intention place constraints on interpretation without, in Chomsky's terms, generating an utterance meaning. Thus a competent speaker must try to anticipate the information requirements of others. If an utterance is apt in context and for certain individuals who know certain things, it will convey an intended comment about an identifiable topic. If it is not apt, there are no rules that can clear things up, and one must ask questions.

In discussing the role of structures in the production and interpretation of novel sentence types (new combinations of linguistic forms) and novel utterance-types (new referring intentions expressed by utterances in context), I have emphasized the expressive function of speech in relation to intentions. The semantic structures that underlie speech forms can be brought to intuitive clarity as the intentional as well as causal foundation of linguistic judgments. For example, one knows intuitively that "John hits Bill" and "Bill hits John" are similar. To clarify this intuition, one must make explicit the structural features which they share—for example, the semantic agent-action-object structure mapped into a feature of word order. Similarly, these sentences are structurally related to another set (for example, "John was hit by Bill") through semantic roles expressed by a passive construction. Intuitions of this type rest on a speaker's knowledge of such productive patterns as expressions of specific intentional structures.

The view that speakers produce novel utterances by analogy is, I think, relevant to the process of acquiring the structures of a language and, having acquired language in this form, selecting or interpreting novel variants of given structures. The child who becomes aware of certain regularities in speech and acquires the intended semantic mapping for those structures, is then able to produce novel utterances that are structurally analogous to those she has heard. Of course, analogical constructions produce surface structure regularities, but they are motivated by underlying semantic structures intended by a speaker. "Mary is riding a tame tiger" is analogous to "Mary is riding a horse," but the speaker who understands or produces this analogy must intend this common structure.

The linguistic structures that place constraints on possible utterance meanings also account for some prior intuitions about the acceptability of possible utterance types. For example, McCawley (1974) noted that while "put the hat on," "put on the hat," and "put it on" are grammatically acceptable, "put on it" is not. McCawley's explanation was that this constraint reflected a purely formal, surface-structure regularity rather than any semantic distinction. Another possibility is that it reflects a distinction between (1) the use of "put on" as a kind of separable verb (analogous to the German *aufsetzen*) to express the fact that something (X) is put on something else (Y), and (2) the use of "put" as a substitute for "place" with a locative preposition in the phrase "on it (Y)."[1] Thus, "put the hat on," "put it on," and "put on the hat" all express the first intention. (One cannot say "put on the table" or "put the table on," except in contexts in which "the table" is the X.) In contrast, "put on it" can be used only to express the second intention, in contexts in which "it" (or its lexical substitute) is the Y. For example, one may say, "She carried the table to the room and put (placed) on it her best china," or "He put on it the sort of interpretation that might excuse his conduct." The extent and precise characterization of these regularities and the semantic structures they express remain to be resolved by linguists. The philosophical point is that intuitions about the acceptability of these possible utterance types has some basis in knowledge of the intentional use of linguistic structures.

It may be useful to distinguish levels in judgments of acceptability based on a knowledge of linguistic structures. At the lowest level, phonetic shapes must be classed as allophones of some phoneme, and combinations of phonemes accepted as, for example, English nonsense ('glik', 'brilk', but not 'lmcha'). At a higher level, phonemic structures may be identified as words or morphemes. 'If and king' is acceptable at this level, whereas 'if and glik' is not (unless 'glik' has been introduced as a special term in some context). At the next level, semantic-syntactic-morphological structure determines whether certain words and morphemes form a semantic unit. For example, taken by itself

1. I am grateful to Lydia Fakundiny for this suggestion.

without any contextual information, one can say that 'if and king' is an incomplete (or even "nonsensical") expression because if 'if' combines with a predicative structure to mark an antecedent condition, while 'and' expresses a relation of conjunction between, say, things, properties, or states of affairs, then 'if' can't form a semantic unit with 'and' or 'and king' because neither is predicative. 'If' can't combine with a predicative structure if there is no predicative structure. Similarly, 'if' is not a thing, property, or state of affairs and therefore can't be combined with 'and'. In short, the semantic structures underlying these forms establish essential conditions for semantic combinations that are not met in this case. (Of course, the expression might be a fragment of an utterance that does satisfy these constraints—for example, "If and, King Tut notwithstanding, only if I find a parking place will I visit the Metropolitan Museum.") On the other hand, 'red and black' does form an acceptable semantic unit because prior conditions for a semantic combination with 'and' are met. More generally, semantic structures place constraints on utterance meaning by restricting the range of intentions that some form can express and perhaps the contexts in which it can be used.

There are also semantically empty or redundant linguistic conventions that may affect judgments of acceptability. Thus, "Mistah Kurtz—he dead" might be relatively less acceptable than the formal "Mr. Kurtz is dead," though both make the same point. This level is controversial, as it involves arguments about description versus prescription, stylistic conventions and subdialects, and even political disputes.

I suggested that the pragmatic topic-comment structure determines, in context, the judgment that some utterance has a complete or incomplete "predicative" structure. Thus, taken out of any context, 'red and black' is an unacceptable, incomplete form at this level, since it does not present a comment about some topic (present some X as Y). However, if it were produced as a completive, say in response to the question "What are your favorite colors?," the question would provide a topic for a complete and acceptable comment structure.

The attribution of a topic-comment structure is, in general, crucial to the interpretation of utterance meaning. For example,

"The rosebush which is in my back yard is blooming" is a sentence that allows at least two different topic-comment analyses, which may, but need not, be marked in an utterance by intonation and juncture. For example, if one is speaking to the nurseryman from whom one purchased a particular rosebush, one may intend to say about that bush that it is in one's back yard and that it is blooming. However, if one is speaking to someone who does not know to which bush one is referring, one will be called upon to provide some identifying description, and in this case one will be saying, about the rosebush in one's back yard, that it is blooming. Further, since such a description will not in fact identify one's intended referent in that context unless there is only one rosebush in the back yard, it will carry that presupposition. The competent speaker must be aware of such pragmatic constraints in expressing some intention in context. Thus the egocentric speaker will produce utterances that are pragmatically defective.

There are, in addition to topic-comment structure, other aspects of a pragmatic level of acceptability. One must make judgments that may be mediated by structural knowledge about the relevance, tone, style, and, in general, appropriateness of an utterance in some context. (See Bauman and Sherzer, 1974, for some ethnographic studies of pragmatic structures.)

I think that claims about the unacceptability of sentences such as "Colorless green ideas sleep furiously" or "My frying pan thinks I'm crazy" reflect implicit ideas about what is logically possible within some context of interpretation. For example, if one believed or determined that frying pans were inanimate objects and therefore could not think, one would stipulate it to be logically impossible for such objects to think someone crazy. Similarly, if ideas are not the sorts of entities that can sleep or do anything "furiously," or have any sort of color attribute, and, moreover, if something green cannot logically also be colorless, one is led to reject the sentence for presupposing what is logically absurd. If, however, one could find a context in which such presuppositions could be met—for example, "frying pans" in Disney cartoons, or metaphorically "green" (jealous) ideas, such utterances would cease to be unacceptable. I would say, however, that this type of judgment is actually logical rather than linguistic. For example, "a circular square" is quite acceptable as a type of linguistic construction, although it describes a logical impossibility. One might think it odd for someone to say, sincerely, "I intend to paint a circular square," but this judgment would be predicated on the logical rather than the linguistic unacceptability of the statement.

The structural model of *langue* for which I have been arguing would account for creativity by positing a system of structures placing constraints on utterances rather than a descriptively adequate system of rules generating all and only grammatical sentences or utterances. This position represents an enriched or expanded version of traditional (Bloomfieldian) structuralism through its emphasis on pragmatic and especially semantic structures. As Chomsky has correctly emphasized, an explanatory theory of competence must do more than describe regularities in linguistic surface structure. Thus, a theory of analogical constructions must characterize the underlying semantic structures that motivate the selection and interpretation of specific forms and constructions.

Structural knowledge underlies linguistic intuitions in the sense that the structural interpretation placed on an utterance establishes, first, a range of possible semantic structures that the utterance can express and, second, a set of conditions affecting the acceptability of the utterance. In this respect, one might speak of "a priori linguistic knowledge" without positing either an innate universal grammar or a generative grammar as a theoretical cause of intuitions. Speakers exercise creativity in finding new ways to use language in context—to create genuinely novel utterances that are not merely tokens of a set of sentence-types described by linguistic rules. My focus has been on the use of structural knowledge, in context, to express a referring intention. In Part 2 I shall clarify the fundamental concept of an "intention" within the context of Husserlian phenomenology.

PART II
AN EMPIRICIST THEORY
OF UTTERANCE MEANING:
PHILOSOPHICAL FOUNDATIONS

CHAPTER 7

Phenomenological Empiricism

There are many possible versions of philosophical empiricism, but they all have in common the premise that perceptual experience is the ultimate source of human knowledge. This claim does not, of course, preclude the possibility that the genetic endowment of human beings sets limits on the structure of human behavior and perception, as well as the pattern of cognitive development, which in turn affect the form and content of human experience. What is essential to empiricism is the assertion that all objects of knowledge (that is, intentional objects) are, in some manner, constituted from the data of experience.

The empiricist position may be contrasted with a metaphysical form of rationalism. Historically, rationalistic philosophers have claimed that there is an a priori form of knowledge, or knowledge that is in some sense "prior" to contingent perceptual experience, in addition to the a posteriori knowledge derived from such experience. Not all forms of rationalism are metaphysical. The distinction between a priori and a posteriori knowledge, or between contingent (factual) and necessary (logical) truths, may be drawn within a phenomenological theory in a way consistent with empiricism in a broad sense. (See "The Law of Contradiction" in Chapter 10 for a discussion.) Thus, phenomenology combines elements of traditional empiricism and rationalism. It is similar to empiricism in its rejection of metaphysical entities and its turn to experience as the source of intentional objects. But it is also similar to rationalism in its acceptance of a distinction between a priori (essential) and a posteriori (contingent) knowledge.

The rationalistic view becomes metaphysical when the objects of a priori knowledge are described as ideal but unobservable entities.[1] I would reject such metaphysical knowledge claims for two reasons. First, one cannot describe the nature of a noumenal entity or "thing in itself" and thus refer to such an entity in a significant way, since any description of entities necessarily characterizes them as phenomena or "things for us." Second, phenomenal objects are of two types: ideal intentional objects and individual (spatiotemporally located) objects. As I shall show, ideal objects are given intuitively as experiential intentional structures. Thus, ideal objects are not unobservable entities that must be posited on the basis of argument or established through a nonempirical form of intuition.

Individual entities, which may properly be said to exist, may be directly given in experience as observable objects, or they may be characterized indirectly as theoretical entities represented by analogy from experiential paradigms. I would hold that knowledge of unobservable individual entities depends on experience in two essential ways: (1) such entities must be characterized as "things for us" through models or analogical constructs, and (2) probable knowledge of the existence of theoretical entities is established through limited experimental evidence.[2] Thus science, rather than metaphysics, is the source of knowledge concerning the nature and existence of unobservable entities.

The crucial difference between metaphysical rationalism and

1. Kant's position is interesting as a form of rationalism that is, perhaps, transitional between metaphysics and phenomenology. He rejected the traditional metaphysical claim to know the nature of Being qua Being, or as a "thing in itself," and in that sense performed a kind of transcendental reduction. However, he used logical (transcendental) arguments as a basis for knowledge claims about an unobservable individual entity—the transcendental ego with its forms of intuition and categories of judgment—and thus remains within the tradition of metaphysics. A phenomenological position would view such transcendental structures as ideal, intentional objects and in this sense would claim a "transcendental experience" as the basis of a nonmetaphysical knowledge claim.

2. Space does not allow a consideration of the unobservable or inferred entities posited by scientific theories. I would emphasize, however, that scientific knowledge of an unobservable reality is limited to inferences from observed patterns of events to a certain specific cause of those patterns. Thus, theoretical entities are individual (rather than ideal) entities characterized in terms of their observable effects by means of some model. They are not metaphysically ideal "things in themselves," nor are they objects of a priori knowledge.

empiricism is the metaphysical claim that universals are, in some unspecified sense, ideal but unobservable entities. Knowledge of such entities is said to be a priori because, though experience may "activate" the knowledge of what Plato called Forms (universals) in some manner, these ideal objects are in no sense constituted within experience from perceptual data, for example, through a process of abstracting from or "idealizing" an individual (perceptual) object. In Chapter 8, I shall present an alternative, empiricist account of universals that clarifies the ontological status of essences as ideal intentional objects constituted within experience. This description, which brings its own intuitive evidence, overcomes the chief defect of a metaphysical theory, which lies in its failure to provide an analysis of the sense in which universals are objectively real. On one hand, universals are said to be unobservable entities rather than objects known or encountered directly within experience. On the other hand, they are ideal rather than individual objects. Thus, they have no space-time location and cannot be understood as causal entities posited in a scientific theory. Until the significance of the claim that universals are both ideal and unobservable entities has been clarified, metaphysical assertions about the reality of universals have no significance.

I shall argue that the distinction between individual and ideal objects can be made, in nonmetaphysical terms, within the context of philosophical empiricism. Though universals cannot properly be said to "exist," insofar as existence implies space-time (or temporal) location and is thus a property of individual objects, their reality lies in their intuitively given presence as specific "idealized" structures or intentional objects that have been constituted by some observer. Intuition is not, then, evidence for the reality of unobservable entities, but rather the direct "seeing" or recognition of specific structures within experience.

The method of intentional analysis that I shall use was, of course, developed by Edmund Husserl, the founder of the phenomenological movement. I shall make frequent reference to his theory, but my main focus will be the elaboration of an empiricist theory of utterance meaning in the context of the theory of language presented in Part I. Thus I shall not be concerned with scholarly disputes about the proper interpretation of the phenomenological position that Husserl intended to hold during a given historical period. I shall develop my own interpretation of Husserlian phenomenology as a form of radical empiricism in a way that, I think, supplements (and at points diverges from) Husserl's position and leads to a coherent and convincing account of utterance meaning.

In my defense of empiricism, I shall not presuppose any narrow interpretation of "experience" as consisting of atomic "sense data" or elementary sensations that must be combined in some manner by an associative mechanism (or a "ghost") in the brain or mind. It is evident that ordinary experience is not fragmented in the way such a model of perception suggests. If one attempts to describe the structures of experience as they are directly given, one recognizes intuitively that the phenomenal world is a closely knit, highly structured system rather than a "chaos" of unrelated sensations. Whether the human nervous system operates by transmitting something analogous to sense data is a matter to be discovered experimentally, by means of a theory supported by indirect evidence, and is thus no part of a phenomenological description. It is possible, of course, to adopt a special analytic attitude, focusing attention on individual sensory aspects of perceptually given phenomena, but such objects are always given within the horizon of the structured system from which they have been abstracted.[3] I shall label the attempt to describe the structures of experience phenomenologically, as they are given, descriptive philosophy or radical empiricism.

The historical debate between philosophical empiricism and metaphysical rationalism is relevant to Chomsky's scientific version of rationalism. Chomsky, of course, does not intend to hold

3. Merleau-Ponty (1945) also rejected "sense data" theories of perception in favor of a phenomenological approach. Although he describes phenomenology as an alternative to empiricism as well as rationalism, he is actually rejecting a particular, historical (British) form of empiricism, rather than the claim that, in some sense, all knowledge is derived from perceptual experience. I think, however, that the link between empiricism and phenomenology should be developed within the context of Husserlian intentional analysis (with its transcendental dimension), rather than in terms of Merleau-Ponty's unclarified realism. In my view Merleau-Ponty misunderstood Husserl and projected onto his transcendental idealism a metaphysical significance that was never intended.

a metaphysical position. Thus, though he speaks of innate linguistic knowledge of a universal grammar, he treats the components of such a grammar as theoretical entities and argues (on the basis of observable linguistic data) for a genetically transmitted linguistic knowledge. The inferred linguistic entities, then, are not posited on the basis of an a priori intuition. Chomsky's strategy has, in fact, been attacked as unscientific or nonempirical in the sense that the hypothesis is not actually empirically disconfirmable. Though I believe there is some merit to this criticism (See Chapter 9, note 3), I shall focus my critical comments (Chapter 9) on another aspect of Chomsky's theory.

Specifically, I do not think that Chomsky adequately explains the nature of a priori knowledge or the linguistic objects of such knowledge, which scientific rationalism posits to account for language acquisition. The linguistic universals that the theory treats as unobservable, inferred entities and that speakers are said to know prior to any experience, must, on the one hand, be understood as genetically transmitted individual objects that cause certain unknown processes to occur during the language acquisition period. But, as I shall show, the theory of linguistic universals must face the philosophical problem of universals and characterize the nature or ontological status of the linguistic concepts that are the common elements in numerically distinct, individual representations or expressions of *langue*. Philosophical analysis makes it plain that such concepts must be ideal objects. Thus, scientific rationalism is subject to criticism for failing to resolve the metaphysical issue raised by a theory of a priori knowledge. The theory must explain how linguistic concepts can be unobservable individual, genetically transmitted objects, and also ideal (nonindividual) entities. If one denies that linguistic universals are ideal concepts, it no longer makes sense to speak of a priori linguistic knowledge. However, a denial that linguistic concepts are individuals undermines the scientific status of the theory as a model of genetically transmitted causal entities, leaving only the metaphysical notion of a priori knowledge of unobservable ideal objects.

I shall hold that the way out of the dilemma is a phenomenological theory of ideal linguistic concepts as observable intentional objects constituted as structures within (and on the basis of) experience. This empiricist model of linguistic knowledge accounts for the possibility of a common or shared language, and it is consistent with the account of language acquisition presented in Part I. It is, however, inconsistent with the claim that linguistic knowledge is innate in the sense that ideal linguistic concepts are genetically transmitted.

In the next chapter I shall begin my defense of phenomenological empiricism by clarifying the nature of universals and exhibiting their basis in perceptual experience.

CHAPTER 8

An Empiricist Account
of Universals

The philosophical problem of universals concerns the ontological status of ideal objects. Plato was the first philosopher to focus on the essential distinction between individual entities, which have space-time location and which are, in the ordinary sense, objects of perception, and universals, or objects of generic reference, which do not have space-time location or other individual perceptual features and which are thus ideal objects. As Plato repeatedly argued, Virtue itself is not a particular instance of virtue, nor is Redness itself a red thing or Tallness a tall thing. Whereas individual objects are discovered through sense perception, universals can only be grasped through (a priori) intuition. In Plato's language, ideal entities are Forms that neither come into existence nor cease to exist. They are eternally self-identical realities in some way connected—for example, through imitation or participation—with the individual objects that are their exemplars. The problem that Plato's distinction has bequeathed to his successors is that of specifying the sense in which universals are real and explicating the relation between ideal and individual entities.

The basic arguments in favor of a distinction between individual objects of perception and ideal objects of intuition are all to be found in Plato's works. It seems clear, as Socrates demonstrates in a number of dialogues, that one must distinguish between individual objects or instances and the general categories or classes of which these things are examples. The former are known through sense experience, but the latter are, it seems, known intuitively, and it is this a priori intuition that enables one to classify or identify objects as identical in some respects. Furthermore, statements about the sensible properties of individual objects are logically contingent, whereas statements expressing intuitions about universals are logically necessary.

Mathematical (geometrical, for example) knowledge most clearly illustrates the difference between perceptually based contingent truths and intuitively based necessary truths. Abstract objects (universals) such as "the" triangle of plane geometry are not objects of perception, and truths about such ideal objects are neither discovered through empirical methods (that is, inductive generalization) nor disconfirmed by counterexamples. Thus, the universal triangle is a plane figure enclosed by three straight lines, each of which is one-dimensional, and the ideal triangle is neither equilateral nor isosceles nor right, nor any other type of triangle; nor does it have any properties of space-time location. In contrast, any physical representation of a triangle is three-dimensional and must be right, isosceles, equilateral, or some other type of triangle. Further, though it is intuitively plain that the generic triangle has three straight lines, it is irrelevant to this intuition that the lines drawn in some representation of a triangle are not absolutely straight. Again, truths about universals are discovered intuitively rather than inductively and are absolutely certain, as no empirical generalization can be. Thus, one may doubt that two particular lines are equal to a third line and to each other, but there can be no doubt that quantities equal to a third quantity are equal to each other. Similarly, the Pythagorean theorem (the square of the length of the hypotenuse of a right triangle equals the sum of the squares of the lengths of the other two sides) is immediately taken to apply to "the" right triangle, and not merely to some particular triangle represented in a construction. For this reason, if the theorem is demonstrated for the generic object, it can be applied to any figure that is an exemplar of that form. It appears, then, that unless one grants the distinction between individual objects of perception and ideal objects of intuition, one must deny the possibility of certain knowledge of mathematical, logical, and philosophical truths.

Plato held the view that only some version of a theory of Forms could account for the possibility of genuine knowledge.

Though Forms themselves have no space-time location and so do not exist as individuals, they are nonetheless real in some sense, and ontologically independent of the individual acts of thought through which they are understood. They are what different individuals think about, the objects of thought. Forms provide a common element of meaning for individually different acts of speech. As Plato put the matter: "if... a man refuses to admit that Forms of things exist or to distinguish a definite Form in every case, he will have nothing on which to fix his thought, so long as he will not allow that each thing has a character which is always the same; and in so doing he will completely destroy the significance of all discourse" (*Parmenides*, 135c).

Nonetheless, Plato was also keenly aware of the difficulties involved in characterizing the ontological status of Forms and their relationship to individuals. During his middle period, especially in the *Phaedo*, Plato seems to have considered an essentially metaphysical account of Forms as ideal but unobservable objects which were somehow real "in themselves," independently of the world as it is given in human experience. Thus, he turned to myth to describe the "other world" of timeless Forms and to characterize intuition as a recollection of what was given before birth in a mystical vision "outside of" this transient world. However, in his later work (beginning with his self-criticism in *Parmenides*), Plato rejected the metaphysical theory of Forms,[1] which is still commonly referred to as "Platonic realism."

An adequate empiricist account of universals would avoid metaphysical realism while recognizing the Platonic distinction between individual and ideal objects. Traditional empiricism, which chose the nominalist route of denying the reality of ideal objects, or reducing statements about universals to statements about classes of individuals, failed to provide an adequate account of generic reference, category formation, and the distinction between necessary and contingent truths. In contrast, the phenomenological version of empiricism which I would defend admits the reality of ideal objects, not as metaphysical entities, but as observable (intentional) structures within experience. I

---

1. See Kates (1969) for an interpretation of Plato on this point.

shall show that this position, which accepts the basic empiricist premise that perceptual experience is the source of all knowledge, is not subject to the philosophical objections against classical (British) empiricism. In arguing for a theory of phenomenological empiricism, I shall not consider the issue of whether my version of phenomenology is consistent at every point with the historical position developed by Husserl or by other phenomenologists.

I shall begin the analysis of ideal objects by examining the claim that there is an intuitively given distinction between acts of individual and generic reference. Consider reference to an individual red hat, or to the particular red color of a particular hat—as in "The red in this hat is too bright"—as distinct from reference to red hats in general or the quality of redness in general—"Red is a color." The traditional empiricist would say that in producing or interpreting such utterances I am actually experiencing, either perceptually or imaginatively, some individual instance or representation, such as a patch of red or a red object, and I am able to interpret the utterance by means of these psychological representations. Husserl agreed that the same "sense-contents" are given in acts of individual and specific (generic) reference, but insisted on an essential distinction between the way in which some individual object is apprehended in each case. As he put it in the *Logical Investigations* (hereafter *L.I.*), there is a difference in the acts themselves. Acts of individual reference are directed toward "the apparent thing itself . . . this thing or that feature, this part of the thing" (vol. 1, p. 340), while acts of specific reference are directed toward a species:

> While the thing appears, or rather the feature in the thing, it is not this objective feature, this feature here and now, that we mean. We mean its *content*, its 'Idea'; we mean, not this aspect of red in the house, but Red as such. . . . a new mode of apprehension has been built . . . constitutive of the intuitive presence of the Idea of Red. . . . this mode of apprehension sets the Species before us as a universal object. . . . [vol. 1, p. 340]

Husserl explicitly rejected a metaphysical theory of universals (though his account of the identity of forms is somewhat misleading). He said that he was strictly concerned with a phenomenological description of intuitively given structures of experience. The experiential fact is that we do make a distinction between individual and generic reference, which, as Husserl said, implies that we direct our attention toward objects of experience in two different ways. The descriptive task is to clarify this distinction as it is given, locating its constitutive ground in the "mode of apprehension" assumed by consciousness. A psychological account of generic reference may succeed in providing a causal explanation for particular acts of experiencing, but that is no substitute for a descriptive account of the object as a universal.

The question, then, is what does it mean to refer to an ideal object, or to make a generic reference? Husserl says it is a type of reference that does not intend any individual object or feature, though it is particular with respect to the qualities or types of features to which it calls attention. But this is a rather "empty" description that, in particular, does not show the genetic origin of ideal objects in the structures of perception.[2] It is at this point, I believe, that empiricism becomes relevant to phenomenology, not to provide a psychological or causal analysis of generic reference, but to explicate the constitutive basis of ideal objects in an act of perceptual consciousness.

In an act of individual reference, one is focusing on an existing object in the sense of one having temporal or space-time location. The individual is a "this" or "that" something, discriminated from everything else and represented (whether through perception, memory, or imagination) as an actual or potential object that can or may exist at a particular point in time. Whether the object is present in memory, perception, or imagination is essentially irrelevant to the temporal specification of any real individual. Thus, in a broad sense psychological entities ("ideas," "memories," etc.) are essentially individual events in time, while physical entities are essentially objects having a

2. In his later work on genetic phenomenology, Husserl paid attention to the passive perceptual processes underlying categorical judgment, but in these studies the essences or noematic *Sinne* are described as being "already there," ready-to-hand, as a residuum of phenomenological reduction, and in this sense their constitutive history is never clarified.

space-time location that is revealed perceptually through a spatial adumbration of the object correlated with systematic changes in the location of the observer's body.[3] Since a physical object is understood as such only through its mode of perceptual adumbration, which is in turn a spatial concept derived from the perspectival relations established through the body of some (real or imagined) observer, one may say that any physical object must be understood as having space-time location. In theory, then, it is always possible to distinguish some individual object, or individual portion of an object, by means of its temporal or space-time location.

In referring to a particular red hat, or to the red color of some red hat, then, one intends a real individual of some type. This individual object may be further characterized as having other properties such as being too bright, being dirty, fading, and so on. However, in referring to an ideal object, such as redness in general, I think one is essentially "bracketing out" the space-time or temporal location (as well as, perhaps, other sensory features) of whatever sense-contents are presented in imagination or perception.

"Bracketing" is a term Husserl used in reference to the "epoché" of phenomenological reduction. In that context, it meant the suspension of certain assumptions about the independent existence of the natural world, freeing the observer to describe things as they were observed, that is, as phenomena. As Husserl emphasized, one in fact continues to believe in the existence of the world placed in brackets, but the crucial point is one does not make use of the assumptions in one's description. In effect, one intends the world strictly as a phenomenon. I think that Husserl's term applies equally to the constitution of any ideal structure. To place a perceptual feature in brackets is to regulate its significance rather than to cease to be perceptually aware of it. Thus, just as one is able to read an expression placed, literally, in brackets, while recognizing that the bracketed expression is not part of the quotation in which it occurs, so one

---

3. See Merleau-Ponty (1945, 1949) for an elaboration of Husserl's "immanence-transcendence" distinction in terms of the notion of "embodied subjectivity."

continues to sense aspects of an object or representation that are not to be taken into account in identifying some object that is intended.

An object of generic reference, then, is ideal in the sense that the space-time location of an exemplar does not "count" in the apprehension or identification of the object intended. Other sensory properties may also be bracketed out, as contingent and irrelevant features of some presentation. For example, a specific patch of red may be bright, another dull, and these features would be irrelevant if one intended to classify a color in terms of hue and intensity but not brightness (value). Similarly, in intending such a color category, one would disregard the qualities of shape and texture distinguishing exemplars. One could also modify the color category—for example, taking into account the lighting conditions—if one were characterizing, say, redness in bright sunshine.

The idealization of the object is immediately obvious in the case of abstract subjects such as geometry. For example, though any physical representation of a triangle must be of a particular type of triangle, of a certain size, employing three-dimensional elements which may furthermore be colored, not quite straight, presented on a particular background, and so on, the generic triangle that one intends in a construction is constituted precisely by bracketing all of these elements. Similarly, one may constitute a single dot as a geometrical point by bracketing out its dimensions; and in the same way constitute a geometrical line as the single dimension that counts in the physical representation. Thus, the universal triangle is a plane figure enclosed by three straight lines, each of which is one-dimensional; and the generic triangle is neither equilateral nor isosceles nor right, nor any other type of triangle, nor does it have any properties of space-time location.

The ability to bracket out sense-contents in this way is no mysterious power of consciousness; it is used constantly in the activity of classifying perceptual information—for example, in reading various scripts or styles of type that present the same letters, or hearing a variety of sounds that present the same phoneme or morpheme. In such cases, we may perceive differences, but we have learned not to take them as distinctive.

That is, we disregard sense-contents that do not count in some context. But while ordinary perceptual classification is an unconscious effect of the system one has learned, logical or abstract categories are deliberately introduced through explicit definitions. Thus, those who have learned geometry are able to give an explicit account of the features that distinguish categories within the system, whereas one ordinarily finds it difficult or impossible to define, say, redness in general, or to define the distinctive features that differentiate one phoneme, or one letter, from another, in a given language. Nonetheless, one may still produce an example, or a series of examples of some type, automatically recognizing the features that count and disregarding those that do not, without this kind of conscious knowledge. Observations of a pattern of judgments (of identity and difference) should reveal the features that are criterial, and thus make explicit the structure of some system of classification.

I might add that the generic objects intended by consciousness are also structures that can be incorporated in a machine program. In effect, a machine can simulate the "bracketing" process I have described. For example, Bates (1976) cites an interesting example of a rule or schema for identifying triangles which is being used in some recent (machine) programs for visual pattern recognition: "How do we teach a program to recognize triangles? . . . The program doesn't store or 'have' triangles at all. Instead, it has a rule, an operation, of the type 'Scan a line that makes three angle turns without breaking and return to the starting point. If you can do that, then there is a triangle'" (p. 30). I would say such a machine does "have" triangles in the form of a procedure for distinguishing features that count from those that do not. Given such a program, the machine in a sense disregards aspects of the sense-contents that are presented. Specific triangles may be isosceles or equilateral, and so on, large or small, black or colored, and of course all are given with a particular space-time location. But none of these features counts in the program. Nor does it count that a physical representation is three-dimensional, because the machine scans in one direction only, thus constituting the geometrical line. If the machine registered more than three turns or deviations in the direction of the line (that is, if the line were not sufficiently straight), the figure would not qualify as a triangle. Again, though this program defines a closed figure as one without breaks, one could alter that definition to allow the machine to identify broken or dotted line representations of triangles, mechanically simulating the interpretation of such gaps as a stylistic device.

This account of universals as structures constituted within experience explains the difference between truths about universals and inductive generalizations about individuals. For example, the Pythagorean theorem states a universal truth about the right triangle. The proof of the theorem does not rely on inductive evidence. Thus, there is no need to repeat the proof with other constructions or representations of right triangles. Since the object of the proof is ideal or generic, the theorem is immediately taken to apply to any possible exemplar. The explanation for this is, I think, that since only distinctive features of a construction are used in a proof, the theorem may be said to be about the idealized triangle and thus about any representation insofar as it is idealized in that way (as a right triangle). For this reason, further examples would be redundant, as all would be constituted the same way. Their individual differences do not enter into the construction or the proof, and so cannot affect the result. On the other hand, the application of a proof is limited by the features that are used, or that count, in a construction. Thus the Pythagorean theorem cannot be applied to all triangles in some generalized form because its proof uses a feature that distinguishes one class of triangles (namely, right triangles) from others.

Ordinary inductive generalizations such as "all men are mortal" or "all swans are white" require empirical confirmation because their subjects ("men," "swans," etc.) have not been constituted in a way that includes or leads deductively to their predicates. The distinctive features in terms of which something is identified as human or as a swan presumably do not include these predicate attributes, nor are they inconsistent with their absence. If there is no proof that something cannot be both human and immortal, or a swan and nonwhite, one must resort to induction to establish what is, or what is probably, the case. (In chapter 10 I shall develop an empiricist account of the distinction between necessary and contingent truths.)

Thus far I have presented an empiricist model of ideal objects as observable structures within experience. Universals, or objects of generic reference, are intentional structures constituted through a conscious or unconscious bracketing of some of the sense-contents of a perceived or imagined object. In the following section I shall consider the function of ideal structures in the process of category formation. That discussion should provide a philosophical clarification of the material on categorical judgment in chapters 3 and 4.

The Formation of Classes

Jakobson's work on distinctive feature theory in phonology provides an empirical model of the phenomenological thesis that category formation is an intentional process.[4] Phonological theory reveals how a number of acoustically different sounds (phonetic shapes) will be "heard" (in Husserl's sense of "apperception") as essentially the same, while other, perhaps very similar sounds, will be heard as essentially different, as a function of the phonological system operating within a language. This means that speakers may very well be able to discriminate sounds by their sense-contents, but they will nonetheless place them in the same category if they share a set of features that are distinctive or that count in a given system. On the other hand, sounds, however acoustically similar they may be, that can be

4. Although the phonemic principle (the function of sounds in distinguishing words) was discovered by a number of independent researchers in the nineteenth century, Trubetzkoy was the founder of phonology. He defined the phoneme as a minimal set of relevant (criterial) auditory and articulatory features that serve the phonemic function. Jakobson developed Trubetzkoy's theory of relevant versus redundant features in his definition of the phoneme as a set of distinctive features.

The best general presentation of Jakobson's distinctive feature theory may be found in Jakobson and Halle (1956), and Jakobson (1968). See also the excellent discussion by Elmar Holenstein (1975) for a historical and theoretical connection between Jakobsonean structuralism and Husserlian (eidetic) phenomenology. Jakobson assumes that distinctive features are organized as binary contrasts or oppositions. However, one may accept a theory of distinctive features without assuming a binary principle. I shall speak of distinctive features as those that distinguish one category from another, without assuming that oppositions (or contrasting features) are always binary.

contrasted through distinctive features, will be placed in different categories.

The sense in which distinctive features count in phonology is a functional one. Phonemes are bundles of features that distinguish morphemes. For example, the English morphemes 'tap' and 'pap' are distinguished by the English phonemes /t/ and /p/. These phonemes, in turn, are contrasted through the distinctive acoustic features of high or low frequency sound (/t/ versus /p/) or, less fundamentally, the distinctive articulatory features dental versus labial stops. Similarly, 'ma' and 'pa' are distinguished by /m/ and /p/, as nasal versus oral consonants, and /t/ and /p/, distinguished from one another through pitch, are distinguished from the high-energy or "compact" (that is, louder) /k/. In contrast, although aspirated and nonaspirated versions of /p/ might be discernibly different to an English speaker, the articulatory feature of aspiration would not be taken by such a speaker as a basis for a categorical phonological distinction. This nondistinctive feature might be sensed, but it would be bracketed in making a phonological judgment. In a language in which aspiration marked a phonemic contrast, however, speakers would be very alert to this particular feature and would classify sounds according to a different pattern. Categorical judgments, in short, reflect an acquired system of distinctive features rather than an unmediated impression of similarity determined by the intrinsic physical properties of the items classified.[5]

It should be clear that the English phonemes /p/ and /t/ are ideal objects. The ideal nature of the phoneme is indicated nicely through the notational convention of representing a phonemic *category* (in contrast to an individual phonetic shape) through slash marks as above. Any particular phonetic shape to

5. For example, whether in acoustic or articulatory terms, there is only a very small difference between an aspirated and a nonaspirated labial stop, or between /l/ and /r/. Yet once these paradigm structures have been acquired, they mediate perception: instances of /l/ and /r/ may be similar in many ways, but they are clearly different in certain ways that count in some systems. Of course, the physical properties of things also influence the kinds of categories that will be formed in a language. For example, Jakobson says that a distinction between /l/ and /r/ is universally acquired later by children and is, among languages, a rarer distinction than, say, that between /m/ and /p/.

which one can point as exemplar is a so-called allophone, an individual variant that counts as an instance of a given phoneme category. Distinctive feature theory says that the basis for classifications of sounds as phonemic variants (or, in Husserlian language, that which motivates the apperception) is the acoustic and/or articulatory structure of those phonetic shapes.[6] The speaker who has acquired a phonological system has in fact acquired paradigms in which all but a set of criterial features are bracketed out. The distinctive features are those which distinguish one phonemic category from another. Unconsciously, a speaker will focus on those features, listen for them, and make phonemic judgments through their presence or absence.

The model of structural classification that Jakobson applied to phonology is relevant to any system of perceptual categories. For example, a great deal of empirical work has been done analyzing and comparing the color terms of various languages, insofar as these encode a system of perceptual judgment. (See Brown and Lenneberg, 1954; Conklin, 1955; Berlin and Kay, 1969; Heider, 1972; Heider and Olivier, 1972; and Brown, 1976.) Human beings are sensitive to three properties of a color stimulus: hue (spectral position), saturation or intensity (chroma), and bright-

6. Jakobson believes that all phonemic judgments reflect a system of structures. For example, if it is true that phonemes are distinguished through a set of binary oppositions, then the English sound that is a nasal, labial consonant is /m/. Whether a given sound is nasal may at times be doubtful, but, in principle, distinctive acoustic features specify the necessary and sufficient conditions of class membership. As Jakobson points out, though, phonemic classifications must also take into account that languages impose a number of very general constraints on the occurrence of particular phonetic features in certain phonetic contexts. In Russian, for example, no word can end with a voiced consonant. This sort of phonetic constraint complicates the task of phonemic description, since phonetic features can serve a distinctive function only in contexts allowing a choice. Thus, the constraint on final voicing in Russian actually (in Trubetzkoy's terms) "neutralizes" the distinctiveness of the voicing contrast in that context. The result is what Trubetzkoy called an "archiphoneme" (Jakobson calls it an "incomplete" phoneme). The theory of archiphonemes is controversial and has not been accepted by all linguists. Despite such theoretical difficulties in describing a phonemic system, it remains true, I think, that phonemic categories are defined by distinctive features and that speakers are able to use such features to classify sounds, although, in actual speech, they must often rely on contextual information rather than phonetic features to interpret an utterance. I am indebted to Linda Waugh for the example and for this account of Jakobson's description of incomplete phonemes.

ness or brilliance (value). It has been estimated that normal individuals can discriminate anywhere from 7.5 million to 10 million colors or visual sense-contents (Optical Society of America, 1953), and yet there are far fewer color terms in any known language. The largest collection of color names in English has 3,000 items (Maerz and Paul, 1930). Only about eight of these terms are common, however (Thorndike and Lorge, 1944). Clearly, a wide range of sense-contents is bracketed out through the selective categories of a particular color system.

Selective attention to certain stimulus conditions is partly a biological function. For example, Eleanor Rosch Heider (1972) found evidence for a universal set of focal colors that are highly salient to human subjects independently of the color lexicon with which they may be familiar. On the other hand, differences in the systems for color classification that are reflected in these lexicons point up the range of variables that may or may not be treated as significant within a given system.

Harold Conklin's (1955) study of Hanunoo color categories is an interesting case of a kind of distinctive feature analysis for a system very different from that of English color terms. Conklin notes that the Hanunoo language lacks a generic term for color, which forced him to use circumlocution in asking questions about specific color terms. He asked subjects, "How is it to look at?" When this question elicited descriptions of spatial organization or form, he narrowed it by specifying "not its shape (or form)" (p. 190). Conklin concluded that Hanunoo color distinctions are made at two levels of contrast, one quite general and the other more specific. There were no disagreements or hesitations about classifications on the general level, but there were some minor variations in more detailed descriptions. The first, or general, level provides the following set of color terms: (1) *biru*: relative darkness (of shade of color) or blackness; (2) *lagti*: relative lightness (or tint of color) or whiteness; (3) *rara*: relative presence of red; and (4) *latuy*: relative presence of light green. It appears that the basic distinctive features in terms of which colors are classified on this general level are light versus dark, wet versus dry, and faint versus intense. Thus, *biru* and *lagti* are opposed as dark versus light, and also as intense (deep, unfading, indelible) versus faint (pale, weak, faded, bleached, or "colorless"). *Rara* and *latuy* are opposed both as intense versus faint and as dry versus wet.[7]

Conklin points out that the Hanunoo are in fact able to discriminate, on the level of sensory reception, between, say, the red, orange, or yellow shades of *rara,* yet these distinctions do not count in the classification of colors as *rara.* What does count is the presence of features of intensity and "dryness"—the colors most similar to those of such "dry" things as yellowed bamboo or hardened kernels of mature or parched corn.

These examples of categorical systems illustrate the nature of the semantic paradigms that condition judgments of identity or similarity. Some categorical judgments, though, involve marginal cases that do not precisely fit any category. For example, if one's paradigm of religion is Catholicism, one might feel that non-ritualistic sects are less clearly "religious" than are ritualistic sects, or if one's paradigm is derived from western religions, one might feel that Zen Buddhism is not quite a religion. In making semantic judgments about items that possess some but not all of the criterial features of a given category, one may be forced to decide consciously which features are or should be distinctive. One might even produce a logical definition as a result of such analysis. For example, one might define religion disjunctively as having sacred rituals or having teachings about the meaning of life or professing belief in a supreme being; or one might produce a conjunctive definition that would reject some candidates as being only quasi-religions. In my view, definitions introduced to decide borderline cases in a systematic way reflect a pragmatic decision and are ways of distinguishing types of cases within some context and for some purpose.

Speakers who have acquired a common set of ideal structures

7. "There is an opposition between dryness or desiccation and wetness or freshness (succulence) in visible components of the natural environment which are reflected in the terms *rara* and *latuy* respectively. This distinction is of particular significance in terms of plant life. Almost all living plants possess some fresh, succulent, and often "greenish" parts. To eat any kind of raw, uncooked food, particularly fresh fruits or vegetables, is known as *paglaty-un* (< *latuy*). A shiny, wet, brown-colored section of newly-cut bamboo is *malatuy* (not *marara*). Dried-out or matured plant material such as certain kinds of yellowed bamboo or hardened kernels of mature or parched corn are *marara.* To become desiccated, to lose all moisture, is known as *marara*" (Conklin, 1955, p. 191).

(linguistic categories) thereby possess a public system of *langue* through which they can overcome the psychologically contingent elements in their experience in expressing and interpreting specific referring intentions. Structures of *langue* condition categorical judgments, as speakers automatically bracket out contextually irrelevant sense-contents in deciding how to classify an item of experience or in following a speaker's intention. At the same time, speakers remain free to create linguistic means of expressing novel categorical (cognitive) structures. Thus, an empiricist theory of universals as ideal intentional structures accounts for both the acquisition and the creative expansion of public linguistic categories.

In the next section, I shall defend this empiricist account of ideal objects against three major objections that have been made to classical British empiricism, showing how the deficiencies in Locke's theory are overcome by a phenomenologically modified theory of universals.

The Arguments against Classical Empiricism

Husserl summarized the case against Locke's account of generic reference or class concepts in *Logical Investigations*. There are three objections that an empiricist account of universals must overcome. The first is that empiricism seems to require some sort of generic image as a general species-meaning underlying acts of specific reference. The problem is that a generic image can contain none of the particular characteristics of individual objects and for this reason is so abstract as to be unimaginable. Further, such an abstract representation, even if it were describable, would not seem at all similar to any individual member of a given class, so that it is hard to see how one could account for class membership through a resemblance between individuals and the generic image. For example, a generic image of a universal triangle could be neither isosceles nor equilateral nor right nor any other particular type of triangle; yet any individual triangle one could imagine or perceive must have some particular and nongeneric features. Thus, it seems that either one must hold that the object of a generic reference is something (a universal) that is not perceived or given as an image, or one must give up the notion of a "general language" in which individual referring acts are mediated by the same general species-meanings.

To this objection I would reply that an empiricist is not compelled to accept either some theory of generic images or a metaphysical theory of universals to account for generic reference. The theory that universals are ideal but observable structures within experience offers a third alternative. The empiricist may argue that any individual image or percept may be treated generically (in effect, constituted as a generic object) simply by bracketing out or disregarding the individual features (sense-contents) that do not count in some context. Thus, for example, the object that is intended in predicative statements about the generic triangle is not an individual representation of a particular type of triangle, nor even an individual composite image, if one were imaginable. But neither is it an unobservable ideal triangle known independently of perception. Rather, the intended referent is an object composed of the features that count in some representation: three one-dimensional line segments determined by a set of three points not on one line and forming an enclosed figure.

Since any truths that may be demonstrated about an ideal object are unconditioned by any properties of the representation (such as its space-time location) that have been bracketed out, one may immediately convert what Husserl called a specific singular judgment into a specific universal form. For example, "The interior angles of a triangle equal 180 degrees" is equivalent to: "For all triangles, the interior angles are equal to 180 degrees." The universal form expresses the attributive statement that insofar as any object is constituted as a triangle, then that object, by virtue of its class membership as a triangle, has the property described in the predicate.

In judgments of class membership, items are classed in a certain way by virtue of their similarity or equivalence to a semantic paradigm. However, such paradigms are not individual objects with all of their contingent features. They are ideal structures in the sense that certain features, including space-time location, are automatically bracketed. An entity judged to be sufficiently similar to an appropriately bracketed paradigm, or that possesses certain criterial features distinctive within a system, will count as a member of a specific class.

The second objection to empiricism that Husserl summarizes concerns the inadequacy of the traditional theory in explicating judgments of class membership. Locke proposed that individual items are classed together if they are perceived to be similar. Husserl counters that similarity relations are unintelligible unless they are understood in terms of identity, but the concept of identity seems to require a theory of ideas. In Husserl's words: "We cannot predicate exact likeness of two things, without stating the respect in which they are thus alike. Each exact likeness relates to a Species, under which the objects compared are subsumed: this Species is not, and cannot be, merely 'alike' in the two cases, if the worst of infinite regresses is not to become inevitable" (*L.I.*, vol. 1, p. 343).

The problem Husserl presents may be put as follows: Suppose a class is understood as composed of individual members that are sufficiently similar to a paradigm and thus in some respects alike. One is then called on to specify what is meant by similarity. Presumably, things that are similar have something in common. If one says that this common element is a self-identical idea (species), one seems to accept a theory of an ideal "one" that is somehow really present in a "many." If, on the other hand, one says that what things may have in common is a similarity (that is, they are all similar to the same paradigm), then, again, one must specify the features these things have in common in terms of which they are perceived as similar. These common elements will then constitute self-identical universals. If one tries to avoid this conclusion by positing another level of similarity, one must then explicate this property, and so on ad infinitum. Husserl concludes from this argument that relations of similarity presuppose an intuition of a common idea or species:

> If two things are 'alike' as regards form, then the Form-Species in question is the identical element, if they are 'alike' as regards colour, the Colour-Species is this element, etc. etc.... It would of course appear as a total inversion of the true state of things, were one to try to define identity, even in the sensory realm, as being essentially a limiting case of 'alikeness'. Identity is wholly indefina-

ble, whereas 'alikeness' is definable: 'alikeness' is the relation of objects falling under one and the same Species. If one is not allowed to speak of the identity of the Species, of the respect in which there is 'alikeness', talk of 'alikeness' loses its whole basis." [*L.I.,* vol. 1, p. 343]

As I see it, the problem for the empiricist is to clarify the meaning of identity without positing any nonempirical intuitions of metaphysical entities. In strictly phenomenological terms, things are judged to be identical in some respect whenever they are judged to be indiscriminable in that respect, that is, when one judges that no observer could make a discrimination of a given type. If one were shown a number of color chips, for example, one might experience varying degrees of difficulty in discriminating them, ranging from relative ease in noticing a difference to inability to make any discrimination, and so to tell the chips apart (other than through their numerical difference as space-time entities). If one were told that two samples that could not be discriminated appeared different under spectrographic analysis, or that some other observer could discriminate the two chips, this would count as evidence that their colors were not identical. In both cases, judgments of identity rest on the criterion of discriminability. To say that two color chips have the same color is not to say that they possess or instantiate a metaphysically self-identical color-species, but simply to say that one is unable to make a discrimination between the two chips by their color and to claim that no other observer could make such a discrimination.

In short, the phenomenological meaning of identity is given by the experiential criterion used in making judgments of identity or difference: the actual or potential indiscriminability, in some respect, of entities. One may, of course, be mistaken in any particular judgment of identity, but this is only to say that some other observer may notice a relevant difference. Indiscriminability is a necessary and sufficient condition for the judgment of identity, and it fully specifies its meaning. Thus I do not agree with Husserl's statement that identity is wholly indefinable: a logically primitive term. If one cannot define identity, then what does it mean to believe or judge that certain objects have identical features? The empiricist criterion of indiscriminability provides an essential clarification of this judgment.

One might perhaps object that the phenomenological notion of identity does not take into account some alleged objective causal basis for judgments of identity. That is, one perceives things to be indiscriminable because they really are identical. And yet, if one asks what is meant by the identity of such causal entities, one finds that once again identity, in this case that of underlying causes, must be explicated in terms of indiscriminability to a possible observer. The causal conditions underlying the perceptual indiscriminability of two sense-contents are understood to be identical only insofar as no other observers could discriminate those causal entities through their effects.[8] In contrast to Husserl, then, I would say that identity is definable, and that the experiential feature of indiscriminability is the primitive notion.

Things may be judged similar in two ways: (1) in the sense that they are identical (indiscriminable) in some respects, or (2) insofar as they are relatively difficult to discriminate. Thus, scarlet and maroon are relatively more difficult to discriminate than, say, scarlet and black. However, if one were faced with an array of fifteen hues ranging from scarlet to maroon at either end, scarlet and maroon would be easier to discriminate from each other than from any of the other chips in the array.[9] Again, scarlet and black color chips might appear relatively more similar to one another than either is, say, to the sensation of running one's hand over velvet cloth because, although it may be equally easy to discriminate between the red and black hue and between

8. The basic implication of this view of identity is that the individual has no privileged metaphysical status. One can conceive of an infinite set of logically possible discriminations in relation to a theoretical observer.

9. One may want to account for similarity as relative difficulty in discrimination in terms of a causal theory—for example, investigating stimulus conditions that produce difficulty for most observers in the absence of special conditions. In this sense, the acoustic or articulatory difference between, say, an aspirated and a nonaspirated p is quite subtle and difficult to detect, but such difficulty may be overcome through the distinctive feature system of a language. If some feature is distinctive in a phonemic system, listeners become very attuned even to relatively difficult discriminations, and in this way one type of similarity becomes less significant than another type, which counts in a given system.

either hue and the tactile sensation, the hues are both visual phenomena. This does not mean they instantiate a metaphysically real visual-phenomena-species, but simply that colors are indiscriminable with respect to the feature of being visually presented.

Given this explication of identity and similarity, the empiricist can provide a straightforward account of the relation between paradigm and exemplar in the formation of classes. Objects are classified as exemplars of a given type when they are perceived as similar to an idealized paradigm. In cases of one type, individual objects are judged indiscriminable from a paradigm in terms of those features that count as distinctive. An individual item that exhibits a sufficient number of such features will be classed accordingly. In cases of a second type, individual items are judged relatively more difficult to discriminate from one paradigm than from other, contrasting paradigms along some specific dimension of comparison. For example, given the Hanunoo system of color classification, some ambiguous shade of grey might be classifiable either as a light, faint color (*lagti*) or as an intense, dark color (*biru*), depending, it would seem, on the relative difficulty involved in discriminating that shade from either of the two paradigms. Again, whereas the Hanunoo system classes red, orange, and yellow as *rara*, our own set of color terms would force a distinction among these colors, and at certain points between two colors there would be undecidable or very difficult cases. In both kinds of cases, there can be degrees of class membership. The essential point is that judgments of class membership are determined by the degree of indiscriminability of individuals with respect to a specific ideal but observable intentional structure.

The third traditional objection to classical empiricism is a continuation of the second. As Husserl puts it, one cannot "dispense with species as objects by having recourse to their extensions" because one must explain what gives unity to the extension. The empiricist claim is that members of a class are unified through their similarity. Things may be similar, however, in a number of different ways, and one must be prepared to say what distinguishes the "circles of similars" among themselves. For example, given a red triangle, a red circle, and a blue triangle, the first two objects are similar in one respect and the red and blue triangle are similar in another way. But the question is, what unifies a given "circle of similars"? The empiricist says these are different *kinds* of similarities. Does this mean that for each "circle" or kind of similarity things are similar in identically the same way? One may ask, for example, if the similarity between the red triangle and circle is identical or similar to the similarity between a red square and a red pentagon. If these are identical similarities, one posits a self-identical universal. If they are only similar similarities, one falls into an infinite regress, since one then wants to know if the similarity of the similarities between the red triangle and circle and the red square and pentagon is itself identical or similar to the similarity of the similarities between, say, a red triangle and circle and a blue triangle and hexagon, and so on indefinitely. This argument recalls Bertrand Russell's (1912) claim that to account for universal properties of quality in terms of similarity is simply to make the relational property of similarity into a universal, as a similarity must either be an identical similarity, or only a similar one, leading to similar similarities of similarities, and so on.

This argument poses no difficulty for a phenomenological empiricism that explicates identity relations in terms of indiscriminability and similarity relations in terms of partial identity or relative discriminability. Thus, a red triangle and a red circle may be judged identical in their specific hue, or they may both be judged more similar to one paradigm (redness) than to any other. The red and blue triangles are more nearly identical or similar with respect to shape or in relation to a generic triangle. In general, although objects are potentially similar in a number of ways, the classification of objects is mediated by idealized paradigms that establish the features that count in judging degree of identity or similarity.

If one asks if the similarity of hue between, say, a red triangle and a red circle is similar to that between a red square and a red pentangle, the answer is that one must examine individual cases and compare them with respect to degree of indiscriminability along the relevant dimension. There may be an indiscriminable (identical) relation of similarity in both cases, or there may not be (for example, if the circle is deep red and the other forms are light red). The point is that one does not encounter an infinite regress, since one has a definite criterion for answering questions about identity or degrees of similarity. This criterion can be applied as long as one is able to perceive or imagine the objects (or "similarities") one is called on to compare.

I conclude that a phenomenological account of universals as ideal structures within experience overcomes the basic objections to classical empiricism without positing any metaphysical entities. I have considered the nature of generic reference and the process of category formation from this perspective, and in Chapter 10 I shall complete the theoretical defense of radical empiricism by explicating the distinction between necessary and contingent truths. In the next chapter, I shall consider the bearing of the philosophical problem of universals on the rationalistic theory of universal grammar.

CHAPTER 9

Universal Grammar

Chomsky's theory of universal grammar (UG) is designed to account for the acquisition of a generative grammar on the basis of innate knowledge. Since speakers are said to have an a priori knowledge of the linguistic concepts incorporated in UG, he has characterized his theory as an elaboration of traditional (17th century) philosophical rationalism. Chomsky (1968) described UG as follows:

> Suppose that we assign to the mind, as an innate property, the general theory of language that we have called "universal grammar." This theory ... specifies a certain subsystem of rules that provides a skeletal structure for any language and a variety of conditions, formal and substantive, that any further elaboration of the grammar must meet. The theory of universal grammar, then, provides a schema to which any particular grammar must conform. ... The innate schema that characterizes the class of potential languages ... defines the "essence" of human language. [p. 76]

According to Chomsky, a child is born with a knowledge of formal and substantive linguistic universals, as well as with an "evaluation procedure" for testing hypotheses about the grammar of a given natural language. Substantive universals, such as "sentence," "phrase-marker," "phonetic (distinctive) feature," "complex symbol," "noun phrase," and so on, provide the theoretical vocabulary or the set of elements that may be included in particular grammars. Formal universals specify the abstract (formal) structure of the rules of any grammar. For example, all transformations are structure-dependent in the sense that they apply to a string of words. All semantic interpretation applies to a surface structure that has been modified by the "trace" (syntactic structuring) left by deep structure operations. All grammars have a syntactic, semantic, and phonological component. And all grammars are systems of rules that assign a pairing of sound and meaning, operating in terms of a basic distinction between underlying and surface structure, and including both phrase structure and transformational rules.[1]

Innate knowledge of universal grammar makes possible and regulates the construction of the specific grammar that can generate the set of possible propositional meanings (in Katz's theory) of possible grammatical sentences (in Chomsky's theory) of a given natural language. One implication of this theory is that the phonological, syntactic, and semantic structures of all languages should be very similar, since the range of empirical possibilities is severely restricted by the schema of universal grammar. As Chomsky (1975) puts it:

> What is learned, the cognitive structure attained, must have the properties of UG [universal grammar], though it will have other properties as well, accidental properties. Each human language will conform to UG; languages will differ in other, accidental properties.... UG will specify properties of sound, meaning, and structural organization. We may expect that in all of these do-

---

1. Chomsky (1968) proposed several specific rules which may be formal universals. For example, he proposed the principle that "certain phonological rules operate in a cycle, in a manner determined by the surface structure" (p. 37), which means that sequences of rules apply in a certain order to bracketed or hierarchically ordered strings. He also proposed the A-over-A principle, which states that "no noun phrase can be extracted from within another noun phrase—more generally, that if a transformation applies to a structure of the form [S ... [A ...]A ...]S for any category A, then it must be so interpreted as to apply to the *maximal* phrase of the type A" (p. 43). This means that if a transformation rule applies to a phrase of the category A, and the string to which the rule has reference contains an A-type phrase included within another A-type phrase, the rule may be applied to the larger but not the included phrase. (For example, "the car in the garage" is a noun phrase that includes the noun phrase "the car." The rule says one can delete "the car in the garage" but not "the car"). Chomsky (1975) proposed a "specified-subject condition" (SSC), which he formulated as follows: "In a structure of the form [...X...[Z - WYV] ...], no rule can relate X and Y if Z is the subject of WYV and is not controlled by X" (p. 150). This rule allows such sentences as "John's friends appeared to their wives to hate one another" and rules out such sentences as "Mary appeared to John's friends to hate one another."

mains, UG will impose conditions that narrowly restrict the variety of languages. [pp. 29–30]

The grammatical categories and rules of which speakers are said to have a priori knowledge are not linguistic structures acquired through experience. Chomsky (1975) makes this point forcibly in the following passage:

> A grammar is not a structure of higher-order concepts and principles constructed from simpler elements by "abstraction" or "generalization" or "induction." Rather, it is a rich structure of predetermined form, compatible with triggering experience and more highly valued, by a measure that is itself part of UG, than other cognitive structures meeting the dual conditions of compatibility with the structural principles of UG and with relevant experience. [pp. 43–44]

Thus, Chomsky's theory characterizes language as, in its essence, an abstract object of a priori knowledge.

Chomsky has made a point of associating his theory of innate knowledge of the formal and substantive universals of universal grammar with 17th century philosophical theories of a priori knowledge. He has, for example, referred to the distinction Gottfried Leibniz drew between two sorts of innate capacities, "powers" and "dispositions." Chomsky argues against the empiricist restriction of innate capacities to "powers" which "require the stimulation of external objects both in order to be activated and in order to receive their perceptual or ideational content; hence which [have] no specific contents of their own," and argues for a rationalistic theory of innate "dispositions." Chomsky quotes Alan Gewirth's (1973) discussion with approval, as a fair statement of his own view:

> Dispositions . . . on the other hand, already have determinate contents which the mind can itself activate, given appropriate external occasions. . . .For ideas to be innate as dispositions means that the mind has quite determinate contents of its own which it is able to activate and perceive; whereas for ideas to be innate merely as powers would mean that the mind has only diffuse mechanisms whose contents are exhaustively derived from the impact of external stimuli. [Chomsky, 1975, p. 215]

Chomsky (1975) describes the following analysis by Gewirth as "exactly to the point," providing a precise contrast between empiricist learning theories and his own (Leibnizean) rationalism:

> Far from being compatible with empiricist and behaviorist learning theories . . . Leibniz's doctrine shows how the mind can itself be the exhaustive source of its linguistic competence, for which external stimuli serve only as occasions for activating what is already dispositionally contained in the mind's own structure. Leibniz's doctrine therefore explains, as the behaviorist theory cannot, the necessity and universality of the linguistic rules for forming and interpreting sentences. [p. 216]

Thus Chomsky insists on a basic difference between his "content" view of innate knowledge and any empiricist learning theory, even one which conceded that the child had innate learning capacities of a general sort, in the Leibnizean sense of "powers." The rationalistic hypothesis entails more than simply innate learning strategies or methods of processing sensory data, such as Willard Quine, Dan Slobin, John Searle, and others have suggested. The claim is for innate knowledge of determinate linguistic structures that are in no sense constructs from experience.

Chomsky has also repeatedly linked his theory of an "active" system of innate "dispositions" (in the Leibnizean sense) with the theories of perception developed by René Descartes and Ralph Cudworth (1838), both of whom argued for innate knowledge of the intelligible universals which may be evoked by sensible things. For example, Chomsky wrote the following in *Language and Mind* (1968):

> There is nothing incomprehensible in the view that stimulation provides the occasion for the mind to apply certain innate interpretive principles, certain concepts that proceed from "the power of understanding" itself. . . . To take an example from Descartes (*Reply to Objections,* V): "When first in infancy we see a triangular figure depicted on paper, this figure cannot show us how a real triangle ought to be conceived. . . . But because we already possess within us the idea of a true triangle, . . . we, therefore, when we see the composite figure, apprehend not it itself, but rather the authentic triangle." In this sense the idea of a triangle is innate.

Surely the notion is comprehensible; there would be no difficulty, for example, in programming a computer to react to stimuli along these lines. . . . Similarly, there is no difficulty in principle in programming a computer with a schematism that sharply restricts the form of a generative grammar, with an evaluation procedure for grammars of the given form, with a technique for determining whether given data is compatible with a grammar of the given form, with a fixed substructure of entities (such as distinctive features), rules, and principles, and so on—in short, with a universal grammar. . . . I believe that these proposals can be properly regarded as a further development of classical rationalist doctrine, as an elaboration of some of its main ideas regarding language and mind. [pp. 72–73]

Chomsky (1971a) has made a very strong statement for innate knowledge of semantic as well as syntactic universals, in opposition to what he admits to be that "part of empiricist theory [which] appears to be true without any qualification: namely, that words which I understand derive their meaning from my experience" (p. 17). Although he admits that, since "experience is required to bring innate structures into operation, to activate a system of innate ideas," (p. 17) there will be some individual and social variations in concepts employed, which must be attributed to experience or to differences in mental capacity, he concludes that:

it is at best misleading to claim that words that I understand derive their meaning from my experience. . . . we can easily imagine how an organism initially endowed with conditions on the form and organization of language could construct a specific system of interconnections among concepts, and conditions on use and reference, on the basis of scanty evidence. . . . There is every reason to believe that the semantic system of language is largely given by a power independent of conscious choice; the operative principles of mental organization are presumably inaccessible to introspection, but there is no reason why they should in principle be more immune to investigation than the principles that determine the physical arrangement of limbs and organs. [pp. 17–18]

Katz (1972) has taken up Chomsky's innateness hypothesis and developed a theory of semantic markers, which he believes reflect the ideal, universal, and objective semantic concepts that combine to form the lexical and structural categories of a language. Chomsky and Halle (1965) asserted that "the significant linguistic universals are those that must be assumed to be available to the child learning a language as an a priori, innate endowment" (p. 4). Katz presents his semantic theory in this context, as part of the theory of "essential linguistic universals" of which speakers have an a priori, innate knowledge. He holds that the "substantive universals at the semantic level," included as components of a hypothetical language acquisition device, will provide the "theoretical vocabulary from which semantic constructs required in the formulations of particular semantic interpretations of grammatical sentences can be drawn (Katz, 1972, p. 33). Using this vocabulary, a descriptively adequate grammar can assign to each expression and sentence of the language its "objective" conceptual and propositional sense.[2] An accurate theory, of course, is one that describes the linguistic categories and rules that "have real counterparts in the causal processes going on in the heads of the speakers" (Katz, 1972, p. 29).

In proposing that speakers have innate knowledge of a set of concepts that define the essence of language, Chomsky and those who have followed his lead have intended a scientific rather than a metaphysical theory of a priori linguistic knowledge. Thus, the theory posits linguistic universals as inferred entities that play a causal role in performance. They are theoret-

---

2. For example, Katz (1972) provides the following model of a dictionary entry a semantic theory could provide: "kill, [+N, +Det _____, +Count, ...]; (Cause) (Become) (Not) (Alive)" (P. 410). He suggests that the English word "chair" might plausibly be analyzed in the following way: "(Object), (Physical), (Non-living), (Artifact), (Furniture), (Portable), (Something with legs), (Something with a back), (Something with a seat), (Seat for one)" (p. 40). He admits that the above analysis is incomplete, since "each of the concepts represented by the semantic markers . . . can itself be broken into components. For example, the concept of an object represented by '(Object)' might be analyzed as *an organization of parts that are spatio-temporally contiguous which form a stable whole having an orientation in space*" (p. 40). Thus, though he endorses the project of discovering the ultimate set of universal concepts in terms of which the semantic interpretation of all possible sentences of a language may be specified by a grammar, he does not claim to have discovered the ultimate "primitive" set of semantic markers.

ical constructs justified on the basis of empirical evidence.[3] Further, the theory proposes a biological basis for innate knowledge. The "prior" knowledge of linguistic concepts belonging to
UG is said to be genetically transmitted.[4] Thus, though Chomsky
(1975) has said that his theory of mind has a "distinctly
rationalist cast," he emphasizes a departure from the
philosophical tradition "specifically, in taking the '*a priori* system'
to be biologically determined" (p. 39).

There has been much discussion of the difficult concept of a
specific genetic basis for linguistic knowledge, or for cognitive
abilities specifically adapted to the task of constructing a model
of the grammar of some language in accordance with the
schema of UG. As I noted in notes 14 and 15 in Chapter 1, there
is presently no genetic theory that can give substance to the idea.
Chomsky (1975) has dismissed this problem, as it simply points
to a gap in contemporary knowledge of genetic mechanisms, but
does not show that the idea has no basis. In any case, this is not
the basic philosophical issue raised by Chomsky's theory of a

3. For example, Katz (1972) asserts that semantic markers, as well as other
components of UG, are "theoretical constructs" posited within a scientific theory
(p. 38). Despite this claim, the theory of UG is not in fact genuinely empirical or
scientific if one can neither verify nor confirm the hypothesis that there is innate
a priori knowledge of linguistic universals. Chomsky (1975) proposed that the
theory be tested by constructing languages that violate postulated principles of
UG to see if they are accessible to human beings (p. 209). The problem with this
suggestion (as I noted in Chapter 1), is that even if one could establish that some
artificial language that violated one of the universals posited by linguistic theory
could not be learned by some speakers, this would not show that those speakers
had an innate a priori knowledge of those universals. There might be some other
explanation for a learning problem (for example, a language might contain
semantically unmotivated rules or rules that simply make no sense in terms of
the experience or cognitive capacities of a child). On the other hand, the fact that
speakers are able to learn a given language does not, in itself, show that they have
innate knowledge of some kind.

4. James Edie (1976) has suggested that Chomsky's account of the genetic
basis of a priori knowledge of universal grammar represents a form of
naturalism and psychologism and that it should be reinterpreted in favor of a
"more sensible kind of aprioristic interpretation which would be natural in a
Husserlian framework" (p. 65). The difficulty with this suggestion is, of course,
that it would have no bearing on what is for Chomsky the central issue: namely,
whether a T-G grammar can be learned in the ordinary sense or whether one
must posit a prior, innate knowledge of universal grammar to account for language acquisition.

priori concepts. The problem concerns what Katz (1972) called "the ancient philosophical puzzle about universals" (p. 39), an issue Katz feels should be "left out of attempts to carry on scientific investigations" (p. 39). Unfortunately, linguistic rationalism itself raises the question about the ontological status of the concepts of which speakers are said to have biologically innate knowledge. Katz (1972) himself has provided an unusually clear view of this issue in the following statement:

> A semantic marker is a theoretical construct which is intended to represent a concept that is part of the sense of morphemes and other constituents of natural languages. By a concept in this connection we do not mean images or mental ideas or particular thoughts.... Concepts ... are abstract entities. They do not belong to the conscious experience of anyone, though they may be thought about, as in our thinking about the concept of a circle. They are not individuated by persons: you or I may think about the same concept. They are not ... elements in the subjective process of thinking, but rather the objective content of thought processes.... Nor are they datable: they cannot possess temporal properties or bear temporal relations.... Concepts and propositions are senses of expressions and sentences. That is, senses are concepts and propositions connected with the phonetic (or orthographic) objects in natural languages.... If the grammar provides an account of the semantic content of each phonetic object in the language, then the pairing of sound and meaning will provide the required individuation [of concepts and propositions] in terms of phonetically specified features of stretches of speech.... This, however, still leaves open the question of what the ontological status of concepts and propositions is, of what kinds of things senses and meanings are. This question will be left without a final answer. [pp. 38–39]

Though Katz would like to defer consideration of the philosophical problem of universals by treating innate linguistic concepts as inferred entities, it is evident from his description that such concepts are ideal objects. In fact, the theory that grammar provides an objective structural and semantic description for all utterances (tokens) of a language requires both Chomsky and Katz to hold this position. It is the ideal nature of linguistic concepts that makes it possible for speakers to say the "same" thing in different utterances on different occasions. More generally, it is only on account of the ideal nature of *langue* that speakers may be said to know the same language.

If, however, linguistic concepts are ideal entities that have neither spatial nor temporal location, how are they to serve as the unobservable, genetically transmitted, individual objects that play a causal role in the language acquisition process? Chomsky's rationalistic theory appears inconsistent because it incorporates conflicting aspects of a scientific model of inferred biological constraints on language acquisition and a traditional metaphysical theory of a priori knowledge of unobservable ideal entities. From an empiricist standpoint, the philosophical difficulty lies in the notion of a knowledge of ideal concepts that are not in some sense observable within, and derivable from, experience. To say that linguistic universals have a genetic basis does not render the theory empirical, because it does not resolve the question of the relation of ideal concepts to experience. In fact, the novel idea of genetically transmitted metaphysical entities (ideal unobservable concepts) only deepens the paradox. If Chomsky truly intends to claim that speakers have a prior, nonempirical knowledge of ideal, unobservable "determinate contents" of UG, then he should present his views about so-called Platonic realism. In particular, he should explain the sense in which ideal unobservable entities are real and clarify the possibility of entities that would seem to be both ideal concepts and individual (causally efficacious) objects of some type.

On the other hand, it is possible that Chomsky intends to say only that there are genetically based constraints on cognition and that these constraints are reflected in universal features of language. There is undoubtedly a causal relation between the genetically determined structure of the human brain and nervous system and the capacity of the human mind to structure experience in determinate ways. Thus, if one could discover certain features exhibited by all languages (or other symbolic forms), one could attempt to test the hypothesis that such features were "essentially" determined by the physical structure of the human brain. Descriptions of abstract universal structures (emptied of empirical content or variations insofar as that is possible) might be taken as representations of what is physically embodied in human beings, that is, of the physical system in its causal operation. One might then reinterpret the language of seventeenth century rationalism by equating unconscious innate or a priori knowledge with that which is physically embodied in the brain insofar as that limits cognitive (and therefore linguistic) structure.[5] Though such a use of seventeenth century language might be misleading, it would avoid the claim that speakers have innate, a priori knowledge of ideal concepts, or that ideal, unobservable concepts are genetically transmitted.

It is not clear from Chomsky's many statements on the subject of innate linguistic knowledge how he would respond to these alternatives. Chomsky (1975) has spoken of innate/unconscious "cognitive structures" rather than "knowledge" because of objections to the phrase "unconscious knowledge." On the other hand, he has resisted efforts to interpret the innateness hypothesis as a broad claim about the limits set by genetic endowment on human thought and perception (which no modern empiricist would deny), as against what has been called his "content" view of innate linguistic knowledge. For example, Chomsky (1978) concludes,

> There seems little reason to suppose, for the moment, that there are general principles of cognitive structure, or even of human cognition, expressible at some higher level, from which the particular properties of particular "mental organs," such as the language faculty, can be deduced, or even that there are illuminating analogies among these various systems. [pp. 218–219]

Moreover, his remarks about innate ideas as "determinate contents" activated by experience, and his references to Descartes and Leibniz are, at best, misleading if he does not intend a theory of genetically transmitted ideal concepts. Again, a clarification of Chomsky's philosophical position might greatly reduce opposition to his version of rationalism.

I conclude that the theory of UG has an unacceptable metaphysical implication if it is interpreted as a claim about a priori knowledge of ideal, unobservable linguistic concepts. To avoid this implication, the theory must be interpreted in a way

5. This interpretation of Chomsky was suggested by Joyce Elbrecht.

that is consistent with a phenomenological form of empiricism. This means, first, that linguistic concepts must be treated as ideal structures within experience rather than unobservable "theoretical entities" and, second, that "innate linguistic knowledge" must refer to biological constraints on linguistic concepts rather than to genetically transmitted intentional structures. If linguistic concepts are understood in this way, it is clear that, by their very nature, they are not theoretical objects of innate knowledge. An empiricist theory of language could speak of an innate basis for language acquisition in a broad sense, however. For example, it is plausible that children at first acquire semantic structures that reflect their biologically determined level of cognitive development, and it is also possible that there are other biological constraints on the sorts of cognitive structures available to the human mind.

An empiricist theory of universals accounts for the acquisition of a common language without positing any metaphysically objective linguistic concepts. The phenomenological description of universals presented in Chapter 8 shows that, in theory, any number of individual utterances may express the same ideal intentional structure. A referring intention (utterance meaning) is expressed in context through a common system of ideal linguistic structures that speakers acquire on the basis of their experience. Thus, in acquiring *langue,* speakers are able to express intentions that transcend the contingent "sense impressions" of private experience.

In the next chapter, I shall show how a phenomenological empiricism is able to overcome psychological contingency in another form, by guaranteeing the authority of statements expressing logical truths.

CHAPTER 10

The Authority of
Logical Truth

In this section I shall further develop the empiricist theory of utterance meaning I have been presenting by showing how this theory can account for the necessity of logical truth and the evident distinction between such necessary truths and contingent empirical statements. I shall contrast phenomenological empiricism with a metaphysical form of rationalism and with classical empiricism and show that the first theory can account for intuitions of logical necessity without positing an a priori knowledge of metaphysically objective ideas and truths, and without falling into a stultifying form of psychologism.

Briefly, a metaphysical theory of necessary truth would say that judgments of logical necessity are grounded in an a priori intuition of ideal, unobservable universals. Empirical knowledge, in contrast, is based on a process of induction from a limited sample of individual cases and involves a simple noting of contingent facts. In Chapter 8 I presented an alternative phenomenological model of ideal intentional objects as observable structures and argued that the necessity of universal (logical) truths lies in a deductive relationship between a certain idealized intentional object and certain properties attributed to that object. For example, a proof of the Pythagorean theorem has as its object a generic right triangle, and, using only the features that count in identifying such an object, shows that the square of the length of the hypotenuse is equal to the sum of the squares of the lengths of the other two sides. From this proof it follows that any object that has the criterial features of that ideal object must also possess those properties arrived at deductively through the proof. In contrast, ordinary inductive generalizations require empirical confirmation since they do not establish a deductive relationship between a given individual subject and a set of predicates.

The model of necessary truth presented thus far remains incomplete until the nature of the crucial "deductive relationship" between subject and predicate has been clarified. What must be explained is the basis of the logical intuition by means of which one asserts that a deductive relationship does hold, and through which one distinguishes between necessary and contingent truths. A metaphysical account is, I think, essentially silent on this point. The claim that logical intuition is somehow primitive, and that it is simply a matter of recognizing what must be, of "seeing" the essential properties of forms and seeing that they are essential (in Descartes's terms, of having a "clear and distinct idea" of essences or universals, including the clear and distinct idea that clear and distinct ideas must be true), is a rather vacuous claim as long as it does not provide a criterion for distinguishing logical intuition from a (contingent) psychological feeling of conviction. In what follows I shall attempt to provide such a criterion, and show how the intuition of logical necessity may be accounted for by intentional structures within experience.

Traditional Empiricism and the Problem of Psychologism

It has long been claimed that empiricism leads to a stultifying form of psychologism in the sense that it accounts for logical necessity in terms of contingent, psychological structures, and cannot distinguish logical intuition from belief. Before presenting my own account of this issue, I shall first summarize Edmund Husserl's influential critique of J. S. Mill's empiricist and psychologistic theory of logical truth and then show how a phenomenological empiricism escapes these criticisms.

In *Logical Investigations*, Husserl develops four arguments against Mill's psychologistic view that logical truths reflect contingent laws of thought, or that they are merely inductive generalizations from "mental facts." The focus of Husserl's discussion is the law of contradiction, $\sim(A \cdot \sim A)$, which says that something (A) cannot simultaneously be and not be the same thing in the same respect. Put another way, the law says that no statement can be both true and false. Mill viewed the law of contradiction as an induction or generalization from the familiar experience of the mental incompatibility of simultaneous *belief* in positive and negative modes or states of being. We experience the incompatibility of, for example, light and darkness, sound and silence, equality and inequality, or succession and simultaneity and generalize from this experience that any positive phenomenon and its negation are distinct phenomena in a relation of extreme contrariety, and thus that one is always absent when the other is present. Mill accounts for the necessity of the law of contradiction in psychological terms: from our constant experience of the incompatibility of positive and negative modes, we form habits of association (for example, between the idea of the existence of a positive or negative mode and belief in the nonexistence of its contrary), such that we find it impossible to believe that contraries can exist as simultaneous modes of an object. The associations are, in turn, accounted for mechanistically in terms of a theory of brain physiology, or arousal of the same area of the brain or nervous system by different stimuli. Thus, the law of contradiction has a merely factual basis in a psychological inability to doubt it or to believe that contrary or contradictory states (Mill does not seem to make a distinction) can co-occur. In *An Examination of Sir William Hamilton's Philosophy*, Mill summarizes his view of the status of the three basic logical laws (contradiction, excluded middle, and identity) and says:

> They may or may not be capable of alteration by experience, but the conditions of our existence deny to us the experience which would be required to alter them. Any assertion, therefore, which conflicts with one of these laws, any proposition, for instance, which asserts a contradiction, though it were on a subject wholly removed from the sphere of our experience, is to us unbelievable. The belief in such a proposition is, in the present constitution of nature, impossible as a mental fact. [Quoted in Husserl, *L. I.*, vol. 1, p. 113]

Husserl's basic objection to this theory is that it makes logical truths contingent. If they merely describe how people happen to think, or the patterns of belief to which their experiences have predisposed them, then there is nothing to prevent these psychological patterns, or the experiences giving rise to them, from changing, even though the corresponding logical law would thereby be disconfirmed. I may not *believe,* for example, that an object that is both red and nonred simultaneously and in the same respect can exist, but if I should ever happen to experience such a thing, I would have to revise my opinion, and the law of contradiction would no longer *seem* necessary. But, as Husserl points out, the law of contradiction does not tell us what we must *think* (or what we do think), but rather, what must be the case. For this reason, we are unwilling to say that logical laws can be disconfirmed. Of course, Mill might still reply to this argument that it simply shows how deep-rooted is our belief in logical laws. We are simply unable to believe that they could be disconfirmed, and so we call them necessary truths, as opposed to descriptions of variable states of affairs we have experienced and know to be contingent. The most Husserl's argument shows is that if one wants to guarantee that logical truths cannot be disconfirmed, one must base them on something other than belief.

Husserl's second objection to Mill's position is that "not every pair of mutually exclusive propositions is a contradictory pair" (vol. 1, p. 112). For example, things are not simultaneously and in the same respect red and green all over, or at least one does not believe that they may be, yet these are not contradictory properties. Thus, something more must enter into the formulation of the law of contradiction than the experience of mutually exclusive, contrary or incompatible states of affairs. Since Mill is not required to accept Husserl's account of what is or is not contradictory, however, this argument does not seem particularly forceful. According to Mill, the coexistence of contrary states *is* contradictory, insofar as one cannot believe in such a possibility. Of course, red and green are contraries in the sense that something may be neither red nor green, but one also sees that something can't be both red and green. I would argue that to say something is simultaneously and in the same respect green and not-green is a contradiction, and one instance of a color that is "not-green" is red (as a function of the distinctive features of our color system), so that by substitution, the same combination of properties that is ruled out under one description (green and not-green) is ruled out under another description (green and red). To recognize that anything one would call a clear case of red would also, as a function of one's color paradigms, be called a clear case of not-green, leads one to recognize that the not-green colors, which may not coexist with green ones, include those that are called red. What the critic must show is that something besides belief is involved in statements about the impossibility of certain states of affairs.

The third point Husserl raises is much more convincing. Against the view that logical laws are descriptions of what people believe, he points out that sometimes some people do hold contradictory beliefs. Does this mean that the law of contradiction holds (as a true description) at some times and not at others, or only for certain individuals? Perhaps one might qualify one's original theory of the laws of logic and say that they describe what people believe when they are paying attention to their thoughts, or when they are not insane, or not hypnotized, or, more generally, when they are "normal." But then what is a normal person? If a normal or sane person is one who does not assert or believe contradictory propositions, one falls into a circle: the normal person is the one who reasons logically, and logic is a description of the way normal persons reason. Finally, if one tries to avoid the notion of a normal person and still acknowledge that some people do hold contradictory views, Husserl says one gets a view of the law of contradiction something like this: "In certain subjective circumstances X (unfortunately not further investigated nor capable of being completely specified) two acts of belief having a Yes-No opposition cannot co-exist in the same consciousness." Husserl comments, "Is this what logicians really mean when they say that two contradictory propositions cannot both be true?" (vol. 1, p. 115). This is a very powerful argument, and I think the most one could say about it, without abandoning the thesis that logical laws describe beliefs, is that any individual who held such beliefs might hold anyone who did not either to reason in a way that was not well founded in experience (for example, believing that contradictory properties might coexist, even though no such state of affairs had ever been experienced), or to reason in such a way as to violate the former's concept of rational, or even human cognition. This would reduce logical laws to a description of the beliefs of some set of individuals, which those individuals held to be normative for "well-founded" or "rational" thought.

Husserl's final argument is also his strongest. He claims that empiricism, and the psychologism to which it leads, are sceptical doctrines, in the sense that they cannot provide a rational justification for being accepted as true. If logical laws are nothing more than descriptions of the beliefs held by some individuals under some conditions, rather than formulations of logical insights, or self-evident truths, then the very empiricist and psychologistic position established on the basis of logical rules of inference is "without rational foundation, is, in fact, a mere assumption, no more than a common prejudice" (vol. 1, p. 116). If one cannot be certain that one's logical premises are true (other than as descriptions of how some people happen to think), one cannot be certain that any "mediate judgments" or "proofs" derived from these premises are true, except in the sense that they are statements one happens to believe. Thus, if one claims that the empiricist and psychologistic position is certainly true, or is more than a chance belief, one violates the premise that logical laws merely describe beliefs; and if one holds to this premise, one cannot claim a rational or logical basis for empiricism. As Husserl puts it, "In other words: the correctness of the theory presupposes the irrationality of its premises, the correctness of the premises the irrationality of the theory (or thesis)" (vol. 1, p. 117). To show that logical reasoning is a function of rational insight, rather than a result of chance (of what people happen to believe), one must provide some objective basis for the necessity of logical truth. In short, one must show that a formulation is logical not because people happen to believe it, but that, on the contrary, people may come to believe in its necessity through an intuition that it is objectively true.

Husserl's answer to psychologism is the claim that truths of reason, or logical truths, can be authoritative for us because they are objectively true. This objective truth can be discovered through an insightful response that brings inner evidence. Inner evidence is not a contingent, experientially derived belief that happens to accompany certain ideas, but rather an experience that "proclaims its truth" and cannot be doubted: "Inner evidence is . . . nothing but the 'experience' of truth. Truth is of course only experienced in the sense in which something ideal can be an experience in a real act. Otherwise put: *Truth is an Idea* . . ." (vol. 1, p. 194). Husserl understood truth, more specifically, as the idea of "*the agreement* between meaning and what is itself present, meant, between the actual *sense of an assertion* and the self-given *state of affairs*" (vol. 1, p. 195). Truth, in short, is said to be the idea of inward evidence. In the case of logical truth, there is an agreement between some assertion and an ideal object or species, and this agreement is experienced in its "primal givenness," much as physical objects are experienced as given in perceptual experience. It is this givenness of the idea which guarantees that, to the extent that one really has insight, "no one's insight can be at variance with our own."

If one interprets this Husserlian statement as consistent with the theory of ideal (intentional) objects discussed in Chapter 8, the implication is that the idea of truth is an ideal or bracketed intentional structure that may be judged present in a set of individual cases, that is, cases in which there is judged to be agreement between the sense of an assertion and a state of affairs. While this may be adequate as an intentional analysis of truth in a general sense, it does not yet answer the question of how we come to know what are the essential properties of some form (ideal object), and so how we come to know what is logically true. For example, the proof of the Pythagorean theorem requires a deductive process. It may be correct to say that we follow this proof through logical intuition, which tells us that the proof is valid, and this intuition may lead, as Husserl claimed, to an experience of the correspondence between the sense of the theorem and some ideal object. But how do we know that our logical intuition about the validity of the proof, which led to the final intuition of truth, is itself reliable? For such intuition to count as evidence, it must show us a correspondence between assertion and some intentional structure. But what assertion, and what intentional structure? Let us say that deductive proof involves a recognition that certain conclusions must be drawn to avoid contradictions (I shall presently argue that this is so). In that case, we must see a correspondence between the sense of the assertion that something follows deductively (or that its denial would involve contradiction) and some intentional structure present within the ideal object under consideration. But this intuitive seeing, which guarantees the truth of a conclusion under certain conditions, cannot be understood without an intentional analysis of the "sense" of the assertions involved. In short, Husserl's remarks fall short of a full explication of logical intuition because he did not analyze the intentional structure of deductive argument and, most fundamentally, of the basic logical law of contradiction.

In the next section I shall attempt to account for logical intuition in terms of the ideal structure of the basic law of contradiction, and show that this structure guarantees the authority of logical truth.

The Law of Contradiction

It seems to me that an empiricist account of the law of contradiction should begin by analyzing what goes on experientially, or imaginatively, when one recognizes or judges that something is a contradiction. If this judgment reflects a specific bracketed experiential paradigm, then by imaginatively varying instances that are or are not judged to be contradictions, one should be able to discover what criteria underlie the various judgments. Suppose, for example, I try to decide whether something may be both red and not-red at the same time. I imagine some instance of a red patch or a red object, stipulating only that it must be something I would judge to be clearly red. Other than that, it may be any sort of object whatever. I then imagine some other object—anything whatsoever—so long as it is a color (purely visual phenomenon) I would judge to be clearly not-red. Holding these two objects before me in my imagination, I try to combine them so that the same intentional object is simultaneously, and wholly or in the same respect, both red and not-red, for example, red and green. I find that I am unable to do so. I can imagine objects that are both red and green, as for example, cloth with red and green lines or patterns, but they are not both red and green in the same respect. Similarly, I can imagine an object that is successively red and then not-red (for example, a neon sign that is first red and then green), but nothing that is simultaneously, and in the same respect, both red and not-red. Finally, I can imagine objects that different observers, or the same observer at different times, might call red or not-red, and I can imagine colors that might not seem clearly red or not-red— for example, shades of purple or orange. I cannot imagine, though, any object that could be seen, by any observer at any time, as both clearly red and not-red, and so I conclude that this is impossible.

From this first example I may observe that although I can imagine the elements of the proposed contradiction, I cannot imagine them in the given combination. One of the elements is always, as it were, kept in brackets, as a sort of unreal or hypothetical element of the total experiential structure. For example, I conjure up an entity as red, and I combine it with a bracketed green color presented alongside of the first entity, *as though* the entity were simultaneously both. Their actual combination, though, is something I am unable to represent. The same sort of process occurs through other sensory modalities as they contribute to an imaginative representation. I can imagine high and low (not-high) tones, and smooth and rough (not-smooth) surfaces, acrid and sweet (not-acrid) tastes or odors, fast and slow (not-fast) movements, and so on, and in each case I encounter limits on the experiential or imaginative structures I am able to represent in combination, simultaneously and in the same respect. In general, features that serve a contrastive function on the same level cannot be combined in an object. For example, red and green appear on the same level as colors in that the feature of being colored may be used to contrast colored objects from noncolored ones (structures that are not visual); but on this level, the features that identify red distinguish it from all other colors, including green. Thus, for a color to be both red and green, it must possess the feature that distinguishes it from green (as red) and also not possess it (as green).

Consider the general form of the law of contradiction: something cannot simultaneously be and not-be the same thing in the same respect, or $\sim(p \cdot \sim p)$. What is the source of the necessity of this truth? I believe that it can never be violated, but then, my belief may be mistaken. I believe that there is life in outer space, but that might be false. Perhaps I do not believe that as strongly as I believe that the law of contradiction is true, but I am unwilling to say that the necessity of the logical truth consists in the strength of my belief. Consequently, I must examine the source of the belief. I find that I am able to imagine the sorts of creatures who might exist in space, and if there is only one natural system, I find it improbable that the system has produced life on only one planet. I am unable to imagine, though, an object that both possesses and does not possess a certain kind of trait. Again, my representation is partially bracketed. I conjure up a case of something that may be anything whatsoever, so long as I can identify it as something. Then, I represent something else that is clearly discriminable from that object, as something that is, in some respect, different. I then attempt to imagine the two in combination, as an indiscriminable single entity that is, in some respect, both one type of object and another, discriminable type; but this is impossible. If they are discriminable, then they are not, in that respect, indiscriminable; and if they are indiscriminable, then, in that respect, they are not discriminable. The most I can do is to bracket one of the discriminable features of an object and to imagine the two objects as though they were in combination, or as though the discriminable feature "did not count" or were not really present. Of course, it is the bracketed presence of the latter feature that enables me to imaginatively represent two types of objects in the first place.

The unimaginableness of a contradiction is not the same as the unimaginableness of entities whose elements cannot be represented. For example, I am unable to imagine the surface of Mercury, but I do not judge the statement that it has a surface to be contradictory. If someone tells me, however, that at a certain space-time location the temperature on the planet's surface both was and was not 150 degrees, I would know this was impossible. In the first case, I simply cannot represent the elements or experiential structures that would, in combination, constitute a fair representation of the surface of Mercury, but I can certainly imagine what the planet might be like: that is, I can create representations that I imagine are fair likenesses, although none of them may turn out to resemble the planet. Nor do I judge it to be a contradiction to say that I cannot imagine the surface of Mercury because the atmosphere creates, for human observers, an entirely new color that cannot be imagined until it has been seen. It is now physically impossible for me to represent the color, but not logically impossible for it to exist: that is, the statement that it exists is not a contradiction, even though I cannot now imagine the color. Certainly I can imagine experiencing new sensory properties, and in fact I occasionally have such an experience. But I cannot, as it were, imagine imagining a contradiction. To imagine experiencing an entirely new color, I simply represent an experience of a color that I judge to be one I have never seen before: an "empty" or unfulfilled case of a type of experiential situation. But to imagine imagining a contradiction I would have to represent an imaginative or perceptual experience of an object that I can represent only by bracketing (though identifying) some distinctive feature, and that is thus unimaginable as such, without the brackets. If I try to imagine, let us say, a temperature that is both 150 degrees and not 150 degrees, what I actually represent is a certain intentional structure: two types of objects—a temperature of 150 degrees and another, different temperature—with the distinctive feature of one (for example, being 150 degrees) both bracketed and identified as the distinctive property of one of the two elements to be combined.

I have been arguing that one recognizes something as a contradiction by virtue of a particular intentional structure. A contradictory state of affairs is one in which some distinctive feature is used to identify or distinguish the terms as described, and then bracketed, to fulfill the condition that the terms are not distinct in that respect.

But, one wants to know, quite apart from what people may or may not happen to believe, must a contradiction be false? Again, what are the intentional structures involved in the judgment that the law of contradiction—which says that if some statement asserts a contradiction, it is false—is itself necessarily true? The answer, I think, lies in the intentional structure of the judgment that something is an object of experience. To identify something as an individual (or a particular type of individual) is to discriminate it from something else. As Hegel put it, individuation is by negation. To identify something as A is to discriminate it from what is not-A; thus, A is what is not not-A ($A = {\sim}{\sim}A$). To say, for example, that something is red is to identify something possessing a distinctive feature in terms of which it can be discriminated from all other colors. The experience of something as a specific red object is conditioned by this perceptual feature. In general, to be an entity in the sense of an object of experience is to possess a distinctive feature that serves a contrastive function.

Now it is intuitively clear that contradictory statements assert a condition that violates the condition for being an object of experience. This is a simple matter of clarifying criteria of judgment and recognizing an identity (Husserl's "correspondence") between two intentional structures. The statement form of a contradiction ($A \cdot {\sim}A$) establishes truth conditions of the following type: For a contradiction to be true, both conditions (that some X is simultaneously and in the same respect A and ${\sim}A$) must be true. But, for these conditions to be met, there would have to be an A that failed to meet the conditions of counting or being identified as an A (that is, there would have to be an object X that both possessed the distinctive feature required to constitute A, or to discriminate it from what is ${\sim}A$, and which, as ${\sim}A$, did not possess that feature, and so was not discriminable from ${\sim}A$). Alternatively, there would have to be an X which was ${\sim}A$, but which met the conditions for being A. Thus, the essential conditions that must be met for the contradiction to be true violate the essential conditions for being an object of experience of a specified type. For some X to be identified as an A, or to count as that type of object of experience, means essentially that it satisfies the conditions for being an A (such as possessing a distinctive feature by which it is discriminated from ${\sim}A$). Similarly, for some X to be identified as ${\sim}A$ means that it does not satisfy the conditions for being A. Since the essential conditions that must be met for a contradictory statement to be true violate the essential conditions for being the specified type of object of experience, an object that would meet those conditions is not a possible object of experience.

Yet, one might ask, couldn't that which violated the condition of being an object of experience still be, nonetheless, an object of experience? This might be contradictory, but how do I know that a contradictory situation cannot be actualized? The answer to this question is, I think, that it is essentially meaningless to say that there is some object of experience that violates the condition for being an object of experience. The essential significance of saying that something is an object of experience is that it has met such conditions. It is essentially meaningless to say that there is some X that is an A but does not meet the essential conditions for being an A, or that there is some X that has met the conditions for being an A but which is not an A. To say that this is essentially nonsense means that it is intuitively clear that such claims violate essential conditions for being judged true, in that they violate essential conditions for experiencing objects of the specified type. It is, in short, a question of *meaning*, rather than a factual question that might be settled by induction. If a contradictory statement is essentially, in its intentional structure, a statement establishing truth conditions that violate the essential (intentional) conditions of a possible object of experience, then no possible object can meet those conditions and the contradiction is, in this sense, necessarily false.

The criterion for judging that something is an object of experience is a common feature in all judgments of that type. That is, all objects of experience are discriminated from something else through distinctive features. The object A is that which is not not-A. In a sense, this intentional structure reflects the nature of human perception, or the biological system that underlies consciousness. Human beings, in common with other sentient organisms, discriminate among the various stimuli that impinge on built-in feature detection systems and organize experience through a set of contrastive (distinctive) features. Some change in the factual nature of perception might occur, which would motivate a change in the criteria for being an object of experience. Such a change, however, would be completely irrelevant to the essential truth of the law of contradiction. That law would still be understood in terms of an essential connection between the sense of a contradictory statement (or the truth-conditions it established) and the intentional structure of an object of experience. Thus, to say that some X is A would mean, essentially, that it meets the conditions for being A; and to say that some X is $\sim A$ would mean, essentially, that it does not meet the conditions for being A.

In general, to say that some X is an object of experience means that it meets the conditions for being an object of experience, whatever those conditions might be. This definition of an object of experience applies to any world, which is to say to any situation structured by a subject-object distinction. Again, the general intentional structure of a contradiction is the requirement that two conditions be met simultaneously by some X: that it be A, and that it be $\sim A$. Essentially, then, the contradiction could be true only if there is some X which counts as A but fails to meet the conditions of being A, or some X which counts as $\sim A$ but which meets the conditions of being A, and one sees intuitively that the essential conditions for a contradiction to be true violate the essential conditions for being an object of the specified type. In short, one cannot constitute as an intentional object (and thus identify as an individual instance) any entity that satisfies the truth-conditions of a contradiction. In this sense, the contradiction cannot be interpreted as true, not for contingent psychological reasons, but because such an interpretation would require an object of experience that failed to meet the essential conditions of being an object of experience, and this is essentially nonsense.[1]

1. Contradictory statements are essentially different from utterances that have no truth-value, such as "and or," since the former are composed of independently meaningful propositional elements P and $\sim P$, either of which may express significant statements and which are given in terms of the significant logical structure of conjunction. Thus, one understands the truth-conditions established by a contradiction while recognizing that these conditions cannot be fulfilled by an object of experience. If it is nonsense to assert that both elements of a contradictory description are simultaneously true, the truth of a contradiction is ruled out for essential rather than contingent reasons, that is, through an intuition directed at the meaning of the logical structure, and in this sense a contradiction is necessarily false. In contrast, something like "and or" lacks any truth-value, since it does not establish any truth-conditions, and one is thus unable to determine whether it is contingently true or false or necessarily true or false, that is, if its meaning is such as to deny the possibility of a claim that it (or its denial) is true.

The pragmatic act of constituting the meaning or intentional structure of a contradictory state of affairs is motivated by an interest in discovering which states of affairs can or cannot exist. The assumption is that if something is a contradiction, it can't exist. Logic has ontological implications, because the limits of logical possibility are also the limits of ontological possibility. But why should this be? Thus far, I have argued that a contradiction violates the condition that makes something an object of experience. An essential, or intentional, relationship between "objects of experience" and "existent objects" or "things in being" remains to be shown.

From a phenomenological, or nonmetaphysical, point of view, the ideal meaning of a thing in being must be constituted from phenomena as they are given in experience. In general, then, things that may be said to exist are possible objects of experience, or things that are given, directly or indirectly, as experiential structures present to some observer. Something may be given directly, as a perceptual or imaginative object, or, if one posits theoretical entities that serve as causes, indirectly through its experiential effects. Looking at the matter linguistically, it makes perfect sense that the term 'existence' or 'being' should be used to refer to some aspect of what is experienced, or that such reference should be mediated by experiential paradigms. As Parmenides put the matter, the way of nonbeing is closed to us. There is no way to talk about that which lies outside of the world, or about that which is not somehow given through experience. Those who disagree must indicate how one is to refer to an instance of something thus beyond the limits of human experience, that is, without making use of any intentional structure derived from experience.

If, then, one grants that the meaning of references to possible things in being can be understood only in terms of intentional structures describing possible objects of experience, it follows that whatever violates the condition of being an object of experience (or, a thing in the world) also violates the condition of being an existing object. In short, a contradictory state of affairs cannot exist.

The position I have developed is not psychologistic in a reductionist sense. I do not reduce logic to contingent psychological laws or account for logical intuition in terms of contingent responses such as association or belief. Logical intuition involves a recognition of what Husserl called a correspondence between certain intentional structures and some state of affairs, rather than the psychological response of believing or disbelieving in the truth of an assertion. Thus, one cannot distinguish between a logical possibility, such as the claim that the world will end in one hour, and a logical contradiction, such as that some object is simultaneously and in the same respect both red and not-red, on the basis of differences in the strength of disbelief in the two assertions. It is likely that most people would disbelieve in both statements with equal force. On the other hand, some people at times do hold contradictory beliefs, and I am even willing to believe that some people may persist in such beliefs even after contradictions are pointed out to them. But I have not defined logical truth in terms of what people may or may not believe to be the case.

I have argued that the recognition of something as a contradiction is a matter of rational insight, which involves "seeing" that the sense of some assertion exhibits a particular intentional structure, which violates the essential condition of being an object of experience and thus a possible thing in being. Within this intentional framework, the idea of the possible being of a contradictory state of affairs is, essentially, nonsense. Now, for anyone who "pays attention" to logical intuition, a logical argument should produce psychological conviction; whereas for those who do not examine the intentional structures of logical assertions, or recognize the link between logic and ontology, such arguments may not have predictable psychological effects. In any case, regardless of the psychological effect of logical demonstrations, the law of contradiction does regulate what can and cannot exist. It is a truth that cannot be disconfirmed because no disconfirming case can be experienced, given that any such case would violate the condition for being experienced, and thus would not count as an object in the world.

On the other hand, it should be evident that, in my view, the law of contradiction is not an a priori truth in the sense of a truth known independently of experience and in no way derived from experience. Experience is the psychological origin of logical knowledge in that it provides the paradigms that are idealized or constituted as intentional structures, and it is through the intuitive recognition of correspondences among these structures that one discovers logical truths. The notion of psychologism has been understood in a number of not always clearly defined ways, and it is sometimes used to describe any derivation of logical intuition from psychological or experiential structures, in contrast to metaphysical theories of a priori, innate knowledge of logical truths. (In fact, many readers of Husserl's *Logical Investigations* found the second volume, in contrast to the first, psychologistic in some general sense.) It may be felt that any empiricist account of logic is psychologistic in this broad sense, and this view may be reinforced by the fact that, in this world, the specific intentional structure of the category of an object of experience reflects a specific causal condition, or a fact about the biological structure of human perception, that could conceivably change in certain ways. However, this possibility does not in any way undermine the necessity of the law of contradiction, or, in general, the authority of logical truth. Though the causal conditions of human experience might change in various ways, it remains true for essential reasons, in any possible world, that no change in experience can violate the law of contradiction. (Husserl might say that a "transcendental condition" regulates the essential possibilities of factual or causal changes.) I may not know what changes are possible, but I can know that it makes no sense to speak of the actualization of a contradictory state of affairs: of the existence of a certain type of object which did not satisfy the essential condition for being that type of object.

The law of contradiction might be called an a priori truth in a special sense. Though it is, on the one hand, an intentional structure constituted from experiential paradigms, it cannot be disconfirmed by counterexample. To say it could be so disconfirmed would be to admit the possibility of an experience that violated the condition for being an object of experience. The necessity of the law is discovered through the logical intuition which is directed toward the ideal, intentional structures of "contradictory statements" and "possible objects of experience."

One sees that contradiction involves a condition that violates the condition for being an object of experience.

Finally, the law of contradiction may be said to define a limit of any human experience for essential reasons. That is, it is taken to be a necessary condition for being human that such a being is "worldly," constituting a set of objective structures that are identified in terms of essential criteria. For that reason, no human being can experience a contradictory state of affairs, or an object that violates the essential conditions for being an object. Thus, the law of contradiction marks the limit of possible or worldly experience, and only that which observes this limit may count as human.[2]

The Law of Contradiction and Logical Deduction

There are a number of systems of symbolic logic that include various symbols and rules of inference, and all of them use nominal definitions of the operational symbols of the system. What guides the logician in the selection of symbols and rules of inference, however, is a desire that logic have an application to the experiential world. The terms and relations included in a system of logic will be those that suggest some semantic interpretation

2. I have focused on the law of contradiction because it is the basic logical structure underlying logical intuition of valid deductive inference. The necessity of the law of excluded middle and of identity may be understood in terms of that of the law of contradiction.

The law of excluded middle ($A \vee \sim A$) says that a statement is either true or false. To falsify this law, one would have to assign the same truth-value to A and $\sim A$, which would create the contradiction $A \cdot \sim A$. Of course, there are multivalued logical systems that do not contain the law of excluded middle, but this does not mean they deny it or assert contradictions. In any system, regardless of the number of essential possibilities or modes of truth allowed in that system, it still remains a contradiction to assert, for example, that something both is and is not possibly or necessarily true. Thus, the law of excluded middle may be seen as a limiting case, for two-valued systems, of the rule that when all of the possibilities of truth within a system are conjoined, the possible truth of a contradiction is ruled out. From this perspective, then, the law says nothing about whether a proposition is *provably* true or false within a system.

The law of identity ($A \equiv A$) says that A is equivalent to itself. Equivalence is defined as a relation of mutual implication ($\supset$). Thus, the identity law says that if a statement is true, then it is true ($A \supset A$). This law could be false only on condition that the antecedent A were true and the consequent A false. Thus, to falsify the law, one would have to assert the truth of the contradiction $A \cdot \sim A$.

of formulas as, for example, propositions or statements about properties of objects; and all logical systems are evaluated in terms of their consistency since it is assumed that any system that is inconsistent cannot have an application to the world. Again, any genuinely rational system of logic is thought to have ontological implications. Further, the notion of consistency and the ordinary notion of deductive proof presuppose the semantic notion of truth.[3] One wants to ensure that the rules of inference of a given logical system are such that, if one's premises are true, one's conclusions must also be true. Logical proof is concerned with showing that inferences are valid in this semantic sense. A system within which it is possible to prove the truth of inconsistent propositions, or in which the same proposition may be shown to be both true and false, is said to be inconsistent. One method of proving the validity of an argument is to show that its premises can be true and its conclusions false only if one assigns inconsistent truth-values to the conclusion. Thus, the necessity of a valid deductive proof—the claim that if the premises are true, the conclusion *must* be true—arises from the circumstance that the alternative (true premises and false conclusions) would be a contradiction: the same statement would be said to be both true and not-true, or false. Logical systems are designed with a view to showing that, under some semantic interpretation of the argument forms as arguments and the statement forms as statements, only true conclusions may be deduced from true premises. The law of contradiction, the basic law of logic, underlies all logical systems because such systems must be consistent in order to have application or lead to a knowledge of truths about the world. Since a contradictory statement cannot be true, one may gain a knowledge of the structure of the world by showing that certain statements about the world *must* be true if other statements are true, in the sense that their denial would lead to contradiction.

3. In a logistic system, a purely formal or syntactic criterion of validity will determine which arguments may be expressed within the system. The syntactic criteria are only useful, however, if they ensure that any syntactically valid argument will become, on some interpretation of the symbols included in the system, a semantically valid argument, that is, one in which if the premises are true, the conclusions must be true.

I shall illustrate the idea of logical validity with the rule of inference or argument form called *modus ponens,* and at the same time point up the function of syncategorematic terms, or words such as 'if . . . then', 'therefore', 'and', and 'or', which can be used only in combination with other words, in expressing ordinary logical inferences. *Modus ponens* is a valid argument form under the truth-conditional definition of material implication, symbolized by ⊃ ("therefore"). That is, under the semantic interpretation of symbols provided by a truth-table definition, if it is true that $p ⊃ q$, and that p, then it must also be true that q. This can be shown easily as follows: if p and q must be either true or false (T or F), then the possibilities are that both p and q are true, or both are false, or p is true and q is false, or q is true and p is false. By definition, to say that $p ⊃ q$ is true is to say that one of these possibilities is eliminated, namely, the condition that p is true and q is false. Under all other conditions, $p ⊃ q$ is assigned a value of true. As has often been observed, such a definition of implication (p therefore q, or if p then q) does not fully capture the ordinary use of these terms, since one would not normally say the relation p therefore q holds in case p is false and q true, or in case both are false (for example, If the moon is made of green cheese, then the stock market is falling). However, this definition does prevent the possibility that p might be true and q false, and it guarantees that all arguments using the definition of material implication (for example, *modus tollens,* hypothetical syllogism, and so on) will be valid.

It does appear to be a part of ordinary usage that one condition is said to imply another when it is believed that the truth of the premise somehow guarantees or leads to the truth of the conclusion, such that the case of a true premise and a false conclusion is ruled out.[4] In any case, under the definition of material implication, to say that $p ⊃ q$ is true is equivalent to

4. A recent investigation of the ordinary psychological processes involved in deductive inference supports this view. It appears that relations of implication are interpreted by ordinary speakers to mean that if the premise is true, the conclusion is true, which rules out the possibility of a true premise and a false conclusion. The subjects tested, however, were more apt to reason from the truth of a premise to the truth of a conclusion (the "confirmation" strategy) than from the falsity of a conclusion to the falsity of a premise (the "disconfirmation" strategy). See Philip Johnson-Laird (1970).

stating that the condition p is true and q false does not hold. This leaves the possibility that both p and q are true, or that p is false (in which case q may be true or false). *Modus ponens* states that if $p \supset q$ is true, and p is true, then q is true, and it is evident that this is the only consistent alternative. If one concluded that q were false (that not-q), one would be saying that the condition p is true and q false both did and did not hold. In other words, under the semantic interpretation of these symbols provided by truth-table definitions, if $p \supset q$ and p, then any substitution instance or case of q must be true, since to say that some instance of q was false would be to assert that some x, as an instance of q under the definition, was true (q), and, as false, $\sim q$: both q and $\sim q$.

In short, the intuitive recognition of potential contradictions distinguishes the logical intuition involved in valid deductive inference from a merely psychological feeling of conviction that some factual statement must be true.

I believe that I have now established the claim that metaphysical assumptions are unnecessary to account for knowledge of logical truths and that an empiricist theory of utterance meaning can establish the authority of necessary truths and avoid psychologism. In Chapter 11, I shall turn from logical to poetic language and show how novel experiential paradigms may be expressed through a metaphorical use of language.

CHAPTER 11

The Constitution of Novel Utterance Meanings: The Metaphorical Function

The literature on metaphor is immense, stretching at least from Aristotle's attempt to define metaphor to the present interest in describing the semantic structure of metaphors. Aristotle defined metaphor as a trope that consists in "giving a thing a name that belongs to something else; the transference being either from genus to species, or from species to genus, or from species to species, or on grounds of analogy" (*Poetics*, 1457b). Thus, metaphor occurs whenever there is a certain kind of verbal substitution. The problem with this sort of definition is that apart from the suggestion about analogy, it does not explain why such substitutions occur, nor does it really circumscribe the conditions under which a verbal substitution will be understood as metaphorical. If someone calls a horse a cow, or a man an ass, or says that a certain rock is an ocean, the utterances will be interpreted, respectively, as a mistake, a literal statement, and a puzzle (as in, "How is a rock like an ocean?"). To ask what metaphor is, I think, is to ask for some characterization that discriminates some substitutions, or uses of terms, from others. Aristotle's remark about analogy has suggested to many that metaphorical substitutions express a resemblance or similarity between two classes of things: the original thing to which the name "belongs" and the new thing to which the name is given. Thus, a substitution of names or terms will count as metaphorical when the thing that is "renamed" is similar to but not literally an instance of the class of things named by that term. And the new meaning of the metaphorical term will lie in the similarity it expresses.

The view that metaphors express perceptions of similarities, or that they are compressed similes, leads to the rather odd conclusion that metaphorical utterances may be taken as making two alternative literal statements, one of which is true and the other false. For example, if one says that a horse is a cow, one might mean quite literally that something which is in fact a horse is a cow, which is false, or one might mean, again literally, that the horse is similar to the cow in some respect, which is true. But then, which is the metaphorical term in this utterance? Does 'cow' actually take on a new meaning when it is used to describe a horse? If it simply means what it ordinarily means, then the metaphorical utterance expresses the literally false statement that a horse is a cow, and it is not clear how to distinguish the metaphorical use of language from simple mistakes or falsehoods. On the other hand, if the new meaning of 'cow' is "like a cow" or "similar to a cow," metaphors seem merely to be elliptical statements that invite confusion. If one wants to say that something is *like* something else, why not say it? What is gained in brevity may be lost in clarity. Moreover, one is in danger of doubling the meaning of every word in the language. Henceforth, 'cow' may mean either having the properties of cows or being similar to a cow, 'ass' may denote having the properties of asses or being similar to an ass, and so on.

This sort of semantic interpretation leads in turn to the problem of distinguishing between saying "A cow is a cow" in the sense that it *is* a cow, and in the sense that it is *like* a cow. Is "A cow is a cow" in the latter sense a metaphorical utterance? But what is it to be a cow? One might argue that something is identified as a cow on condition that it is sufficiently similar to some paradigm case of a cow. On that criterion, there is no difference between *being* a cow and being *like* a cow, and so there is no way to distinguish between a literal and a metaphorical version of "A cow is a cow." Of course, one could add some further semantic conditions to the case of being only metaphorically like a cow, as for example lacking some sufficient condition of "cowness," so that a statement is metaphorical if false on one interpretation (actually being a cow) and true on another (being like a cow). In that case, "A horse is a cow," in the sense of being like a cow, might count as metaphorical since horses cannot literally qualify as *being* cows. Obviously this whole approach is unwieldy and implausible.

The view that metaphor is a shorthand way of saying that something that is not literally an X is literally like an X is implausible because it does not explain why anyone would ever wish to use such a device. One could say a horse is a pig or a dog or a giraffe (as an animal), or a car or a train or a plane (as transportation), or a tree or a flower or a peach (as living matter), and so on. Anything may be viewed as similar to anything else, along certain dimensions. If a metaphor simply says one thing is similar to another, it appears to be a very general and imprecise way of saying what one means. Of course, this is not the way people talk. If one wants to say a horse is similar to a cow, one will, to avoid confusion, say exactly that, or "Horses and cows are both animals." Further, the idea that metaphors express similarities conflicts with the view that only "dead" metaphors can be literally true, or, in a sense, "say what they mean," and that living metaphors provide a particularly concrete and vivid way of saying what cannot be said another way. However, the alternative view, that metaphorical terms do not take on a new meaning that constitutes a literally true statement, but in fact continue to mean what they ordinarily mean, does not seem to differentiate metaphorical utterances from false statements.

What is needed is some sort of meaning attached to a metaphorical term which does not reduce a metaphorical utterance to a statement that is literally true or false. Max Black (1962) has developed I. A. Richard's view that, as Black puts it, "In the simplest formulation, when we use a metaphor we have two thoughts of different things active together and supported by a single word, or phrase, whose meaning is a resultant of their interaction" (p. 228). Richards (1936) called the metaphorical term a "vehicle" conveying a certain complex meaning or "tenor" (p. 96). For example, if "The horse is a cow" were a metaphor, the vehicle would be "cow" and the tenor a new meaning resulting from the interaction of the original meaning of "cow" and that of the new object (a horse) to which it is used to refer. Black illustrates this "interaction" theory with the metaphorical utterance "Man is a wolf." The metaphorical term 'wolf' is a vehicle for a new meaning, resulting from the interaction of ideas about wolves and ideas about men. One knows the term is being used metaphorically because if it were taken literally, it would be not only false but absurd. Thus, the context points to a new use of the term, not to express some objectively given similarity between men and wolves, but, in a sense, to create a perception of similarity, inviting one to recognize what men have in common with wolves. The term 'wolf' has both a literal meaning and a set of "associated commonplaces" such as "vicious," and some of these associated meanings apply to men. Black rejects the view that metaphorical expressions are "poetic" substitutes for some literal statement (such as "Man is similar to a wolf") on the grounds that similarities are not objectively given. He says we often use metaphors and so assert relations "in cases where, prior to the construction of the metaphor, we would have been hard put to it to find any literal resemblance between M (metaphoric expression) and L (literal expression). It would be more illuminating in some of these cases to say that the metaphor creates the similarity than to say it formulates some similarity antecedently existing" (p. 227). Thus, the metaphorical term 'wolf' in "Man is a wolf" conveys something like the meaning "vicious animal," which is created through the interaction of the original meaning of 'man' and 'wolf'. 'Wolf' does not mean being similar to a wolf; nor does it denote some objective similarity between man and wolf. Rather, the use of 'wolf' to describe man expresses one of many potential similarities between men and wolves, and it is this specific similarity that the metaphorical term means in that context.

The difficulty with the "interaction" theory of metaphor held by Richards, Black, and others[1] is that it does not really prevent one from interpreting a metaphorical utterance as a statement that is literally true, given the new tenor of the metaphorical

---

1. W. B. Stanford (1936) offered a similar definition of metaphor, which influenced Susanne Langer's theory of the expressive symbol: "Metaphor is the process and result of using a term (x) normally signifying an object or concept (a) in such a context that is must refer to another object or concept (b) which is distinct enough in characteristics from (a) to ensure that in the composite idea formed by the synthesis of the concepts (a) and (b) and now symbolized in the word (x), the factors (a) and (b) retain their conceptual independence even while they merge in the unity symbolized by (x)" (p. 101).

term. But then it is not clear why one should say things metaphorically rather than literally, or how one is to explain the felt difference between living and dead metaphors. Black tries to avoid this dilemma by asserting that the similarities named by metaphor are not "objective," or that they are created rather than discovered. If this is so, then, for example, the metaphorical term 'wolf' does not mean "similar to a wolf," but if it is applied to men, it takes on the meaning "similar to a wolf in some respect, namely, whatever men and wolves have in common." At least, this is the only plausible interpretation I am able to make of the rather vague distinction between objective and subjective, or created and discovered, similarities. The similarity between men and wolves must be objective at least in the sense that one may recognize similarities once the comparison is made. Had these similarities not been at least potentially available to an observer, one would be unable to interpret the expression "Man is a wolf." But then, if some metaphorical use of a term makes a similarity explicit, and the term takes on a new meaning, then once it takes on this meaning, it would seem to constitute a statement that is literally true. For example, one could say that "Man is a wolf" makes the true statement that man is similar to a wolf in being vicious. And, if this is what the expression means, why should one not simply say "Man is vicious"? In fact, the sentence "Man is a wolf" is ordinarily interpreted as simply meaning something like "man is vicious," without any thought of vicious *wolves*. It is, like "Men are sheep" and "The river runs" and "Time flies," a dead metaphor that makes a literal statement. Of course, one could stipulate that "Man is a wolf" is only a genuine or living metaphor on condition that one does think of wolves in uttering it, but this requirement does not avoid the problem of explaining why anyone should think of wolves at all, if it is possible to say something much more direct such as "Man is vicious."

Thus far, there seem to be two alternative ways of characterizing metaphorical utterances. The first is that through the "metaphorical function" of expressing created or discovered similarities, certain terms actually take on a new meaning. Once a metaphorical term takes on a new meaning, it serves as a semantic component in a literal statement made by the utterance. And, given this shift in meaning, the metaphorical statement is literally true. The difficulty with this theory is that it does not really distinguish metaphors from ordinary true statements. The second possibility is that metaphorical terms do not take on a new meaning, and thus that metaphorical statements are literally false. According to this view, the very absurdity of the statement keeps one from taking it at face value, so that one is actually called on to reinterpret the utterance as a literally true statement about a newly discovered relation of similarity. If one holds both the original and the new metaphorical meaning of the term in mind, the expression maintains its tension as a living metaphor that is false under one interpretation and true under another.

I would hold that an adequate theory of metaphor must define the characteristic function served by metaphorical language, and that this function must distinguish a metaphorical from a nonmetaphorical or literal utterance. The claim that the metaphorical function is expressing created or discovered similarities may be criticized on the grounds that it does not distinguish metaphorical utterances from true or false (literal) statements. That is, one can construct statements expressing relations of similarity that are literally true or false and that are in no sense metaphorical; and, if one places some interpretation on a metaphor by which it becomes a literally true statement, there is common consent that the term ceases to function as a living metaphor.

What is called for, then, is a theory of the metaphorical function that distinguishes metaphorical utterances from ordinary true or false statements and that satisfies one's intuitive sense that metaphorical language serves a specific purpose. It must be this purpose, in fact, that determines the judgment that some utterance is to be taken literally or metaphorically and that enables one to grasp the difference between a living and dead metaphor.

Semantic Theories of Metaphor

The theory that metaphorical terms express a relation of similarity between some referent and some class of things that is conventionally named by those terms focuses on what Charles Morris (1938), following Peirce, called a semantic relation between signs and their referents. Thus, what I would call semantic theories of metaphor hold that metaphorical terms are signs having connotation (intension) and denotation (extension), and consider the question of whether the referent of a metaphorical expression is or is not a member of the class connoted by the term. If a metaphorical term retains its original literal connotation, and is used to refer to something that does not meet the criteria associated with the term, or that is not literally denoted by the term, then the statement made by the metaphor is false. Alternatively, if a metaphorical term takes on a new connotation (for example, signifying some property that a referent has in common with a specific class of things of which it is not a member), then if it is used to refer to something denoted by the term under the new interpretation, the statement made by the metaphor is true. Thus, if one says "Man is a wolf" in the sense that the class of men is included in the class of wolves, the statement is false; but if 'wolf' connotes, for example, any vicious creature, the statement is true on condition that men are in fact vicious or capable of viciousness.

I have criticized the theory that metaphorical language may be identified through the "special metaphorical function" of expressing created or discovered relations of similarity because it does not distinguish metaphorical utterances from literally true or false statements. One can express relations of similarity in literal, nonmetaphorical language. For example, one can easily say that men and wolves are similar in some respect, or similar in being vicious, or that men are as vicious as wolves, or as timid as deer, or that they follow leaders like sheep. None of these expressions is metaphorical, but they all refer to some similarity between men and some other animal species that one might not have observed had the comparison not been made. It would seem, then, that the distinction between a metaphorical and a literal utterance cannot be captured within a narrowly semantic theory that considers only the denotative and connotative relation between a sign and its referent.

Susanne Langer has a more complex semantic theory of metaphor that attempts to distinguish metaphors from literal statements by means of Peirce's distinction between icons and symbols. According to Peirce (1897), "an *Icon* is a sign which refers to the Object that it denotes merely by virtue of characters of its own, and which it possesses, just the same, whether any such Object actually exists or not," and "a *Symbol* is a sign which refers to the Object that it denotes by virtue of a law . . . which operates to cause the Symbol to be interpreted as referring to that Object" (p. 102). Langer (1942, 1953) has suggested that metaphors are iconic or, in her terms, expressive or presentational symbols.[2] In general, Langer's claim is that metaphor is a form of presentational (iconic) symbolism because there is a relation of similarity between the original literal connotation of the metaphorical term and some property that is not literally denoted by the term. For example, if one says about some fire that it flares up, one is speaking literally of some property denoted by the term 'fire'. But if one says about some king that his anger flares up, one is speaking metaphorically to express a perception of similarity between some property of fire (literally connoted by "flares") and some property of the king's anger that is not literally an instance of flaring. If one were to take the statement literally, it would be false. The metaphorical term, however, acts as a presentational symbol to present or show an intuitively given property that it means by virtue of its intentional similarity. As Langer (1942) put it, "In a genuine metaphor, an image of the literal meaning is our symbol for the figurative meaning, the thing that has no name of its own" (p. 139).

Langer argues that her theory of presentational symbolism distinguishes between literal and metaphorical utterances and also shows how metaphor has contributed to the historical development of new general meanings in a language. First, metaphors convey their meaning (connotation) iconically. They mean by resembling, and this meaning is conveyed through an intuitive recognition of a relevant similarity. Metaphorical language differs in this respect from ordinary literal statement,

2. Langer has developed a theory of expressive symbols which, she says, connote expressive or presentational meaning and denote some instance of what she calls a "feeling." Presentational meaning, on this account, lies in the immediately grasped similarity (or "congruence") between the form of a symbol and some aspect of human feeling or sentience. Thus, presentational symbols are iconic.

which conveys a meaning that has been established by convention. If one interprets a metaphor in literal terms, assigning to it its conventional meaning, the utterance is false. However, metaphor actually expresses a new meaning that is presented directly through its semantic form. This presentational meaning is then available to be made explicit through analysis. For example, one might ask what it is that a flaring fire and the anger of a king have in common. One answer is that both are capable of intensifying or bursting out in sudden, fierce activity. One has thus defined a new general property that two classes of things have in common, and this property might be attributed to the term 'flares' as a second, more general, connotation. Given such a redefinition, "His anger flared" would make a literal (true) statement. Langer argues that it is through such a process of articulating the common properties underlying the intuitions of similarity originally expressed through metaphor that general literal meanings have evolved during the history of a language. As she puts it, general terms may be "faded metaphors."

I think Langer's approach is fruitful to an extent in its attempt to distinguish metaphorical utterances from literal statements. As numerous critics have observed, however, Langer has been less than successful in clarifying the exact nature of expressive symbols and has in fact abandoned some of the claims she made in her earlier work.[3] Since the focus of Langer's work on presentational symbolism has been art forms rather than metaphor, a full discussion of her theory and its difficulties is not feasible in this book. I shall summarize only what I think are two central, related problems in her remarks on metaphor as a means of introducing an alternative, pragmatic model of metaphor.

The essential difference between Langer's theory of metaphor and the other semantic theories I have summarized lies in her claim that metaphors do not make literal statements. Expressive symbols are, she says, nondiscursive: the meaning of such sym-

3. Langer (1957) acknowledged Nagel's (1943) criticism that so-called presentational symbols do not have "meaning" in the ordinary sense "known to semanticists," and for this reason she changes her terminology. *Expressive symbol* becomes *expressive form*, and presentational *meaning* becomes *import*. (See Langer, 1957, Chapter 9.) For discussions of some difficulties in Langer's theory see Arthur Szathmary (1954), Ernest Nagel (1943), Morris Weitz (1954), and Paul Welsh (1955).

bols is understood intuitively rather than through analysis. If one were to take a metaphorical utterance literally, it would be false; and if one analyzes the relation of similarity that the symbol presents, one in effect creates a new general meaning and thus a new statement that is literally true. Thus, if one says "Man is a wolf" in the literal sense that man is *Canis lupus,* the statement is false. If one asks what men and wolves have in common and judges the statement to assert that "Man is vicious," the statement is perhaps literally true. But the metaphor as expressive symbol is neither true nor false. As Langer says, its presentational meaning lies in the intuitively given (but not explicitly articulated) similarity between the connotation of the term ('wolf') and its referent ('man').

Unfortunately, Langer's theory does not really say what expressive meaning is. First, it does not explain why, as Langer herself acknowledges, it is commonly thought that metaphors and art forms (as expressive symbols) convey a kind of truth. What is needed is some explanation of this form of truth that shows how metaphors can be significant in their own, nonliteral terms, even though they are unlike ordinary (true or false) statements. Second, Langer's account of the similarity expressed by metaphor does not establish an essential difference between two kinds of *meaning.* What, for example, is the difference between the type of meaning expressed by "Men are wolves" and "Men are animals"? Since men and wolves and animals are all categories of the same semantic type—that is, all empirical categories—"Men are wolves" and "Men are animals" would seem to differ, as statements about similarities, only in their truth-value, and, as two different kinds of statements, only in the direct versus indirect (or explicit versus implicit) expression of a similarity. Presumably, "Men are similar to wolves" or "Man is vicious" would make explicit the meaning presented but not stated in "Man is a wolf," just as "His anger suddenly intensified" would capture the meaning expressed by "His anger flared." Of course, if one can "say what one means" in such a clear, explicit way, expressive symbolism must serve as a less satisfactory method of communication. Its real value would lie in its historical role in the development of new general concepts.

In sum, semantic theories of metaphor that focus on the question of whether the referent of a metaphorical term is or is not denoted by that term are not able to distinguish metaphorical utterances from ordinary, true or false statements while accounting for the irreducible significance and truth of figurative speech. Langer's theory, though it attempts to define a nonliteral form of expression, ends by characterizing the meaning of metaphorical utterances in terms of an indirectly expressed relation of similarity between some literal connotation and a referent. On that account there is no essential difference between the meaning conveyed implicitly by a "figure of speech" and that expressed by an explicit statement of similarity.

A Pragmatic Theory of Metaphor

I have been arguing for a pragmatic theory of utterance meaning: for the view that the meaning of an utterance is determined by the referring intention of a speaker, that is, by the pragmatic relation established between speaker and linguistic sign. Only such a pragmatic model can adequately characterize the metaphorical function as a specific type of referring intention that constitutes a distinctive, nonliteral form of utterance meaning.

A speaker who uses language metaphorically is carrying out a specific function: using signs that have a certain literal, empirical connotation to frame some empirical object(s) in a way that creates a new intentional object without making an empirical statement. I shall claim that metaphors express ideal, nonempirical structures which frame novel aspects of experience.

The difference between an empirical statement and a metaphor can be made explicit by several examples. If one asserts, "Man is a wolf," one might be making the empirical claim that all men have a certain physical structure by virtue of which they are members of the class *Canis lupus*. To explicate the meaning of this claim, one would set out certain empirical (observational) criteria that, if fulfilled, would serve to verify the claim. Similarly, one might make the empirical statement that some fire is flaring, or that someone is blind, or that some door is creaking, in each case as an assertion about a physical property of the fire, the eyes, or the door in question. The empirical criteria that might govern verification of these assertions would be intended to establish a correlation between a specific set of observations and a specific causal state of affairs.

Alternatively, one may say things like "Man is a wolf," "Tempers flared," "Blind mouths!" (Milton's "Lycidas"), or "The morning light creaks down again . . ." (Edith Sitwell's "Aubade") in an entirely nonempirical sense. What is necessary for "Man is a wolf" to work as a metaphor is that we understand 'wolf' in the straightforward, empirical sense of *Canis lupus* (rather than the more general sense of, say, "vicious animal"), and that we intend the intuitively given object "man-as-wolf." In short, we are asked to "see" men in terms of wolves, or to frame our experience of men in terms of the wolf paradigm. What we "see," man-as-wolf, is a very specific experiential paradigm that is shown or framed by the metaphor. Similarly, "Tempers flared" serves as a metaphor if we are able to see tempers in terms of the empirical paradigm of a flaring fire. The metaphor shows us tempers-as-flaring-fires; it indicates, then, a very specific, paradigmatic way of experiencing tempers. As I shall presently show, "Man is a wolf" and "Tempers flared" are ordinarily not experienced as living metaphors, though it may be possible to revive them in the way I have suggested.

Milton's image of "blind mouths" has perhaps not died completely for the ordinary speaker. Milton was speaking from a religious context about mouths that cannot utter the Christian word (as "revelation"). As metaphor, the utterance presents mouths-as-blind-eyes (one can imagine a striking painting on this theme). Again, what is given to intuition is the paradigmatic structure: (unconverted) mouths in terms of, or as, blind eyes. Sitwell's paradigm is somewhat less obvious, so she has thoughtfully provided the reader with the following comment: "In a very early dawn, after rain, the light has a curious uncertain quality, as though it does not run quite smoothly. Also it falls in hard cubes, squares, and triangles, which, again, give one the impression of a creaking sound, because of the associations with wood" (Sitwell, 1926, quoted in Philip Wheelwright, 1954, p. 116). And yet, one does not grasp the metaphor, even after

220

reading the comment, unless one is able to experience a specific intuitively given structure: morning-light-as-creaking-(wooden)-object. It may be that such a paradigm is difficult to grasp and unlikely to pass into common usage because the specific experience of morning light that Sitwell frames as "creaking" is in fact a product of a rather unusual sensibility, and therefore "creaking" may not suggest to the ordinary reader a sort of wooden contraption working with difficulty. Nonetheless, once one reads the poet's comment, one is able, I think, to imagine that elusive quality of light-as-creaking-(wooden)-object.

The specific experiential paradigms framed by metaphorical language are nonempirical in the sense that they do not establish categories of physically real objects posited as the causes of specific sets of observations. Thus, there are no observational criteria governing verification of metaphors, and metaphors are not taken as literal, empirical claims about some physically real or causal state of affairs. Of course, the terms used to carry out a metaphorical intention must be intended in some literal empirical sense, but such connotations are used to create new paradigms rather than to make an empirical claim. For example, wolves, flaring fires, blind eyes, and creaking wooden objects are all types of physical objects that can be identified through certain observations. However, the paradigmatic structures man-as-wolf, tempers-as-flaring-fires, mouths-as-blind-eyes, and light-as-creaking-(wooden)-object are ways of seeing rather than classes of physical objects.

My claim, then, is that the meaning of a metaphor lies in the specific, nonempirical paradigm framed by the utterance. If one interpreted a metaphor as a literal, empirical statement, it would, of course, be false. However, the referring intention behind metaphorical language is not that of making an empirical statement, so it is inappropriate to assign a truth-value determined by an empirical interpretation of such an utterance. On the other hand, one may say that a metaphor has a kind of intuitive (nonempirical) truth in the sense that it shows or frames an intentional structure that one can "see." Thus, just as one may say, without making any sort of causal claim, that one truly sees a certain pattern as triangular or sees a certain patch as red (or judges a flow of water to be cold), so one may grasp intuitively an experiential structure that constitutes the significance of a metaphor.[4]

Although metaphors and other sorts of intuitively verified utterances are similar, there are at least two differences between them. First, metaphorical paradigms do not have analytic definitions, laying out necessary and sufficient conditions for category membership. Thus, one can explicate the literal (though nonempirical) meaning of the claim that something appears triangular, or as a color, and so on, whereas such things as the "wolfness" of men or the "creakiness" of light are, like redness and coldness and saltiness, primitive, experientially given qualities of things. Furthermore, metaphorical utterances simply frame experiential paradigms without asserting any a priori or necessary relations among ideal structures, as is the case, for example, with the literal and necessary truth-claims made in geometry. In short, a metaphor simply presents a specific paradigm that frames a primitive quality of experience which we either grasp or fail to grasp in a moment of intuition.

The second distinctive feature of a metaphorical utterance is that it establishes its nonempirical meaning by means of signs that are understood in a certain literal empirical sense, such that one may read a metaphor as a false empirical statement. Of course, just as one may wish to discover whether, for example,

4. I am, of course, using "intuition" in the way it is used by phenomenologists, as an immediate recognition or grasp of some structure. For example, we may recognize intuitively that two different figures have a common triangular structure, just as we may "see" that some argument uses the rule *modus ponens*. Intuition, understood in this way, does *not* mean a vague feeling or premonition.

I would hold, in one sense, that, for example, man-as-wolf is an ideal intentional structure that can be recognized or "seen" in some instance in essentially the same way that one may recognize the structure of the triangle or the number four, or the intentional structure of "redness" or "coldness" in general. Thus, there is no causal, empirical claim involved in the assertion: it seems to me that some object is triangular or red or cold, or that something is an instance of man-as-wolf, or temper-as-flaring, or light-as-creaking, etc. Such claims are true if we have such intuitions. But if we make the empirical claim that some object really is red or cold or triangular (in the sense that any number of observers could make certain measurements or would record certain observations, or in the sense that I am perceiving rather than imagining or hallucinating or dreaming about some object), then we must state verification criteria and provide observational evidence that an experience is correlated with a specific causal state of affairs.

one's intuitive recognition of an instance of redness or coldness has an empirical (causal) basis, one may also want to find some empirical basis for the possibility of seeing the "wolfness" in men or the "creakiness" in light, and so on. In the first instance, one would have to provide an empirical definition of redness, coldness, etc., as physical causes of certain perceptual responses. Using such empirical concepts, one could then make the empirical claim that something was actually red or cold and that it was for that reason experienced as such. But if one alters the empirical content of a metaphorical term in this way, one destroys the intuitive significance of the metaphor. Thus, if one asks what men and wolves have in common (how they are similar), and decides they are vicious, one may reinterpret "wolfness" as viciousness. In that case, the new literal, empirical content of the statement "Man is a wolf" is "Man is vicious." Although the latter statement may clarify the empirical or causal basis of the intuition of man-as-*Canis-lupus*, it does not have the same kind of meaning: "Man is vicious" is an empirical claim that attributes an empirical property to men; "Man is a wolf" *(Canis lupus)* is an intuitive presentation of the paradigm man-as-wolf.

The other metaphors I have discussed thus far may also be analyzed to discover some empirical basis for the possibility of a specific intuition. Wheelwright (1954) has suggested that the greatest metaphors are "archetypes" that are "drawn from correspondences that lie deep within the heart of nature herself" (p. 117). Perhaps these "correspondences" are common empirical properties linking classes of things ordinarily kept distinct, and if so, this must be the truth of the widespread feeling that metaphors somehow "name" similarities. "Flaring tempers," for example, plays with the ancient view that human life or spirit is in some respect a flame that may "burn out" in death. If one asks what tempers and flaring fires have in common, one may discover a common property of suddenly intensifying or bursting out in activity. Such a discovery, in turn, leads one to add a second meaning to 'flares,' in terms of which "tempers flared," like "Man is a wolf," may be taken as a literal empirical statement. Yet, just as the primitive experiential paradigm of the wolfness in man is intuitively distinct from the more general and analytic concept of viciousness, so is the specific flaring quality of temper distinct from the abstract notion of sudden intensification. Empirical analysis may succeed in developing new general concepts, but when such concepts are read back into metaphors as new literal meanings, not only is the metaphor destroyed but the original intuitive paradigm is usually lost.

The intuitive distance between living and dead metaphors may be easier to grasp in phrases that have not yet become clichés. Thus, Milton's "Blind mouths" still has intuitive force as an image of mouths-as-blind-eyes, though the phrase "eyes" which speak/do not speak" has grown trite. On the other hand, Milton's poetry tends to be so didactic that it is hard not to reduce his image to a literal statement about mouths that do not speak the word of Christ and thus do not minister to the flock. In contrast, Sitwell's "creaking light" almost eludes analysis. Yet, if one asks what morning light and creaking wooden machines or objects have in common, one may decide that they both have an uncertain, hesitating quality (as Sitwell suggests). Nonetheless, the literal statement that morning light is uncertain or hesitant is so abstract that one could have little idea what is meant by it, or what kind of uncertainty is being attributed to light, without the clarification provided by the specific paradigm of a creaking wooden contraption.[5]

I have been arguing that a distinctive type of metaphorical meaning can be understood only in pragmatic terms, as a function of a use of signs with a given literal empirical connotation, not to make a literal empirical statement, but rather to frame a new, nonempirical intentional object. The empirical connotations attributed to the terms of a living metaphor are such that, if one reads the utterance as a literal statement, it is false. The truth of metaphor, however, lies in its intuitive presentation of that specific experiential paradigm that constitutes the significance of the utterance. I shall try to clarify the primitive, irreducible quality of metaphorical paradigms by developing the contrast between living and dead metaphors.

5. After reading this chapter, John Bowers suggested that good metaphors may be precisely those that resist empirical analysis, so they cannot become hackneyed, whereas bad metaphors are so easily reduced to an empirical statement that they are poor from the beginning.

Metaphorical Creativity:
Living and Dead Metaphors

A number of theorists, including Ernst Cassirer and Susanne Langer in this century, have claimed that metaphor is an important historical source of new terms in a language. I think this claim is plausible because one may analyze a metaphor by searching for some empirical property that two classes of things have in common. The effect of this analysis is to discover a new, general property that may in turn provide a new literal (and metaphorically extended) sense for terms. However, if such a new literal sense is read back into a metaphor so that it becomes a literally true empirical claim, the original term ceases to function metaphorically. In short, the metaphor simply dies.

Langer (1942) illustrated the process through which a metaphor may take on a new extended meaning in the following example:

> If a metaphor is used very often, we learn to accept the word in its metaphorical context as though it had literal meaning there. If we say: "The brook runs swiftly," the word "runs" does not connote any leg-action, but a shallow rippling flow. If we say that a rumor runs through the town, we think neither of leg-action nor of ripples; or if a fence is said to run around the barnyard there is not even a connotation of changing place.... Now we take the word itself to mean *that which all its applications have in common,* namely *describing a course.* [p. 140]

As Langer suggests, the word 'runs' has a number of literal empirical connotations which a speaker may select in various contexts to complete a literal statement. Thus, if one says, "The river runs down the mountain," one will ordinarily be interpreted as making the literal statement: "The river moves swiftly down the mountain" or "The river describes a course down the mountain." In neither case is one speaking metaphorically. One might try, however, to reconstitute such a statement as a metaphor (and in doing so, Langer believes, recover the historical origin of a general concept) by selecting an interpretation for 'runs' that would make the utterance false as an empirical statement. For example, one might intend by 'runs' something like "rapid leg motion." Under that interpretation the utterance might make the false statement "The river flows with a rapid leg motion down the mountain." Langer's claim would be that, if this were the original metaphorical significance of the utterance, it "presented" an implicit relation of similarity between running legs and flowing rivers that, when analyzed, produced the more general concept of rapid motion. Once this meaning is made explicit, the metaphor is dead.

I would agree in general with Langer's claim that a metaphor dies when analysis reveals some general property that can be defined and read back into the utterance so as to make explicit a relation of similarity between two classes of things. However, I have already expressed my disagreement with Langer's view of metaphor as "presentational symbolism."[6] Langer treats metaphors as *implicit* empirical statements, arguing that one is able to perceive an unstated similarity between two classes of things (such as flowing rivers and running legs) and that the meaning of a metaphor lies in this similarity. Once this implicit similarity is made explicit, the utterance states rather than presents its meaning, and thus is no longer metaphorical. There is no essential difference, however, between the kind of meaning that is stated or presented (for example, between river-as-running and river-as-moving-rapidly). In contrast, I have argued that metaphors are neither implicit nor explicit empirical statements, but that they serve the very different function of framing specific, concrete experiential paradigms (for example, river-as-running), and that they are true insofar as one is able to

6. I think Langer's theory suffers from an excessively narrow version of empiricism, which does not allow her to distinguish between experiential structures as such (that is, ideal intentional objects) and individual objects posited as physically real, causal entities and defined in terms of empirical (observational) criteria. Thus, she is unable to make an essential distinction between empirically and intuitively verified truth-claims. On her account, intuition (of "significant forms") cannot really have its own truth, since she treats intuition naturalistically as a kind of vague perception that can be "clarified" through empirical analysis. Whereas the meaning of an expressive form lies, for Langer, in an actual similarity between two classes of things, I would claim that it lies precisely in the new paradigmatic (intentional) structure that is created and presented to intuition. The difference between these two approaches becomes even more striking in the analysis of nonverbal art forms.

"see" the structure presented. If one then asks an empirical question about a general property of two classes of things, one may develop a new general concept (such as "rapid motion"), but this concept, though it may provide a causal explanation for a specific intuition, is essentially different from the original paradigm. The new literal statement that this concept determines is not an explicit statement of what was implicit in the metaphor, but is rather a completely different kind of statement. And, as paradigmatic objects of intuition, the general (empirical) structure river-as-moving-rapidly is quite different from the primitive (nonempirical) paradigm river-as-running.

In my view, the effect of successful metaphor is to create new, irreducible paradigms that frame a specific primitive quality of experience. These paradigms may be used in turn to focus our attention on or "name" that quality whenever we encounter it. This is ordinarily a function served by poetry, or by art in general. And, as Langer notes, such paradigms may stimulate reflection on those general or abstract properties that classes of different things may share, and in this way new general terms may enter a language as "faded metaphors."

For most speakers, talk about running rivers is entirely literal. The explanation is that the most salient feature of a running river is its speed, and it is possible to make a literal reading of the statement as pointing to this feature. Thus, it is unlikely that anyone would think of the specific image of a runner. Once a term is redefined to allow such a literal, empirical claim, it is difficult for speakers to suspend this sense and restore the original experientially primitive paradigm that constituted its metaphorical significance.

Metaphorical language is appropriate whenever one believes that some conventional term will not convey exactly that aspect of an experience one wants to frame. One must constitute new experiential paradigms when those available, the conventional semantic structures of a language, are inadequate for some communicative needs because they are too general, or too abstract or analytic, or because they simply do not focus sharply on the specific quality one wishes to indicate. For example, if one wanted to draw attention to some specific subtle qualitative aspect of river's motion, one might say the river "rushed head-

long" or "stumbled over rocks." A "rushing" river may also literally "run" ("move rapidly"), but the image of rushing, like that of
a runner, is less abstract than the concept of something (a river, a
train, an auto engine) that runs in a general sense. After a new
paradigm has been established as an experiential structure, it
may be possible once again to analyze the metaphorical utterance to discover some general empirical property common to
two classes of things. The original paradigm, however, is not the
semantic equivalent of the new empirical concept.

The irreducibility of the new experiential paradigms created
through metaphor becomes much clearer in the case of genuine
or living metaphors. Consider T. S. Eliot's invitation to visit
"Streets that follow like a tedious argument/Of insidious in-
tent/To lead you to an overwhelming question. . . ." What sort
of analytic comparison might be suggested by this metaphor?
(As the "streets" themselves are "metaphysical," the utterance
might be viewed technically as a simile within a metaphor. However, the comparison is hardly analytic, and the general effect is
metaphorical.) An "interpretation" might go something like this:
the "streets" one follows are exhausting, and they seem to lead
inevitably to some trap or place from which one will not be able
to escape, and this sense of entrapment in turn causes one to ask
some disturbing or compelling question, which is not specified.
Further, the image of streets is used to refer to something else,
perhaps the temporal course of life (as in "paths" of life), so the
entire structure says that living itself is exhausting and seems to
lead inevitably to some trap and to some question about that fact.
I hope it is evident that the interpretation is illuminated by the
poem more than the poem by the interpretation. The interpretation refers to a fairly general experiential structure (being
exhausted by living and feeling anxious about the future), while
the poem refers to a specific experience of some referent (a
lifetime?) in terms of an experience of traveling on streets which
are like arguments experienced in a particular way (as tedious
and insidious). Analysis of the poem might help one discover the
referent of the metaphor, but the "point" lies in the complex
experience which is presented rather than in some analytic comparison it might suggest.

The difference between the form of semantic creativity exhibited in metaphor and the ordinary sort of referential creativity may be seen through a few examples. Consider the difference between the hackneyed description of a person as "deep" or "shallow," and a (critical) characterization of a self-absorbed woman as caught up in "the rushing torrent of her self." Perhaps at one time the terms "deep" and "shallow" captured an experience of a person as "containing" a kind of "reflective space" wherein ideas and experiences were considered from several angles, producing responses that could not easily be predicted, or, alternatively, (of a person) as responding with very little reflection to the most obvious and immediate aspects of any situation, in a highly predictable way. The common metaphorical image would be the self or consciousness as a "container" of thoughts, though consciousness is not given as a spatial entity. Today, talk about a person's depth ordinarily makes no reference to a spatial paradigm, but simply conveys an estimate of the degree of intensity or thoroughness with which a person has considered a subject. Similarly, one says "What's on your mind!" or speaks of the "contents" of consciousness, in the simple sense of what is being thought about. When one uses such terms in their extended metaphorical, or literal, sense, one is using established empirical paradigms within a language to identify a referent. In using metaphors, one is recombining those established paradigms to create new ones. Thus, metaphorical utterances do not refer simply to some individual object or state of affairs, they actually force one to reexperience a familiar paradigm, and so constitute a new way of experiencing things. Thus, if talk about the depth of a person were metaphorical, it would refer to or frame a new experience of a person in terms of a spatial paradigm. One would be called on to reexperience one's ordinary notion of what it is to be a person. Similarly, spatial metaphors about consciousness in general, insofar as they are still understood as metaphors, present a particular experiential paradigm of consciousness.

To say that a woman is caught up in "the rushing torrent of her self" (as one critic recently said about a fictional character) is to present one sort of referent, perhaps a woman attempting to free herself from psychological inhibitions, in terms of another paradigm, namely a rushing torrent. More specifically, one is framing the self that is being liberated as a rushing torrent. The new paradigm that the utterance creates, liberated-self-as-rushing-torrent, is the intentional structure expressed by the metaphor. If one wanted to analyze the metaphor, to discover what may have motivated the choice of that image, one might find that the liberated self (under an essentially romantic or negative interpretation of freedom, as unlimited behavior or will) and the rushing torrent are both forces that move recklessly and possibly destructively down a predictable or unvarying path. Thus, to say that one is caught up in the rushing torrent of one's self is to suggest that the self has become a force that is both out of control (hence reckless) and, strangely, in control, leading one down an unvarying path that is its chosen direction. The self has become a force, but not a blind one. It is a force of unlimited will, and it wills the satisfaction of its desires. This particular metaphor was applied, quite appropriately, to a fictional character who was pursuing what Freud called polymorphous perversity. The reader will have noticed that I am still characterizing the "self" of the metaphor in metaphorical terms as a force that moves down a path. If one dispenses with any such metaphor and simply compares a self to a "rushing torrent," one might isolate the common feature of a pattern of reckless, possibly destructive activity. If the metaphorical expression took on an extended literal meaning of this sort, then it could be used simply to refer to someone whose behavior revealed a predictably reckless and possibly destructive pattern. The range of possible referents of such an utterance is very great. One might, for example, refer in this way to a person who routinely failed to watch for traffic before crossing a street, or who deliberately left fires burning all night. On the other hand, if one retains the metaphorical sense of the utterance, one is not referring to one of many instances of reckless behavior, but framing a new paradigm: an experience of some liberated self in terms of the paradigm of a rushing torrent, and this experiential structure cannot be shown or presented in any other way. The metaphor is successful insofar as it makes one reexperience the familiar paradigm of the self in some new way and fruitful to the extent that it invites reflection on the implications of following a rushing torrent.

Interestingly enough, there is another expression often

applied to some individuals which undoubtedly started out as a similar sort of metaphor. One may speak of a person who is very energetic and who moves and acts in sudden and unpredictable (and possibly destructive) ways as a "whirlwind," ordinarily with no thought of the natural force it once evoked. To say that someone is a whirlwind is simply to comment on the unpredictability and energetic suddenness or impetuousness of someone's movements. It is a simple literal reference, which (if I have not revived the metaphor) ordinarily fails to present a specific paradigm of some person as a body of furiously rotating wind. Again, once a metaphorical term is understood in a new, extended sense, the force of the metaphor is usually lost.

The area in which the creative function of a metaphor is most fully carried out is, of course, poetry. In ordinary communication one takes it for granted that a listener shares semantic paradigms or categories that are similar enough to one's own to ensure that approximately the same range of referents will be specified by some expression. One takes the meaning of things for granted. It is precisely the meaning of things that a poet may not take for granted. A poet's focus is on reexperiencing, redefining, casting off old paradigms and presuppositions about how things are given, making the world seem strange rather than familiar, and at the same time bringing it closer as an experiential structure directly given in a certain way through the poem. Poetry does not make statements; it creates paradigms, or it takes the paradigms of a language and recreates or renews them. I would argue that although a poet uses a number of devices, of which metaphor is one, in constructing a poem, the poem as a whole should be viewed as similar to metaphor in its artistic purpose of framing an experiential paradigm in a new way or creating a new paradigm.

I have suggested elsewhere[7] that in fact all art forms perform the same general function of creating paradigms. For example, an observer familiar with a certain set of semantic paradigms and having a certain range of experiences (requirements that may vary greatly from one work to another), might view Goya's horrifying painting *Saturn Devouring One of His Children* as framing a specific experience of time that comes rather close to the

---

7. "Meaning in Art: A Pragmatic Approach" (manuscript in preparation).

Shakespearean line about "this bloody tyrant, Time" (Sonnet 16, line 2). This example may suggest the sorts of relationships between verbal and nonverbal signs that a pragmatic theory of reference is able to uncover.

The Metaphorical Function: Conclusions

I have argued that narrowly semantic theories of metaphor are unable to distinguish metaphorical structures from ordinary literal (empirical) statements, and that this distinction can only be captured by a pragmatic model of the metaphorical function. Semantic theories, which consider the relation between a sign and its referent, have typically described a "metaphorical function" as indicating some property that two classes of things have in common. The limitation of this approach is that a metaphor must then be judged to be a literally false empirical statement if the referent is not denoted by the metaphorical term; or a literally true empirical statement if the meaning of the term has been extended so that it does denote its referent. Since these are the only alternatives possible within a semantic framework, there is no essential difference between metaphors and literally true or false empirical statements.

Langer attempts to avoid this difficulty by claiming that metaphors have no truth-value, since they present a relation of similarity (between the connotation of a term and some referent) in an implicit, perceptual form rather than through an explicit (conventional) statement. According to Langer, however, there is no essential difference between the semantic content of a metaphorical and a literal (empirical) statement, only a difference in the form or mode of presentation. Thus, once adequate general concepts have been developed, a metaphor may be reexpressed analytically so that its originally implicit meaning becomes explicit. Once again, Langer's semantic model does not reveal an essential difference between metaphorical and literal utterances. If one can "say what one means" in literal terms, there would seem to be no good reason to use imprecise and possibly misleading figures of speech.

A pragmatic model of speech, which focuses on the relation between speaker and linguistic sign, reveals a number of possible speech acts or, in my terms, referential acts, that can be carried out in speech. In each case, the meaning of an utterance is determined by the referring intention of a speaker, who uses signs with a specific semantic structure to carry out a specific referential function. From a pragmatic perspective one may distinguish the referential act of empirical statement from an essentially different metaphorical intention.

My position has been that metaphor involves a use of signs that are intended with a specific empirical (literal) connotation to describe some empirical object(s) as a means of expressing a new, nonempirical semantic structure. This structure is an experientially primitive, nonanalytic, intuitively given paradigm that has no empirical meaning in the sense of positing a physical object. That is, such "ways of seeing" as are conveyed by Sitwell's "creaking light" or Eliot's "streets that follow like a tedious argument" do not have empirical truth-conditions as descriptions of some individual state of affairs. They simply present for intuitive recognition a specific, qualitatively primitive aspect of possible human experience. To interpret the utterance meaning of a metaphor one must use the paradigm which it creates to frame a structure of experience. The metaphor is "true" in a nonempirical sense insofar as we are able to grasp or "see" that intentional structure.

If one attempts to analyze a metaphor in empirical terms, to discover some objective, causal basis for a specific intuition, one may develop a new general concept that describes, in literal terms, what two classes of things (such as light and creaking objects, or streets and tedious arguments) have in common. However, such a concept is not the semantic equivalent of the original metaphorical paradigm; and if the empirical content of a metaphorical term is altered through such analysis, the utterance becomes a literally true, empirical statement that has lost its metaphorical significance.

A pragmatic theory of metaphor may be evaluated through linguistic intuitions. I have claimed that one is intuitively aware of a difference between a metaphorical utterance and a literal empirical statement, or between a living and a dead metaphor. We are able to use metaphor when appropriate, and to speak in literal terms when metaphor is not appropriate. A theory of metaphor, then, is adequate if it distinguishes a metaphorical function from other pragmatic speech acts and if this function clarifies our ordinary ways of speaking.

Furthermore, a pragmatic account of metaphor clarifies the structural and possibly also historical relationship between living and dead metaphors. I conclude that the pragmatic model succeeds in making all of the functional distinctions necessary to account for those semantic distinctions we recognize intuitively in our use and interpretation of metaphorical language.

By framing new experiential paradigms speakers supplement the stock of conventional paradigms when these are inadequate to convey a specific referring intention or novel utterance meaning. Thus, the metaphorical expansion of meaning increases the expressive powers of a language. The relationship between ordinary metaphor and poetry lies precisely in this creative activity.

CHAPTER 12

Conclusion

The basic question that has been raised in this book is, What must a speaker know to produce and understand novel but acceptable and contextually appropriate utterances? To answer this question I developed an empiricist theory of utterance meaning, in opposition to the rationalistic theory proposed by Chomsky.

There is both experimental and theoretical support for the view that speakers acquire language in the form of a system of structures. Speakers exercise creativity in discovering new ways of using language in context to produce novel utterances that are not generated by rules. At the limits of the expressive possibilities within a historical language, speakers may extend a system of language by creating new structures through metaphorical and poetic speech, as well as through logical analysis and analogical extension of existing categories.

The basic implication of philosophical empiricism for a theory of meaning is that perceptual experience is the source of all linguistic significance. Empiricism however, is not adequate to account for utterance meaning unless it accepts a phenomenological, and nonmetaphysical, distinction between individual and ideal (intentional) objects. Thus, I have proposed a radical form of empiricism which describes the essential concepts of language as ideal experiential paradigms or structures that speakers use to communicate specific referring intentions in context.

As an element of linguistic and psycholinguistic theory, philosophical rationalism has, I believe, led to a great deal of confusion about the nature of scientific research. The implication of an empiricist theory of utterance meaning for current scientific investigation of language is that such research should focus on the descriptive and experimental study of communicative competence. The questions to be decided are not, What descriptively adequate generative grammar does a speaker acquire, and how is it acquired on the basis of innate knowledge? The significant and truly productive questions are, What linguistic structures are acquired, and what is the cognitive basis for linguistic knowledge?

References

Austin, John. 1962. *How to Do Things with Words.* Cambridge, Mass.: Harvard University Press.

Bates, Elizabeth. 1976. *Language and Context.* New York: Academic Press.

Bauman, Richard and Joel Sherzer., eds. 1974. *Explorations in the Ethnography of Speaking.* London: Cambridge University Press.

Berlin, Brent and Paul Kay. 1969. *Basic Color Terms.* Berkeley: University of California Press.

Black, Max. 1962. "Metaphor," in *Philosophy Looks at the Arts,* ed. J. Margolis. New York: Scribner's.

Bloom, Lois. 1970 *Language Development: Form and Function in Emerging Grammars.* Cambridge, Mass.: M.I.T. Press.

———.1973. *One Word at a Time.* The Hague: Mouton Press.

———.1974. "Talking, Understanding and Thinking: Developmental Relationship between Receptive and Expressive Language," in *Language Perspectives: Acquisition, Retardation and Intervention,* ed. R. L. Schiefelbusch and L. Lloyd. Baltimore: University Park Press.

———.1975. "Language Development," in *Review of Child Development Research,* vol. 4, ed. F. Horowitz. Society for Research in Child Development. Chicago: University of Chicago Press.

———.1976. "An Integrative Perspective on Language Development." Keynote address, Stanford Child Language Research Forum, Stanford University.

———.1978. "The Semantics of Verbs in Child Language." Invited address, Eastern Psychological Association Annual Meeting, Washington, D.C.

Bloom, Lois, Peggy Miller, and Lois Hood. 1975. "Variation and Reduction as Aspects of Competence in Language Development," in *Minnesota Symposia on Child Psychology,* vol. 9, ed. A. Pick. Minneapolis: University of Minnesota Press.

Bloomfield, Leonard. 1933. *Language.* New York: Henry Holt.

Blumenthal, Arthur. 1967. "Prompted Recall of Sentences." *Journal of Verbal Learning and Verbal Behavior* 6:203-6.

Blumenthal, Arthur, and Robert Boakes. 1967. "Prompted Recall of Sentences," *Journal of Verbal Learning and Verbal Behavior* 6:674-76.

Bowerman, Melissa. 1973. *Learning to Talk: A Cross-Linguistic Study of Early Syntactic Development.* Cambridge: Cambridge University Press.

——.1976. "Semantic Factors in the Acquisition of Rules for Word Use and Sentence Construction," in *Normal and Deficient Child Language,* ed. D. and A. Morehead. Baltimore: University Park Press.

Braine, Martin. 1962. "Piaget on Reasoning: A Methodological Critique and Alternative Proposals," in *Thought in the Young Child,* ed. W. Kessen and C. Kuhlman. Monographs of the Society for Research in Child Development, vol. 27, no. 2.

——.1974. "Length, Constraints, Reduction Rules, and Holophrastic Processes in Children's Word Combinations," *Journal of Verbal Learning and Verbal Behavior* 13:448-56.

Bransford, J. D., and M. K. Johnson. 1972. "Contextual Prerequisites for Understanding: Some Investigations of Comprehension and Recall," *Journal of Verbal Learning and Verbal Behavior* 11:717-26.

——.1973. "Considerations of Some Problems of Comprehension," in *Visual Information Processing,* ed. W. G. Chase. New York: Academic Press.

Brown, Roger. 1957. "Linguistic Determinism and the Parts of Speech," *Journal of Abnormal and Social Psychology* 55:1-5.

——.1958. "How Shall a Thing be Called?" *Psychological Review* 65:14-21.

——.1973. *A First Language.* Cambridge, Mass.: Harvard University Press.

——.1976. "Reference: In Memorial Tribute to Eric Lenneberg," *Cognition* 4:125-53.

——.1978. "A New Paradigm of Reference," in *Psychology and Biology of Language and Thought,* ed. G. Miller and E. Lenneberg. New York: Academic Press.

Brown, Roger, and E. Lenneberg. 1954. "A Study in Language and Cognition," *Journal of Abnormal and Social Psychology* 49:454-62.

Bruner, Jerome. 1966. "On Cognitive Growth, II," in *Studies in Cognitive Growth,* ed. Jerome Bruner, Rose Olver, and Patricia Greenfield. New York: Wiley.

Bruner, Jerome, Rose Olver, and Patricia Greenfield, eds. 1966. *Studies in Cognitive Growth.* New York: Wiley.

Chafe, Wallace. 1970. *Meaning and the Structure of Language.* Chicago: University of Chicago Press.

References

Chao, Yen Ren. 1968. *Language and Symbolic Systems.* Cambridge: Cambridge University Press.

Chomsky, Noam. 1957. *Syntactic Structures.* The Hague: Mouton Press.

———.1959. Review of B. F. Skinner's *Verbal Behavior* in *Language* 35:26–58.

———.1965. *Aspects of the Theory of Syntax.* The Hague: Mouton Press.

———.1966a. *Topics in the Theory of Generative Grammar.* The Hague: Mouton Press.

———.1966b. *Cartesian Linguistics.* New York: Harper & Row.

———.1968. *Language and Mind.* New York: Harcourt, Brace & World.

———.1970. "Deep Structure, Surface Structure, and Semantic Interpretation," in *Studies in General and Oriental Linguistics,* ed. R. Jakobson and S. Kawamoto. Tokyo: TEC Co.

———.1971a. *Problems of Knowledge and Freedom.* New York: Vintage Books.

———.1971b. "Recent Contributions to the Theory of Innate Ideas," in *The Philosophy of Language,* ed. J. R. Searle. London: Oxford University Press.

———.1972. *Language and Mind,* enlarged edition. New York: Harcourt, Brace, Jovanovich.

———.1975. *Reflections on Language.* New York: Pantheon Books.

———.1978. "On the Biological Basis of Language Capacities," in *Psychology and Biology of Language and Thought,* ed. G. Miller and E. Lenneberg. New York: Academic Press.

Chomsky, Noam and Morris Halle. 1965. "Some Controversial Questions in Phonological Theory," *Journal of Linguistics* 1:97–138.

———.1968. *The Sound Pattern of English.* New York: Harper & Row.

Church, Alonzo. 1956. "Propositions and Sentences," in *Readings in the Philosophy of Language,* ed. J. Rosenberg and C. Travis. Englewood Cliffs, N.J.: Prentice-Hall, 1971.

Church, Joseph. 1961. *Language and the Discovery of Reality.* New York: Vintage.

Clark, Eve. 1970. "How Young Children Describe Events in Time," in *Advances in Psycholinguistics,* ed. G. B. d'Arcais and W. J. Levelt. Amsterdam: North-Holland Publishing.

———.1971. "On the Acquisition of the Meaning of *Before* and *After,*" *Journal of Verbal Learning and Verbal Behavior* 10:266–75.

———.1973a. "What's in a word? On the Child's Acquisition of Semantics in His First Language," in *Cognitive Development and the Acquisition of Language,* ed. T. E. Moore. New York: Academic Press.

———.1973b. "Nonlinguistic Strategies and the Acquisition of Word Meanings," *Cognition* 2:161–82.

———.1974. "Some Aspects of the Conceptional Basis for First Language Acquisition," in *Language Perspectives,* ed. R. L. Schiefelbusch and L. L. Lloyd. Baltimore: University Park Press.

———.1975. "Knowledge, Context, and Strategy in the Acquisition of Meaning," in *Developmental Psycholinguistics: Theory and Applications,* ed. D. Dato. Georgetown University Round Table on Language and Linguistics. Washington, D.C.: Georgetown University Press.

Clark, Herbert. 1970a. "Comprehending Comparatives," in *Advances in Psycholinguistics,* ed. G. B. d'Arcais and W. J. Levelt. Amsterdam: North-Holland Publishing.

———.1970b. "The Primitive Nature of Children's Relational Concepts," in *Cognition and the Development of Language,* ed. J. Hayes. New York: Wiley.

Cole, Michael and Sylvia Scribner. 1974. *Culture and Thought.* New York: Wiley.

Conklin, Harold. 1955. "Hanunoo Color Categories," in *Language in Culture and Society,* ed. D. Hymes. New York: Harper & Row, 1964.

Cromer, Richard. 1974. "The Development of Language and Cognition: The Cognition Hypothesis," in *New Perspectives in Child Development,* ed. B. Foss, New York: Penguin Books, Inc.

Cudworth, Ralph. 1838. *Treatise Concerning Eternal and Immutable Morality.* New York: Andover Press.

Derwing, Bruce. 1973. *Transformational Grammar as a Theory of Language Acquisition.* Cambridge: Cambridge University Press.

Donaldson, Margaret, and George Balfour. 1968. "Less Is More: A Study of Language Comprehension in Children," *British Journal of Psychology* 59:461–72.

Donaldson, Margaret and Roger Wales. 1970. "On the Acquisition of Some Relational Terms," in *Cognition and the Development of Language,* ed. J. R. Hayes. New York: Wiley.

Edie, James. 1976. *Speaking and Meaning.* Bloomington, Ind.: Indiana University Press.

Fillmore, Charles. 1968. "The Case for Case," in *Universals in Linguistic Theory,* ed. E. Bach and R. T. Harns. New York: Holt, Rinehart & Winston.

———.1971. "Some Problems for Case Grammar," in *Report of the 22nd Annual Round Table Meeting on Linguistics and Language Study,* ed. R. O'Brien. Washington, D.C.: Georgetown University Press.

Fodor, Jerry, and Thomas Bever. 1965. "The Psychological Reality of Language," *Cognition* 1:83–95.

Fodor, Jerry, and Thomas Bever. 1965. "The Psychological Reality of Linguistic Segments," *Journal of Verbal Learning and Verbal Behavior* 4:414–20.

Fodor, Jerry, and Merrill Garrett. 1966. "Some Reflections on Competence and Performance," in *Psycholinguistic Papers,* ed. J. Lyons and R. Wales. Edinburgh: University of Edinburgh Press.

References

——.1967. "Some Syntactic Determinants of Sentential Complexity," *Perception and Psychophysics* 2:289-96.

Fodor, Jerry, and Jerrold Katz. 1963. "The Structure of a Semantic Theory," *Language* 39:170-210.

Fodor, Jerry, and Jerrold Katz, eds. 1964. *The Structure of Language: Readings in the Philosophy of Language.* Englewood Cliffs, N.J.: Prentice-Hall.

Fraser, Colin, Ursula Bellugi and Roger Brown. 1963. "Control of Grammar in Imitation, Comprehension and Production," *Journal of Verbal Learning and Verbal Behavior* 2:121-35.

Garrett, Merrill, Thomas Bever and Jerry Fodor. 1965. "The Active Use of Grammar in Speech Perception," *Perception and Psychophysics* 1:30-32.

Geschwind, Norman. 1970. "The Organization of Language and the Brain," *Science*, Nov. 27, 1970, pp. 940-44.

Gewirth, Alan. 1973. "The Sleeping Chess Player," *New York Review of Books*, February 22, 1973, p. 38.

Gleitman, Lila, Henry Gleitman and Elizabeth Shipley. 1972. "The Emergence of the Child as Grammarian," *Cognition* 1:137-64.

Gordon, David and George Lakoff. 1971. "Conversational Postulates," in *Papers from the 7th Regional Meeting of the Chicago Linguistic Society.* Chicago: Chicago Linguistic Society.

Gough, P. B. 1965. "Grammatical Transformations and Speed of Understanding," *Journal of Verbal Learning and Verbal Behavior* 4:107-11.

——.1966. "The Verification of Sentences: The Effects of Delay of Evidence and Sentence Length," *Journal of Verbal Learning and Verbal Behavior* 5:492-96.

Greene, Judith. 1972. *Psycholinguistics.* New York: Penguin Books.

Greenfield, Patricia and Joshua Smith. 1976. *The Structure of Communication in Early Language Development.* New York: Academic Press.

Gregoire, Antoine. 1937. *L'apprentissage du langage.* Paris: Librairie E. Droz.

Grieve, Robert, Robert Hoogenraad, and Diarmid Murray. 1977. "On the Young Child's Use of Lexis and Syntax in Understanding Locative Instructions," *Cognition* 5:235-50.

Harner, Lorrain. 1976. "Children's Understanding of Linguistic Reference to Past and Future," *Journal of Psycholinguistic Research* 5:65-84.

Healy, Alice. 1978. "Poor Communication in Psycholinguistics: Review of Four New Textbooks," *Journal of Psycholinguistic Research* 7:477-92.

Healy, A. F. and A. G. Levitt. 1978. "The Relative Accessibility of Semantic and Deep-Structure Syntactic Concepts," *Memory and Cognition* 6:518-26.

Heider, Eleanor Rosch. 1972. "Universals in Color Naming and Memory," *Journal of Experimental Psychology* 93:10–20.

Heider, Eleanor Rosch, and Donald Olivier. 1972. "The Structure of the Color Space in Naming and Memory for Two Languages," *Cognitive Psychology* 3:337–54.

Higgins, E. Tory. 1977. "The Varying Presuppositional Nature of Comparatives," *Journal of Psycholinguistic Research* 6:203–22.

Hockett, Charles F. 1958. *A Course in Modern Linguistics.* New York: Macmillan.

———.1968. *The State of the Art.* The Hague: Mouton Press.

———.1973. *Man's Place in Nature.* New York: McGraw-Hill.

Holenstein, Elmar. 1975. "Jakobson and Husserl: A Contribution to the Genealogy of Structuralism," *The Human Context* 7:61–83.

Hörmann, Hans. 1971. *Psycholinguistics,* trans. H. H. Stern. Berlin, N.Y.: Springer-Verlag.

Hubel, David. 1963. "The Visual Cortex of the Brain," *Scientific American* 209 (November 1963): 54–62.

Hubel, David, and T. N. Wiesel. 1962. "Receptive Fields, Binocular Interaction and Functional Architecture in the Cat's Visual Cortex," *Journal of Physiology* 160:106–54.

———.1963. "Receptive Fields of Cells in Striate Cortex of Very Young, Visually Inexperienced Kittens," *Journal of Neurophysiology* 26:994–1002.

———.1965. "Receptive Fields and Functional Architecture in Two Non-Striate Areas (18 and 19) of the Cat," *Journal of Neurophysiology* 28:229–89.

———.1968. "Receptive Fields and Functional Architecture of Monkey Striate Cortex," *Journal of Physiology* 195:215–43.

Husserl, Edmund. 1900. *Logical Investigations,* 2 vols., trans. J. Findlay. New York: Humanities Press, 1970.

Huttenlocher, Janellen. 1974. "The Origins of Language Comprehension," in *Theories in Cognitive Psychology: The Loyola Symposium,* ed. R. L. Solso. Potomac, Md.: Lawrence Erlbaum Associates.

Huttenlocher, Janellen, Karen Eisenberg, and Susan Strauss. 1968. "Comprehension: Relation Between Perceived Actor and Logical Subject," *Journal of Verbal Learning and Verbal Behavior* 7:527–30.

Huttenlocher, Janellen, and Susan Strauss. 1968. "Comprehension and a Statement's Relation to the Situation It Describes." *Journal of Verbal Learning and Verbal Behavior* 7:300–304.

Hymes, Dell. 1971. *On Communicative Competence.* Philadelphia: University of Pennsylvania Press.

Inhelder, Bärbel. 1962. "Some Aspects of Piaget's Genetic Approach to Cognition," in *Thought in the Young Child: Monographs of the Society for Research in Child Development,* vol. 27, no. 2, ed. W. Kessen and C. Kuhlman.

References

———.1978. "Language and Thought: Some Remarks on Chomsky and Piaget," *Journal of Psycholinuistic Research* 7:263–68.

Jakobson, Roman. 1968. *Child Speech, Aphasia and Phonological Universals.* The Hague: Mouton Press.

Jakobson, Roman, and Morris Halle. 1956. *Fundamentals of Language.* The Hague: Mouton Press.

Johnson-Laird, Philip. 1970. "Linguistic Complexity and Insight into a Deductive Problem," in *Advances in Psycholinguistics,* ed. G. B. d'Arcais and W. J. Levelt. Amsterdam: North-Holland Publishing.

Kates, Carol. 1969. "Heidegger and the Myth of the Cave," *The Personalist* 1:532–48.

———.1976. "A Critique of Chomsky's Theory of Grammatical Competence," *Forum Linguisticum* 1:15–24.

———.1977. "Linguistic Relativity and Generative-Semantic Grammar," *Forum Linguisticum* 2:133–56.

Katz, Jerrold J. 1972. *Semantic Theory.* New York: Harper & Row.

Katz, Jerrold J. and P. M. Postal. 1964. *An Integrated Theory of Linguistic Descriptions.* Cambridge, Mass.: M.I.T. Press.

Kuczaj, Stan. 1975. "On the Acquisition of a Semantic System," *Journal of Verbal Learning and Verbal Behavior* 14:340–58.

———.1977. "The Acquisition of Regular and Irregular Past Tense Forms," *Journal of Verbal Learning and Verbal Behavior* 16:589–600.

Lacey, Hugh. 1974. "The Scientific Study of Linguistic Behavior: A Perspective on the Skinner-Chomsky Controversy," *Journal of the Theory of Social Behavior* 4:17–51.

Langer, Susanne. 1942. *Philosophy in a New Key.* Cambridge, Mass.: Harvard University Press, 1973.

———.1953. *Feeling and Form.* New York: Scribner's.

———.1957. *Problems of Art.* New York: Scribner's.

Lemmon, E. J. 1966. "Sentences, Statements, and Propositions," in *Readings in the Philosophy of Language,* ed. J. Rosenberg and C. Travis. Englewood Cliffs, N.J.: Prentice-Hall, 1971.

Lenneberg, Eric. 1967. *Biological Foundations of Language.* New York: Wiley.

———.1971. "Of Language, Knowledge, Apes, and Brains," *Journal of Psycholinguistic Research* 1:1–29.

Leopold, Werner. 1948. "Semantic Learning in Infant Language," in *Child Language: A Book of Readings,* ed. A. Bar-Adon and W. Leopold. Englewood Cliffs, N.J.: Prentice-Hall, 1971.

Lewis, M. M. 1937. "The Beginning of Reference to Past and Future in a Child's Speech," in *Child Language: A Book of Readings,* ed. A. Bar-Adon and W. Leopold. Englewood Cliffs, N.J.: Prentice-Hall, 1971.

———.1951. *Infant Speech,* 2d ed. London: Routledge.

Leiberman, Philip. 1968. "Primate Vocalizations and Human Linguistic Ability," *Journal of the Acoustical Society of America* 44:1574–84.

Luria, A. R. 1959. "The Directive Function of Speech in Development and Dissolution," pt. I, *Word* 15:341–52; pt. II, *Word* 15:453–64.

Lyons, John. 1971. *Introduction to Theoretical Linguistics.* Cambridge: Cambridge University Press.

McCawley, James. 1968. "The Role of Semantics in a Grammar," in *Universals in Linguistic Theory.* ed. E. Bach and R. T. Harns. New York: Holt, Rinehart & Winston.

———.1974. "[Dialogue with] James McCawley," in *Discussing Language,* ed. H. Parret. The Hague: Mouton Press.

McMahon, L. E. 1963. "Grammatical Analysis as Part of Understanding a Sentence." Ph.D. dissertation, Harvard University.

McNeill, David. 1966. "Developmental Psycholinguistics," in *The Genesis of Language,* ed. F. Smith and G. Miller. Cambridge, Mass.: M.I.T. Press.

———.1970. "Language before Symbols: Very Early Children's Grammar," *Interchange* 1:127–33.

MacCorquodale, Kenneth. 1970. "On Chomsky's Review of Skinner's *Verbal Behavior,*" *Journal of the Experimental Analysis of Behavior* 13:1–17.

MacWhinney, Brian, and Elizabeth Bates. 1978. "Sentential Devices for Conveying Givenness and Newness: A Cross-Cultural Developmental Study," *Journal of Verbal Learning and Verbal Behavior* 17:539–58.

Maerz, Aloys, and M. Rea Paul. 1930. *A Dictionary of Color.* New York: McGraw-Hill.

Malinowski, Bronislaw. 1936. "The Dilemma of Contemporary Linguistics," in *Language in Culture and Society,* ed. D. Hymes. New York: Harper & Row, 1964.

Mei, Tsu-Lin. 1961. "Subject and Predicate: A Grammatical Preliminary," *The Philosophical Review* 70(2):153–75.

Merleau-Ponty, Maurice. 1945. *Phenomenology of Perception,* trans. C. Smith. New York: Humanities Press, 1962.

———.1949. *The Structure of Behavior,* trans. A. Fisher. Boston: Beacon Press, 1963.

Miller, George, and Kathryn McKean. 1964. "A Chronometric Study of Some Relations Between Sentences," *Quarterly Journal of Experimental Psychology* 16:297–308.

Morris, Charles. 1938. *Foundations of the Theory of Signs.* Chicago: University of Chicago Press.

Nagel, Ernest. 1943. "Book Review: *Philosophy in a New Key.*" *Journal of Philosophy* 40:323–29.

Nelson, Katherine. 1973a. "Some Evidence for the Cognitive Primacy of Categorization and Its Functional Basis," *Merrill-Palmer Quarterly of Behavior and Development* 19:21–39.

References

——.1973b. "Structure and Strategy in Learning to Talk." *Monographs of the Society for Research in Child Development,* vol. 38, nos. 1–2, serial no. 149.

——.1974. "Concept, Word, and Sentence: Interrelations in Acquisition and Development," *Psychological Review* 81:267–85.

Olson, David. 1970a. *Cognitive Development: The Child's Acquisition of Diagonality.* New York: Academic Press.

——.1970b. "Language and Thought: Aspects of a Cognitive Theory of Semantics." *Psychological Review* 77:257–73.

Optical Society of America, Committee on Colorimetry. 1953. *The Science of Color.* New York: Crowell.

Palermo, David. 1973. "More about Less: A Study of Language Comprehension," *Journal of Verbal Learning and Verbal Behavior* 12:211–21.

Peirce, Charles. 1897. In *The Philosophy of Peirce: Selected Writings,* ed. Justus Buchler. London: Routledge & Kegan Paul, 1956.

Piaget, Jean. 1937. *The Construction of Reality in the Child,* trans. M. Cook. New York: Basic Books, 1954.

——. 1946. *Play, Dreams and Imitation in Childhood,* trans. C. Gattegno and F. Hodgson. New York: Norton, 1962.

Pitcher, George. 1964. "Propositions and the Correspondence Theory of Truth," in *Readings in the Philosophy of Language,* ed. J. Rosenberg and C. Travis. Englewood Cliffs, N.J.: Prentice-Hall, 1971.

Putnam, Hilary. 1968. "The 'Innateness Hypothesis' and Explanatory Models in Linguistics," in *Boston Studies in the Philosophy of Science,* vol. 3. New York: Humanities Press.

Quine, Willard. 1969. "Propositional Objects," in *Ontological Relativity and Other Essays.* New York: Columbia University Press.

Richards, I. A. 1936. *The Philosophy of Rhetoric.* Oxford: Oxford University Press.

Rosch, Eleanor. 1975. "Cognitive Representations of Semantic Categories." *Journal of Experimental Psychology: General* 104 (1975):192–233.

Rosch, Eleanor, and Carolyn B. Mervis. 1975. "Family Resemblances: Studies in the Internal Structure of Categories." *Cognitive Psychology* 7:573–605.

Rosch, Eleanor, Carolyn B. Mervis, Wayne Gray, David Johnson, and Penny Boyes-Braem. 1976. "Basic Objects in Natural Categories," *Cognitive Psychology* 8:382–439.

Russell, Bertrand. 1912. *The Problems of Philosophy.* New York: Holt & Co.

——.1919. "On Propositions: What They are and How They Mean," in *Problems of Science and Philosophy. Proceedings of the Aristotelian Society,* suppl. vol. 2, pp. 1–43.

Saussure, Ferdinand de. 1916. *Course in General Linguistics,* ed. C. Bally and A. Sechehaye, trans. W. Baskin. New York: Philosophical Library, 1959.

Savin, Harris, and Ellen Perchonock. 1965. "Grammatical Structure and the Immediate Recall of English Sentences." *Journal of Verbal Learning and Verbal Behavior* 4:348-53.

Schallert, Diane. 1976. "Improving Memory for Prose: The Relation between Depth of Processing and Context, *Journal of Verbal Learning and Verbal Behavior* 15:621-32.

Schlesinger, I. M. 1971. "Production of Utterances and Language Acquisition," in *The Ontogenesis of Language: Some Facts and Several Theories,* ed. D. Slobin. New York: Academic Press.

Searle, John. 1965. "What Is a Speech Act?" in *The Philosophy of Language,* ed. J. Searle. Oxford: Oxford University Press, 1971.

Sinclair, Hermina. 1969. "Developmental Psycholinguistics," in *Studies in Cognitive Development,* ed. D. Elkind and J. Flavell. Oxford: Oxford University Press.

———.1970. "The Transition from Sensori-Motor Behavior to Symbolic Activity," *Interchange* 1:119-26.

———.1978. "Conflict and Progress," in *Psychology and Biology of Language and Thought,* ed. G. Miller and E. Lenneberg. New York: Academic Press.

Sitwell, Edith. 1926. *Poetry and Criticism.* New York: Holt.

Slobin, Dan. 1963. "Grammatical Transformations in Childhood and Adulthood." Ph.D. dissertation, Harvard University.

———.1966. "Grammatical Transformations and Sentence Comprehension in Childhood and Adulthood," *Journal of Verbal Learning and Verbal Behavior* 5:219-27.

———.1970. "Universals of Grammatical Development in Children," in *Advances in Psycholinguistics,* ed. W. J. Levelt and F. d'Arcais. Amsterdam: North-Holland Publishing.

———.1971a. "Developmental Psycholinguistics," in *A Survey of Linguistic Science,* ed. W. Dingwall. College Park, Md.: University of Maryland Press.

———.1971b. *Psycholinguistics.* Glenview, Ill.: Scott, Foresman & Co.

Smith, Frank and George Miller. eds. 1966. *The Genesis of Language.* Cambridge, Mass.: M.I.T. Press.

Stanford, W. B. 1936. *Greek Metaphor: Studies in Theory and Practice.* Oxford: Basil Blackwell Press.

Strawson, P. F. 1971. "Identifying Reference and Truth-Values," in *Semantics: An Interdisciplinary Reader,* ed. D. Steinberg and L. Jakobovitz. Cambridge: Cambridge University Press.

References

Swinney, David, and David Hakes. 1976. "Effects of Prior Context upon Lexical Access during Sentence Comprehension," *Journal of Verbal Learning and Verbal Behavior* 15:681–89.

Szathmary, Arthur. 1954. "Symbolic and Aesthetic Expression in Painting," *Journal of Aesthetics and Art Criticism* 13:86–96.

Thorndike, E., and I. Lorge. 1944. *The Teacher's Word Book of 30,000 Words.* New York: Bureau of Publications, Teacher's College, Columbia University.

Thorndyke, Perry. 1976. "The Role of Inferences in Discourse Comprehension," *Journal of Verbal Learning and Verbal Behavior* 15:437–46.

Tremaine, Ruth. 1975. "Piagetian Equilibration Processes in Syntax Learning," in *Developmental Psycholinguistics: Theory and Applications.* Georgetown University Round Table on Language and Linguistics (1975). Washington, D.C.: Georgetown University Press.

Trubetzkoy, N. S. 1939. *Principles of Phonology,* trans. C. Baltaxe. Berkeley: University of California Press, 1969.

Vygotsky, Lev. 1934. *Thought and Language,* trans. and ed. E. Hanfmann and G. Vakar. Cambridge, Mass.: M.I.T. Press, 1962.

Wason, P. C. 1965. "The Contexts of Plausible Denial," *Journal of Verbal Learning and Verbal Behavior* 4:7–11.

Weiner, Susan. 1974. "On the Development of *More* and *Less,*" *Journal of Experimental Child Psychology* 17:271–87.

Weiser, Ann. 1974. "Deliberate Ambiguity," in *Papers from the 10th Regional Meeting of the Chicago Linguistic Society.* Chicago: Chicago Linguistic Society.

Weitz, Morris. 1954. "Symbolism and Art," *Review of Metaphysics* 7:466–81.

Wells, Rulon. 1971. "Distinctively Human Semiotic," in *Essays in Semiotics,* ed. J. Kristeva, J. Rey-Debovo, and D. Umiker. The Hague: Mouton Press.

Welsh, Paul. 1955. "Discursive and Presentational Symbols," *Mind* 64:181–99.

Werner, Heinz. 1948. *Comparative Psychology of Mental Development,* trans. E. B. Garside. Chicago: Follet.

Wheelwright, Philip. 1954. *The Burning Fountain.* Bloomington, Ind.: Indiana Univ. Press.

Wilcox, Stephen, and David Palermo. 1974/1975. "'in,' 'on,' and 'under' revisited," *Cognition* 313:245–54.

Yngve, Victor. 1975. "Toward a Human Linguistics," in *11th Regional Meeting of the Chicago Linguistic Society: Parasession on Functionalism.* Chicago: Chicago Linguistic Society.

Index

PRAGMATICS AND
SEMANTICS

Designed by Richard E. Rosenbaum.
Composed by The Composing Room of Michigan, Inc.
in 10 point Baskerville V.I.P., 2 points leaded,
with display lines in Baskerville.
Printed offset by Thomson/Shore, Inc. on
Warren's Number 66 Antique Offset, 50 pound basis.
Bound by John H. Dekker & Sons, Inc.
in Holliston book cloth
and stamped in All Purpose foil.

Library of Congress Cataloging in Publication Data

Kates, Carol A   1943–
   Pragmatics and semantics.

   Includes bibliographical references and index.
   1. Communicative competence.   2. Languages—Philosophy.
3. Pragmatics.   4. Semantics.   I. Title.
PS37.5.C64K3   415   80-16742
ISBN 0-8014-1288-9